WELFARE IN WORKING ORDER

edited by
James Mc Cormick
Carey Oppenheim

INSTITUTE FOR PUBLIC POLICY RESEARCH

Contents

Foreword

1998 is an appropriate year to consider the future of welfare provision in the United Kingdom. It is not only the 50th anniversary of the introduction of the Beveridge reforms. It is also the 150th anniversary of Prudential which, throughout its history, has been closely associated with the development of welfare provision.

For this reason I am delighted that Prudential has sponsored this report which considers two key aspects of reform. Although the report represents the views of its authors and does not constitute Prudential Policy, it is vital that a company such as Prudential Corporation plc plays its role in ensuring that the debate about such a fundamentally important issue is informed. "Welfare and Work" makes a significant and accessible contribution to that debate.

Peter Davis
Group Chief Executive
Prudential Corporation plc

About the Contributors

James McCormick is Research Director of the Scottish Council Foundation, a network promoting independent thinking in public policy. He was a Research Fellow with the IPPR from 1993 to 1997, where he worked for the Commission on Social Justice and on related welfare projects.

Carey Oppenheim is is a Senior Lecturer in social policy at South Bank University and will be on secondment at IPPR as a Senior Research fellow in social policy from 1998.

Holly Sutherland is Director of the Micro-simulation Unit in the Department of Economics, Cambridge University.

Gerald Holtham has been Director of the IPPR since 1994. Before joining IPPR he was chief economist with Lehman Brothers. He has also worked for the OECD in Paris and the Brookings Institute in Washington.

Ken Mayhew is Fellow in Economics at Pembroke College, Oxford. He is editor of the Oxford Review of Economic Policy and Oxford Economic Papers. He spent two years on leave from Oxford as Economic Director of the National Economic Development Office.

Peter Ingram is Lecturer in Economics at the University of Surrey. Previously he was a Senior Adviser at the Confederation of British Industry.

Marilyn Howard is a freelance social policy analyst, currently researching disability benefits and welfare to work, chiefly for the Disablement Income Group. Until the General Election she was a Researcher to Alan Howarth CBE MP; previously she was Social Security Policy Officer for RADAR and the Disability Alliance.

Acknowledgements

The authors would like to thank the many people who have contributed to IPPR's ongoing research on welfare reform by reading early drafts of these papers and attending seminars, in particular:

Brian Arrighi, Gordon Borrie, Bryn Davies, Stephen Davies, Dan Finn, Karen Gardiner, Tony Gray, Gerry Holtham, Damian Leeson, Ruth Lister, Ken McIntyre, Cliodhna McMullin (Toronto), Michael Mendelson (Toronto), Andy Mitchell (Toronto), Sue Monk, Eddie Phillips, Ann Richmond (Victoria), Peter Robinson, Helena Scott, Holly Sutherland, Robert Walker and Steve Wilcox.

Thanks are also due to the Prudential Corporation plc both for funding the wider research programme on which this publication is based and contributing to the development of policy ideas.

The views and proposals published here are those of the authors, they are not necessarily those of IPPR, its staff or trustees.

Preface

During 1997, IPPR prepared a series of papers on options for reforming the state of welfare in Britain. Following a number of seminars bringing together representatives of the pensions industry, academics, politicians and policy experts, interim papers from the series were sent to government departments and task forces which had invited submissions on various aspects of welfare reform. This book presents the final series of papers and sets out our priorities for change for people of working age and the retired. The chapters deal with the following topics:

- Welfare to Work: What it means for Taxes and Benefits
- Brokering the New Deal: Design and Delivery
- The Long-term Unemployed: What More Can Be Done
- Disability Benefit Reform
- Prospects for Pension Reform

Further work will continue in 1998 on other aspects of the welfare state. In advance of the work of the Royal Commission on Long-Term Care, a future publication will focus on how the principles of equity and affordability can be applied in practical terms to care provision. Our starting point in all this work is that, despite huge changes in society since the Beveridge settlement was struck, the case for intelligent intervention by government remains obvious. The task ahead is neither to hasten the end of the welfare state nor to "go beyond" it. Instead we need to go beyond the euphemisms routinely used by its would-be undertakers on the Right and work out how collective action can address the shortcomings of the private market in areas of social insurance and income support.

The first three chapters address reform for people of working age, in particular the government's New Deal programmes for the long-term jobless. The first presents an analysis of how the tax and benefit systems could be changed to support the aims of welfare-to-work. Drawing on the results of modelling specially commissioned for this project from Cambridge University, Carey Oppenhiem presents a number of costed options which are assessed for their likely impact on the unemployment and working poverty traps. This analysis demonstrates that government has a menu of options. Intelligent reform of the tax system must consider the distribution of tax allowances. Oppenheim illustrates how the transition into work could be eased: through allowing people to earn more before benefits are withdrawn less steeply; through targeted increases in Child Benefits; reduced social housing rents; or a combination of these. The chapter makes the important distinction between strategies that assist people to get jobs in the first place and those that help people to keep them and eventually move free of means-testing – the difference between getting one foot on the first rung of the earnings ladder and getting both feet on the second rung. An adequately ambitious welfare-to-work programme must focus on job retention as well as job entry rates.

Even with a more effective social security system that encourages people to earn, appropriate opportunities to work must be available. The New Deal is Britain's first dedicated welfare-to-work programme, bringing substantial new resources to bear on long-term unemployment among target groups. Implemented against a background of falling unemployment among under-25s, the New Deal has every chance of succeeding. Yet it is far from clear that delivery of the programme to the most excluded communities will be effective without fresh thinking on the infrastructure of employment services. As the second chapter argues, a uniform national approach is a recipe for disappointment in precisely those localities which need the New Deal to work most.

This chapter addresses the problem of low expectations – among target groups in communities which have long since grown suspicious of employment and training schemes that have failed to deliver, and among employers who will be wary of recruiting individuals who do not appear to be job-prepared, even if they do bring with them a wage subsidy. Drawing on original fieldwork in the Canadian provinces of British Columbia and Ontario, as well as local initiatives in Britain, James McCormick argues that a network of alternative employment brokers should be recruited in different locations. They must have the capacity to earn the trust of New Deal participants and the reputation among employers for their ability to screen and match applicants to vacancies. Making welfare-to-work succeed in the least promising areas will require existing agencies to contract with new ones and will need a strong commitment by the government continually to re-evaluate the outcomes. The guiding principle according to this analysis is to keep the New Deal simple and sell it well.

The third chapter considers further how extensions to currently announced New Deal programmes could help to deal with foreseeable difficulties. The decline in the numbers of young people who have been out of work for a long time releases funds for other long-term jobless. The best programmes may well differ in different parts of the country given the uneven state of the labour market. Gerry Holtham, Peter Ingram and Ken Mayhew argue that in areas of low labour demand, the local government sector may be an indispensable source of new employment if the various options which the New Deal offers in principle are to be available in practice. The authors examine how an earlier IPPR proposal to tackle long-term unemployment might be incorporated in the New Deal to enhance its reach.

Marilyn Howard's chapter on disability policy rests on the boundary between working age and retirement. For the older, long-term unemployed in particular, the dilemma is how a more appropriate balance between incapacity, early retirement and welfare-to-work can be struck. Exploring in detail how the New Deal for Disabled People could encourage activity, this chapter outlines how individual plans would result in a more sensitive assessment of ability, from being ready to work with assistance in the workplace through to those who are unable to work again. It proposes a targeted package of in-work benefits and Employment Service support through "Jobmatch Plus". If extended as part of the New Deal, this could offer a genuine choice to those who are most at risk of ending up trapped on incapacity benefits despite their ability to undertake some work.

Patterns of risk, cost and reward are constantly shifting. How does this impact on our approach to retirement? The fifth chapter in the series notes that in the time of William Beveridge living well beyond the official retirement age was a risk to be insured against. Today, it is a predictable event to be saved for, increasingly out of individual earnings and savings. But we should be wary of concluding that all retirement income should be met through more efficient individual savings schemes. It cannot. There will certainly be people whose own earnings are too low or irregular to build up a decent second-tier pension and others whose contributions will simply not earn the level of pensions they had expected (or hoped for). While we strongly support the government's focus on stakeholder pensions which will extend security and value for money to the lifetime lower-paid, reform to the first-tier is just as important. If the state is to retain its capacity to redistribute in favour of groups who were unable to make adequate provision for their retirement (rather than simply choosing a higher level of consumption during working age), methods of transferring income through state pensions must be rather more effective than they are today. The basic state pension has enormous symbolic value and should be retained as the pay-as-you-go foundation of retirement income. But it cannot continue to be of diminishing significance both to the affluent retired and to the poorest (who increasingly rely on means-tested top-ups).

In the final chapter, James McCormick sets out a number of strategies for tackling retirement poverty, both today and in the future. No new savings scheme or welfare-to-work programme can raise the incomes of the "third nation in retirement" – those pensioners who have little if any income in addition to their state pension. A number of one-off and ongoing changes are explored. While the scope for redistribution is largely appropriate to the first-tier, the paper does propose one means of "gearing up" the modest contributions of the low paid to second-tier pensions by reducing the rate of tax relief to the basic rate of income tax and converting some of the savings into pensions credits. Low wage earners who have done badly out of changes to SERPS by previous governments might be considered the priority group for such assistance. Any such change should be part of a wider review of how tax relief is used. We would expect a new government to set targets on product performance if tax advantages are to be continued.

The fourth chapter on disability benefit deals with an issue of considerable topicality. Here and in general, our approach to welfare reform is guided by a central principle. We do not require that all individuals have equal access to retirement income or earnings. We do seek, through policy intervention, to deliver a decent minimum to everyone retired or disabled. For retirement, we should then encourage additional provision in line with ability to pay, and use various incentives to assist those who are least able to do so. If there is any fiscal room for manoeuvre it is the working poor (and some groups of non-employed, including the disabled) who should benefit, instead of paying higher tax relief to the highest paid. This does not of course resolve the particular issue of how high the basic state pension and benefits should be if they are to relieve poverty and avoid providing the same or greater support for the affluent.

We should not, however, apply the same principles when it comes to other goods which are socially provided at present, like health care and school-level education. Here, we would argue that individuals should have access to rather more than a basic minimum. As far as resources allow, our goal is equal access to high quality services. In a free society, individuals are entitled to top up with private provision, but there should be no guarantee of state resources in order to facilitate that; those should be reserved for raising quality in the public sphere. We are, therefore, deeply sceptical about recent proposals to move the whole welfare state towards funded accounts covering individual needs. Although these might be useful devices in the areas of retirement income and long-term care needs, their extension to health, housing and education would not raise standards or widen choice to those who face the poorest services. Innovative ways of increasing saving and improving universal services are badly needed and these will be the subjects of other, future studies. One idea to be explored is that of a a long-term "Community Fund" established with public resources invested commercially to finance the year-on-year expansion of health and education needs above the rate of GDP growth.

The centre-left has rediscovered some old truths about welfare. People need to have a sense of ownership over their own savings and a sense of security over their future prospects if we are to strike a better deal for the lifetime poor. There is another verity that remains powerfully apposite. As we become better at tackling the old risks identified by Beveridge, new risks emerge: lone parenthood, long-term unemployment, long-term care needs. Because none of us knows what risks we shall have to face in the future, we cannot afford to give up on the welfare state, without a damaging growth of misery and exclusion and a serious loss of social cohesion. While reforming it will always be unfinished business, a more effective welfare state is both necessary and achievable.

Gerald Holtham
IPPR
January 1998

Executive Summary

Welfare reform poses a key challenge for government. In the past, opinion has been divided in favour of incremental change to the benefits system and more radical reform to the balance between cash benefits and services, means-testing and universality. Motives for reform have been diverse: reduce the benefits bill, reduce the length of time on benefit, improve the quality of care, promote work as the best form of welfare. At various stages in our lives, some welfare strategies are more appropriate than others. Yet much discussion of the welfare state has been based on 'snapshot' measures leading to inadequate or inappropriate proposals.

This book is the result of a research project co-ordinated by IPPR. It presents a map of the main reform options. From people of working age who need to get jobs and keep them, to today's retired poor who need higher incomes, the IPPR provide new answers to some of the key dilemmas.

- How should the tax and benefit systems be changed to promote a secure balance between work and care responsibilities?
- Can the New Deal build trust among the long-term unemployed and confidence among employers?
- How should long-term and hidden unemployment in the economic blackspots be tackled among those outside the New Deal?
- How can more disabled people be helped to move out of the 'incapacity trap'?
- How should state pensions be reformed to relieve poverty in retirement, both now and for tomorrow's pensioners?

1. Welfare-to-work: What it means for taxes and benefits

This chapter explores who should be the 'targets' of welfare-to-work programmes. It identifies the key barriers to getting jobs in the first place and goes on to look at how they can be overcome by improving incentives in the tax and benefit systems. While there is little hard evidence to support a full-blown 'dependency thesis', a more sophisticated notion about the variety of factors which would enable people to take jobs is needed. Poverty among people of working age is not confined to the registered unemployed. Churning at the foot of the income ladder occurs as people move from out-of-work benefits to work and back again. Families with children, particularly lone parents, are less likely to move up the ladder and stay up. While it offers no guarantees, employment and self-employment for most 'work-poor' households remains the main route out of poverty. A lasting strategy to promote work must address economic inactivity as well as registered unemployment; be tailored to different types of household (through reformed child benefits, childcare and flexible working for example); and focus on in-work support which will enable people to make the move to the second rung of the 'welfare to work ladder' – to keep the jobs they have gained.

The goals of welfare to work

A serious approach to placing work at the heart of welfare reform will focus on prevention as well as cure. The goal should be to help people move further than in-work poverty. This will contribute towards a second objective of maintaining a sustainable social security budget (a more important indicator than its overall level). While there is no financial crisis looming in the benefits system when measured as a proportion of national wealth, welfare to work strategies are one way of containing growth in the means-tested elements of the system. Four key barriers to moving into work are discussed:

- Financial disincentives such as high marginal tax-back of benefits;
- Care responsibilities such as the availability and affordability of providing alternative care for children or elderly relatives;
- Bridging or transitional difficulties, including the gap between coming off benefits and getting the first pay packet;
- Attitudes towards work, covering self-perceived capacity and confidence.

The results of three significant tax-benefit changes are presented. They were modelled for this book at Cambridge University. The options are:

- Simplification and integration of in-work benefits including a low income mortgage benefit;

- A non means-tested approach which reduces social housing rents, increases Child Benefit for the under 5s, raises the tax threshold and introduces a national minimum wage;
- A participation income alongside the existing national insurance scheme.

Two other reforms are explored – Earned Income Tax Credits (EITCs, a variant of which is to be introduced in Britain) and the merging of Income Support and Family Credit. The combined effect of simplifying means-tested benefits, reducing costs and improving non-means tested benefits offers one promising way forward. EITCs may be an acceptable tool for directing resources towards the working poor but they do not send a specific signal about the advantages of working. Nevertheless a child tax credit which unifies financial support for families with children in and out of work and claws back some support from more affluent households is worth further consideration.

In addition, a range of smaller scale reforms would ease the transition into work. These include greater flexibility over how couples share the 'earnings disregard' to ease the problem of work-poor households; the extension of low-interest credit facilities; and 'fast-track' qualification for benefits to encourage claimants to take a job without risking their security if it does not work out. A comprehensive strategy will also consider how people use benefits as a springboard into work. While incentives must be clearer, low benefits do nothing to help those with the poorest employment prospects get jobs.

Access to affordable childcare must be another core component of welfare to work. While support with childcare costs should be available to those undertaking education and training as part of the New Deal for Lone Parents, careful consideration should also be given to proposals for childcare vouchers now with a generous affluence test for those below nursery age.

Compulsory or voluntary?

If benefit sanctions for non-participation in the New Deal are too punitive, there are risks of pushing some of the unemployed further away from the labour market and of damaging employer confidence. In addition to high quality Gateway activities before entry to the New

Deal, there should be a safety-net of hardship payments. There are strong grounds for being cautious about compulsory participation for lone parents:

- Evidence from North America suggests that compulsion is counterproductive, failing to increase lone parents' earnings, unless programmes offer childcare guarantees;
- Successful programmes tend to be more expensive;
- In contrast the voluntary JET scheme in Australia found no difficulty in recruiting enough participants;
- Benefit sanctions inevitably punish children who have no power to control the actions of their parents.

Welfare reforms have to take into account the trade-offs lone parents make in balancing the employment, time and needs of their children. Public policy needs to strike a balance between supporting part time opportunities for work, education and volunteering – in other words supporting a broader notion of *welfare to activity* rather than only paid work.

2. Brokering a New Deal: Design and Delivery

The New Deal is Britain's first dedicated welfare to work programme. It brings substantial new resources to bear on the problem of long-term unemployment, implemented against the background of falling unemployment and strong government commitment to raise employment levels for those out of work the longest. This chapter considers the prospects for the New Deal succeeding – especially in areas where labour demand is weakest. Drawing upon fieldwork conducted in Canada and the UK, it argues that Britain's programme has a number of key advantages which international models have lacked. Where this country may face a problem is in designing an appropriate infrastructure to deliver the New Deal. Insufficient attention has been paid to innovative delivery methods which will reach the most excluded communities. A 'one size fits all' approach - more likely to emerge by default than by intent - would be a sure recipe for disappointment.

Persuading Employers

Welfare-to-work will not be judged simply by how many people are moved off means-tested benefits. The aim must be to ensure that expectations are raised in suspicious communities, and that employer scepticism is addressed rather than ignored. The clear evidence from North America and Australia is that employers will quickly become wary of recruiting individuals who are not job-ready, irrespective of how large the wage subsidy or training credits they bring with them. While much attention has been given to securing a high level of participation among benefit claimants, the take-up rate among employers will be equally important. Unlike under-25s on benefit, employers cannot be compelled to provide jobs for every New Deal participant. First impressions last. It is therefore essential that a high quality programme of job preparation and pre-vocational training is delivered through the Gateway stage of the New Deal. The more individually-tailored and action-oriented the Gateway is the better. A guiding principle throughout the programme should be to 'keep it simple and sell it well'.

Brokers

A network of alternative employment brokers should be recruited in different locations to deliver the key options. Such brokers will often be local, trusted and have a track record for success in working with some of the most 'difficult to reach' client groups. They should have the flexibility to tap into the shadow economy, offering those engaged in cash in hand trading a route into mainstream work or self-employment. The Employment Service should prepare to establish local agreements with brokers who have a reputation for providing employers with the high quality screening and matching service that they require for even lower-skilled vacancies.

The development of a purchaser-provider split for employment services carries the potential risk of cherry-picking by providers. If an incentive system along the lines of that emerging in North America and Australia were to develop in the UK, with funding driven by performance outcomes, the more employable clients would be the most attractive. Instead this chapter argues that there is a convincing case for contracting with non-profit brokers on a limited basis. The Employment

Service offers a national network to deliver 'active labour market policies' which many countries lack. But in those places where the labour market is failing, the capacity of the public Employment Service is weak and could be strengthened through carefully-managed brokering partnerships. Provided the substance and design of the New Deal can be adjusted over time, then the higher the level of investment, the greater its impact should be.

3. Beyond the New Deal: Tackling long-term unemployment

The New Deal was designed to tackle long-term unemployment among under-25s and has been extended to assist lone parents and people with disabilities (who have not necessarily been registered as unemployed). As the level of unemployment falls, especially among young people, older workers living in areas where the demand for labour is weakest continue to face the longest periods of unemployment. In this chapter, the authors revisit an earlier IPPR proposal to create jobs in such localities in the light of developments in the labour market and government policy. They contend that falling unemployment coupled with its highly uneven distribution means that government can both afford to be more selective in how it applies new resources and needs to be so.

The original proposal was targeted at those who have been out of work for more than 12 months. They would be eligible for a part-time job in the local authority sector, either extending current services or helping to deliver new ones. The balance between working in the care sector, environmental maintenance and leisure services would vary between authorities. Jobs would be paid at the going rate and last for one year. To overcome the barriers faced by families with children, every participant would find themselves better off. Aware of the risks attached to wage subsidies from government – deadweight, displacement and substitution – the authors argue that the contracting process would have to specify the additional output that would result. Reactions to this proposal were mixed. Because most of the new jobs would be created in non-traded activities, concern about unfair international competition is largely misplaced. However, being registered unemployed for the required 'waiting period' should not be the only way into the programme.

Given the distribution of non-employment in Britain, any member of a household without an earner in the previous 12 months should be eligible. This would reach many of the partners of unemployed claimants as well as some who were moved from unemployment to incapacity benefits and who would like to work part-time. Moreover, the programme could be extended to other areas of the public sector (including the health services) which would benefit from higher levels of employment. Other criticisms concern the impact on incentives for existing employees: some work fewer hours than proposed by this programme even though they would like to increase them; longer-established employees might find themselves taking home the same pay as new recruits with less experience; and the 'better off in work' condition for new workers might again leave existing low-paid workers on lower incomes.

Potential risks

As the New Deal unfolds, a number of difficulties may have to be addressed. The risks include:

- Turf wars between TECs/LECs, local authorities, the Employment Service and the voluntary sector over who should have lead responsibility for delivering New Deal programmes. This would have obvious effects on overall efficiency;
- Deadweight, substitution and churning especially in the private sector employment option;
- In some economic blackspots there are too few private employers for government to pay a wage subsidy to in the first place. In Northern Ireland, Merseyside and the North-East of England, there are two vacancies for every 13 unemployed. In the East Midlands and the South East there are two jobs for every five claimants;
- An imbalance between money for job entry (wage subsidies) and job retention (training credits).

Flexibility

The government's welfare-to-work strategy should therefore be flexible enough to respond to the very different labour market conditions – and prospects – across the UK. Even if applied sparingly, in areas of unusually high unemployment only, the updated IPPR proposal could reduce substitution and enhance the quality of public services. It could either be delivered as part of an extended New Deal or piloted through the Employment Zones announced at the end of 1997 using resources already available through the windfall levy. In either case, the programme would fill a clear gap in the range of policies to tackle the hardest edges of long-term unemployment.

4. Disability Dilemmas: Welfare to work or early retirement?

People aged between 50 and pension age are particularly likely to be disabled. So should disabled people be viewed as simply long-term unemployed (requiring a welfare to work response) or as early retired (without any expectations of a return to work)?

To date policy responses have tended to be confused, based on a benefits system based purely on compensating people for their inability to work and discouraging any contact with the labour market. Welfare to work initiatives emphasise work rather than early retirement and so could ultimately identify better ways of helping disabled people who want to work. However, in the short term, these initiatives may serve to highlight the limitations of the current benefits system, and may limit their success. Alternatives could be tested. The over-50s should be encouraged to take up part time work through the proposed 'Jobmatch Plan' an extension of one of the existing Employment Service schemes. The three principles for welfare reform outlined by the Prime Minister in January 1997 are developed in relation to disability policy.

Local opportunities

An active welfare state could be, underpinned by an interactionist perspective encompassing both individual needs and external barriers. An earlier assessment of 'employability' could be devised examining someone's abilities and capacity to work, with the active support of the Employment Service and Benefits Agency. It could help employers meet their Disability Discrimination Act (DDA) responsibilities, leaving early retirement as the last and not first option. Agencies should focus on external barriers to employment faced by disabled people.

Employability

Opportunities and responsibilities could extend local work opportunities through Neighbourhood Match and Employment Zones, providing incentives to employers to locate in deprived areas and recruit disabled workers. Building motivation is an alternative approach to responsibility than using sanctions. An enabling government could develop disability and income policy across public and private sectors, developing greater consistency of definition, assessments and structures to achieve more flexible and secure incomes using the DDA itself as a baseline for these developments. More consistency between policies for income security, DDA employment and appropriate service provision is essential.

Concerns about the growth of the disability benefits budget could be addressed by considering the nature and distribution of the risks of becoming disabled and through a better understanding of the contributory factors. Both public and private sectors stand to gain from carefully targeted intervention deigned to reduce the nature of risk. Policies could be accompanied by 'disability impact statements' including any disabling effects of policy itself.

5. Prospects for Pensions Reform

We used to assume that being old meant being poor. Pensioners today are no longer as likely to be poor, largely due to rising incomes from occupational pensions. But income inequality in retirement has grown significantly. We can now talk of Three Nations in Retirement, with a low-income third relying only on state pensions continuing to fall further behind the rest. The Government Actuary Department expects the trend to accelerate over the next thirty years. There is no crisis of affordability for British state pensions. As long as the first-tier pension remains linked to prices, the combined National Insurance rate needed to fund future entitlements is likely to fall. There is instead a problem of adequacy. Without reform, the Basic State Pension (BSP) will be of diminishing importance both to the poorest (whose incomes will increasingly depend on means-tested top-ups) and the most affluent.

The First-Tier Pension

Proposals by the last government to switch the BSP from pay-as-you-go to a funded benefit raised the familiar dilemma of double payment for the current generation of workers. Such proposals rely on changing the tax treatment of pension contributions or issuing gilts to cover government liabilities. Even if these were politically feasible, it is by no means clear that any economic boost from funding the first tier as second tier pensions would justify the upheaval. It would also remove the key government instrument of redistribution in retirement. The BSP should therefore remain as an unfunded first-tier pension. But its structure could be changed. Contribution gaps currently mean that part-time workers earning below the Lower Earnings Limit (LEL) may work for years without accumulating pension entitlements. They could be closed by widening the contributory base to include workers currently excluded from paying National Insurance, allowing them and their employers to pay a low entry rate. This option would alter the contributory basis but it would not tilt the benefit structure in favour of the low paid. Nor would an across-the-board increase reduce inequality. In the longer term the accrual rate for the BSP could be changed with an enhanced rate for the lifetime low-paid and a reduced rate for the highest earners.

To assist today's retired poor or those who are at risk of retiring on low incomes soon, more immediate targeting could be achieved on the basis of income or age. Some form of Minimum Pension Guarantee could be introduced, targeting increases on those who retire on the lowest incomes. It would be more effective than another campaign to secure higher take-up of means-tested benefits. Government should also consider the case for a late endowment to the over-75s who had no opportunity to benefit from SERPS and Home Responsibilities Protection. This could be a one-off payment to include the oldest and poorest pensioners.

We are unlikely to make progress towards an improved first-tier pensions unless we also recognise the need to restore confidence in second-tier pensions. They are designed to redistribute income across the individual's lifetime rather than from higher to lower income groups. Lower earners are therefore likely to earn a lower second pension although there is considerable scope to improve the return on low contributions through much-reduced administration costs. The link between second-tier contributions and benefits must be clarified: contributors have to feel that their own savings are secure and that others are making an effort to save for their own retirement in line with their capacity to do so (rather than their willingness).

Second-Tier Pensions

There are two key tasks of any sustainable pensions reform. It must address the problem of uneven access to a decent second pension, and encourage a higher savings rate. SERPS was designed to include employees with low and irregular earnings. However, it has been hollowed out by reductions in the value of benefits. Those employees who remain in SERPS are most likely to be low-paid, part-time women workers. The benefits they can expect are unlikely to be enough to float them free of means-testing in retirement. Any case for closing SERPS cannot be made simply on the grounds of cost since existing commitments will still have to be paid out in forty years. But there is a convincing case for closing SERPS for the under-50s if a better value alternative can be found. A National Savings Pension Plan might be the natural successor to SERPS combining security with low costs for those on lower incomes.

Less than half the workforce are in an occupational scheme. Many of the others are contributing only to SERPS or making sufficient contributions to a personal pension. Around four in ten employees are therefore on course for an inadequate second pension if they qualify for one at all. There is evidence of a clear gap between expected retirement incomes and current patterns of saving.

Continuing to rely on voluntary encouragement to take out a pension is unlikely to address the problem. The benefits of funded second pensions should therefore be shared more widely. Nevertheless, if the only contribution to a fund is the contracted-out rebate (worth less than 5% of earnings), the final pension will be wholly inadequate. The savings rate must be raised over time. There are two approaches. One depends on a higher target proportion of earnings - 10% rather than 5% for example - while the other would specify a target amount which would be enough to provide all with a combined retirement income free of means-testing. Once this amount has been saved, it is not clear why the state should require further savings through pensions, although it can encourage further contributions. A fixed contribution rate across working age would bear hardest on young families with the heaviest financial commitments. It should be possible to devise target contribution rates, with 'milestones' after every five years for example, allowing lower levels to be compensated for later. Contribution credits for some groups of the non-employed should be paid by government on an annual basis rather than as a one-off supplement on retirement. Carers and disabled people unable to work would be included. The short-term unemployed need support to find jobs rather than credits to second pensions although some groups of long-term unemployed (especially the over-50s) might qualify for credits in return for other forms of activity to reflect the particular labour market barriers they face. A decision on the value of credits should be taken according to the level of tax relief received by earners. Government should decide how it wishes to support the unpaid work of carers compared to paid work.

Different schemes

Occupational Pensions have traditionally been Final Salary Schemes on a defined benefit basis. They place a premium on length of service and often add discretionary benefits. However they have penalised early leavers and are probably not suited to younger employees who can expect to change job more frequently. Money Purchase pensions usually specify the contribution required rather than the target benefits. Money Purchase pensions receive less in employer contributions than Final Salary schemes and the investment risk is passed to the individual rather than the employer. We should have neither an in principle preference for Final Salary or Money Purchase schemes. Both have a role to play.

In addition, stakeholder pensions could include a new range of Industry Pensions enabling employers to form sectoral or locality-based affinity groups to run pension funds. These would widen choice and lower costs for those who have no access to an occupational scheme. The need for a genuine sharing of the costs and risks of pension schemes between contributors, employers and government must be grasped. As employee contributions increase, employers should also be required to contribute a higher amount to their employees' pension funds.

Regulation

Pension-planning requires a uniquely long-term commitment to secure the full effects of fund growth. Tax relief on contributions should be retained and interest accrued rather than switched to benefits. Its focus should be sharpened however. Tax relief should be available on contributions up to a new fixed sum (perhaps £6,000 a year) and restricted to the basic rate regardless of income tax band. Tax reliefs for high earners are unduly generous set against the minimal support for the low paid. They require support if low contributions are to be 'geared up'. Government should consider targeting relief to the low paid in the form of an Earned Income Pension Credit, paid into their new funded pension accounts. Those earning between £62 (the Lower Earnings Limit) and twice that amount might be eligible.

This reform should be part of a wider review of tax treatment of pensions. Schemes which impose unacceptably high charges and penalise early leavers still receive state subsidies. Tax relief should be earned rather than assumed. Government should therefore instruct the regulator to publish in league-table format a range of accepted performance indicators and agreed targets. Persistently poor performers would lose their status as approved products as long as savers could move to a more secure scheme without penalty.

1. WELFARE TO WORK:

Taxes and Benefits

by Carey Oppenheim

with computer modelling

by Holly Sutherland

Introduction

Welfare to work lies at the heart of the government's strategy for reforming welfare. It encompasses a wide range of policy areas: social security, taxes, education, training, wage levels and job creation. Government initiatives begin from a difficult starting point - many of the socio-economic and policy changes of the last two decades have made entering work more risky. The growth of low wages and insecure jobs, the polarisation between work rich and work poor households, rises in real housing costs, the patchy network of childcare, the growth of the tax burden and extensive means-testing have all acted as important barriers to joining the labour market.

This Chapter begins from first principles. It assesses the extent of the problem - the length of time people are reliant on income support and why they come off benefit; it explores the goals of a welfare to work policy; it identifies the key barriers to paid work and goes on to look at ways of overcoming them by exploring ways of improving incentives in the benefit and tax systems; and the role of an active benefits system more generally.

The Government's Policies on Welfare to Work

The government has committed itself to a number of policies under the aegis of welfare to work. They are:

- *The New Deal for the Young Unemployed* costing some £3.5bn over the lifetime of the Parliament is the major plank of the government's welfare to work strategy. It has a target of getting 250,000 unemployed (six months plus) young people aged 18-24 out of unemployment. All of them will be offered counselling/guidance by Employment Service advisors and independent careers advice as part of the 'gateway' to the New Deal. 'Gateway' is a job preparation phase offering job search, careers advice and guidance, lasting for up to four months. Young people with particular disadvantages or special needs can access the New Deal options without having to wait for six months. A four-pronged programme is on offer: employment in the private/public sector with a wage subsidy of £60 a week, work experience for 'benefits plus' (£15 per week) in the voluntary sector or as part of the Environmental Task Force and access to full-time education/training on an approved course. The first three options require day release for an accredited educational/training qualification and will last for six months on a full-time basis. The fourth may last for up to 12 months. This part of the New Deal is mandatory: sanctions for certain groups who refuse all the options are similar to the current job seekers allowance.[1] At the end of the six months period further guidance and help will be available. A self-employment option will be introduced later in 1998. A follow-through service will monitor the progress of participants and offer further help if they go back to unemployment. Help with childcare will be available either in the form of the childcare disregard for in-work benefits or help with childcare payments/facilities. The programme is being piloted in 12 Pathfinder areas from January 1998 and will be extended nationally in April 1998. The New Deal will be delivered by the Employment Service in partnership with other organisations such as local authorities, TECs/LECs, voluntary organisations and private companies.

- *The New Deal for the Young Unemployed People* is to be extended on a piloted basis to the long-term unemployed (one year plus) aged 25-34 later on in 1998, at a cost of £250m.
- There are two options for the long term unemployed (two years duration plus) aged over 25: either employment in the private sector subsidised by £75 a week or access to an employment-related course leading to an accredited qualification for up to 12 months. Employment Zones, directed towards people who have been unemployed over a year (and aged over 25), are to be set up in five areas. In partnership they must provide 'Neighbourhood Match' (a form of intermediate labour market), Business Enterprise (support for self-employment) and 'Learning for Work'.
- *A New Deal for Lone Parents* will cost an additional £200m. It will be voluntary. Lone parents whose youngest child is in the second term of primary school are to be invited for a job centre interview to develop an individual plan of action to combine job search skills, training and childcare with a personal caseworker.

Lone parents will also have access to the Employment Service Programmes for the Unemployed. They will get fast track family credit and child maintenance payments. This has been piloted in eight parts of the country from July 1997 and extended to the whole country from April 1998. The childcare disregard for those on in-work benefits is raised to £100 for those with two children or more and available until the child is aged 12. A further £150m from the National Lottery will be available to create a network of after-school clubs. The New Deal for the Unemployed will supply 50,000 trained childcare workers over the lifetime of the Parliament to increase childcare support.

- *A New Deal for Disabled People* will encourage disabled people into the workforce at a cost £200m.
- The establishment of a statutory national minimum wage by the Low Pay Commission (possibly with a lower rate for the under-25s).

What is the problem?

There has been extensive documentation and analysis of the scale and growth of poverty in the UK. According to the DSS's latest Households Below Average Income (HBAI) in 1993/94, 10.9 million people below pension age were living below half of average income (after housing costs) - a commonly accepted definition of poverty (DSS, 1996). The composition of the poorest tenth (decile group) of the income distribution provides a useful indicator of the causes of poverty (see table 1.1). The unemployed accounted for 34% of the bottom decile, 'other' (predominantly lone parents not in paid work and the chronically sick and disabled) accounted for 22%, the self-employed for 18% and those in part-time work for 10%. Evidently unemployment is a key cause of poverty, but so too is economic inactivity. Some kinds of work, notably self-employment and part-time employment, do not provide guarantees of escaping poverty.

Table 1.1
Composition of the bottom decile 1993/94
(after housing costs)

Self-employed	18%
Single/couple in full-time work	2%
One in full-time work, one in part-time work	1%
One in full-time work, one not working	5%
One or more in part-time work	10%
Aged 60+	9%
Unemployed	34%
*Other	22%

*includes long-term sick and disabled and non-working lone parents
Source: DSS, Households below average income, a statistical analysis 1979 - 1993/94, London HMSO.

In 1995, 7.7 million people below the age of 60 were living on income support. Looking at patterns of reliance on income support more closely (see table 1.2) shows that lone parents were the largest group, accounting for nearly two-fifths of working age claimants; the unemployed came a close second making up 35% (of those of working age on income support). People with a disability are the most likely to stay on income support for two years or more (70%), closely followed by lone parents (61%).

Table 1.2
Numbers on Income Support below age 60 by group and duration (May 1995) (000s)

	Total numbers	of which children	% recipients on IS for 2 years+
All below aged 60	7,662	3,113	49%
Disabled	1,306	373	70%
Lone Parents	2,983	1,927	61%
Unemployed	2,710	657	33%
Other	663	156	46%

Source: Derived from DSS (1996), Social Security Statistics 1996, HMSO, Tables A2.09 and A2.32

By and large these statistics do not tell us in any detail for how long people are on benefit/low incomes. More recently, research has focused on the dynamics of poverty. This material has an important value in allowing us to look at which groups are likely to move off benefit quickly and the factors that either pull people off or push them on to benefits.

DSS-commissioned research explored the length of time on income support in more depth (Shaw et al, 1996). It found that 40% of income support claimants leave benefit within one year. Certain characteristics are associated with those who are likely to get off benefit quickly. Among the unemployed the following were associated with quick exits from income support: being under 40, white, female, better educational/vocational qualifications, access to a telephone and driving licence and recent previous work experience. By contrast, poor health, language difficulties, having two or more children and being in rented/housing association accommodation all hindered movement off income support for the unemployed. Interestingly, once primary characteristics were taken account of, the length of time on income support had no effect on the likelihood of exiting from benefit for the unemployed. A similar analysis for lone parents showed that those who were over 40, had a driving licence, no pre-school children and lived in areas with relatively low levels of unemployment were more likely to leave income support. Surprisingly, the same research found that educational qualifications and work experience had no significant effect on the chances of leaving income support. They also found that as with the unemployed, duration on income support did not have an effect on exit rates. Both these findings contrast with work by Jenkins (1996) which found that educational qualifications and previous work experience raised the exit rates of lone parents and that there was a duration effect for this group.

Material from the British Household Panel Survey shows that there is considerable movement at the bottom of the income distribution, but it is very often of the revolving door kind - from unemployment to low pay to unemployment again. Although people in poverty do move from the bottom rung of the ladder, a large proportion do not move up very far (see table 1.3). Close to half (43 per cent) of the sample had some experience of a low income over the period - they spent at least one year out of the four in the bottom three deciles. Around 10-

15 per cent of the sample experienced low incomes continuously - they were in the bottom three deciles in all four years. Lone parents and pensioners were least likely to be able to move from the lowest levels of income in contrast to households with someone in employment or self-employment or in receipt of disability benefits. The chances of moving up the income ladder decreases with the length of time spent at the bottom it (this does not control for differences in characteristics).

Table 1.3
Destination of those moving up out of the bottom of the 1991 income distribution for the year 1994

Position in 1994 1991	Those in bottom 10% 30% in 1991	Those in bottom in
Second decile	40%	n/a
Third decile	18%	n/a
Fourth decile	14%	38%
Fifth decile	(8%)	23%
Top five deciles	21%	38%

Source: Households below Average Income, A statistical analysis 1979-1993/94, HMSO, 1996:

This analysis is confirmed by the work of Jenkins and Jarvis (1997). They found that low income 'escapers' were disproportionately childless couples and single adults and that getting a job or a new partner who was in paid work were two important routes out of low income. But the authors highlight the churning of incomes with high proportions of low income escapers finding themselves on 'the down escalator to low income' again. Research on the duration of low pay adds an important dimension to the question of escaping from low income. Gosling et al (1997) found that 68% of people who were low paid in 1991 were still low paid a year later. Women with low qualifications were likely to be low paid over the whole of their working lives. They found that poor education, the employment sector and importantly job tenure (particularly for women) were principal explanations for the persistence of low pay.

    In combination this evidence has a number of important policy implications for welfare to work. First, *individual access to employment and self-employment is a central plank of a strategy to tackle poverty.* Second, *it is crucial to address economic inactivity as well as unemployment* both in terms of benefit incentives and access to programmes for employment preparation, and job search. Third, *the presence of children acts as a barrier to paid work because higher in-work income is needed to cover higher costs, caring tasks have to be organised and it is more difficult to take risks about paid work given greater responsibilities for others.* This suggests that policies for child benefit, flexible childcare and work patterns remain important components of a welfare to work strategy. Fourth, the degree of churning between being out of work and low pay indicates the importance of policies which are focused on the second rung of welfare to work - that is, helping people out of low paid, low skilled, short-term employment, even if this will inevitably be the entry point for some. This will reduce the risks of people finding themselves back on the down escalator to unemployment. Thus, welfare to work needs to encompass policies which are not only about taking the risk of entering paid work but also enable people to move off and beyond in-work benefits. Policies which are geared to improving qualifications, providing access to training for those in low paid work, improving the continuity of paid work (maternity/parental leave are important in this context) and increasing job tenure are all important dimensions of this strategy.

The research also raises questions about the nature of 'dependency'. Explaining why some groups of claimants are on benefit for long periods of time is at the centre of dispute between those who see poverty as rooted in structural/economic explanations, and those who emphasise cultural reasons related to individual lifestyle. Each has different implications for the kinds of solutions that are sought. For example, the former tend to emphasise tax/benefit disincentives - that is, after taking account of withdrawal of benefits, Marginal Tax Rates, work-related costs and housing costs it is not worth working. The latter tend to focus on personal motivation and welfare dependency - that with greater length of time on benefit claimants are less inclined to search for work and take the risk of taking a job. Recent work on lone parents found no evidence for a dependency effect among lone parents (Bryson et al, 1997). Early pregnancy, single parenthood and the length of time spent being a lone parent were not associated with greater likelihood of being a claimant. Neither were young or single lone mothers less inclined to enter paid work. The main barrier restricting entry into paid work was the age of the youngest child. This confirms the work by Shaw et al (1996). The evidence to sustain a 'dependency' thesis is at best uncertain. However, *we do need a more sophisticated notion about the variety of factors which enable people to take paid work which encompasses financial disincentives alongside more tailored help with job search, support on entering work and easing the transition into work.*

The goals of a welfare to work policy

How should we frame the goals of welfare to work policy? Active labour market policies are being pursued in many OECD countries but various goals are embodied in such schemes. It is helpful to clarify the overlapping aims of policy:

- Enabling individuals to move off out-of-work benefits and eventually in-work benefits;
- Tilting labour demand in the direction of disadvantaged groups
- Improving employability;
- Increasing opportunities for individuals to participate in a range of forms of paid work and a range of activities such as education, voluntary work, caring responsibilities, in addition to paid work
- Increasing social inclusion;
- Maintaining a sustainable social security budget.

The most frequently stated aim of a welfare to work strategy is to reduce what has increasingly been called 'welfare dependency' ie, reliance on out-of-work benefits principally income support, job seekers allowance, housing benefit, council tax benefit and passported benefits (such as school meals and prescriptions). In fact the debate tends to be over-simplified - that people who are on benefits are 'dependent', while those who are in work are 'independent' of state subsidy. In reality the entry jobs that the unemployed/economically inactive are likely to enter are predominantly low paid and as a result are often topped up by in-work benefits. *Even with the introduction of a national minimum wage, under our existing social security system, in-work benefits will continue to have an important role.* As Jane Millar puts it:

> For many people the 'choice' is not between earnings
> and independence on the one hand and benefits and
> dependency on the other, but between varying degrees of
> earnings and benefits and other income. (Millar,
> 1994:89)

This is not to say that it makes no difference whether claimants are
reliant on income support or family credit - it clearly does. It is certainly
more desirable that people keep in contact with the labour market and
that their earnings can make some contribution to their overall income.
Moreover, the evidence suggests that claimants prefer to rely on family
credit than income support - the combination of earnings and benefits
appears to be less stigmatising (Ritchie and Morris, 1994).

At the very least a welfare to work programme should help to move
people off out-of-work benefits. However, beyond this limited goal,
*policy needs to focus on both preventing people returning to income
support in the short term and moving people above the first rung of the
labour market ladder, or free of in-work benefits. This is particularly
important if the aim is to reduce exclusion in the long term, rather than
simply to achieve a more efficient process of churning or a reduction in
the number of claimants irrespective of their destination.*

The second and third goals of tilting new job opportunities towards
the disadvantaged and improving employability are central to the
government's New Deal. These are dealt with in other chapters in this
book. The fourth goal is to increase opportunities to both paid work
and other activities. Welfare to work debates in the past have tended
to simplify the work choices that might be available (McLaughlin,
1994). In fact there are a number of choices of paid employment: full-
time/part-time employment, self-employment on a full or part-time
basis, permanent or temporary work, casual or seasonal work. *At the
very least social security and other policies should allow people to
combine a variety of forms of paid work.* For example, many lone
parents choose to work for 16 hours and no more, not only because
of benefit traps but also because it allows them to work a short week
and have more time with their children. *More broadly, welfare to work
policies could encourage other forms of participation such as*

education/training (welfare to learning), voluntary work, caring for children/elderly/sick and disabled. Social security policies would then be concerned with participation rather than a narrowly defined work test (Atkinson, 1995).

A fifth goal is to increase social inclusion. There is ample evidence of the importance of paid work to reduce material hardship and to have benefits which are not solely related to income. Bryson *et al*'s (1997) study of lone parents found that those who had paid work had increased fringe benefits, greater access to credit and access to social networks. It is therefore not surprising that paid work is beneficial for both the psychological health of individuals and communities:

> To be employed is an important part of what it means to be an adult in our society: it means to have an occupational identity with a recognised and valued social role (Jackson, 1994).

The Wise Group Schemes in Glasgow and Newham have a wider agenda on welfare to work, attempting to create intermediate labour markets which combine raising employability with the regeneration of local areas (McGregor et al, 1997). These provide one of the models for the Government's Employment Zones. The long-term unemployed are trained and employed on insulation programmes, rehabilitation of local housing and community safety schemes. Robinson (1997) questions whether such programmes are best carried out by temporary labour and points to the dangers of ghettoising the long term unemployed in marginal parts of the labour market. However, there are important bonuses in such schemes, the local community is involved extensively and there are tangible outcomes from the programmes, not least for the participants whose chances of securing an unsubsidised job thereafter are relatively high. This approach is in tune with the French discussion of this area of policy which describes a transition from passivity to integration, rather than passivity to activity (Evans et al, 1995), embodying a more all-encompassing approach which is not confined to the shortest route to a job. *This broader approach points to the importance of how we evaluate different welfare to work schemes including not only the specific employment outcomes, but also the impact on educational gains, health benefits and community regeneration.*

Finally, welfare to work is looked to as a source of generating social security savings. Gardiner (1997) estimates that a welfare to work programme has the potential to save 18% of the total social security budget. She estimates that for each unemployed person who is in employment for one year there is a saving (in terms of benefits and tax payments) of £5,849. For a non employed person, partner and children the savings are greater – £8,039, and for a lone parent the savings are lower - £2,039 (lone parents are likely to work lower hours, pay less tax and still be reliant on benefit top-ups). Evidence from Australia shows that in the medium term social security savings were achieved, though these were offset by the costs of other parts of the work programme (Saunders, 1995). The two core issues at stake are the sustainability of the social security budget rather than its overall level, and the desirability of this form of spending. The Social Security Select Committee estimates that social security spending will be 11.7% of GDP in 2000/2001, down from 12.6% in 1994/95. However they suggest that 'this is not an indication of the trend rate of social security growth after this period.' This suggests that there is *no 'crisis' looming but that welfare to work is one strategy for containing growth in social security spending.*

Barriers to paid work

The decision to enter paid work is a complex one, especially for those with sole responsibility for children. The barriers which prevent people taking a job range from financial incentives to skills and education, employment opportunities and caring responsibilities. The DSS's *Moving off Income Support: barriers and bridges* (Shaw et al, 1996) pinpoints a range of factors which claimants themselves identify as preventing them from leaving income support (see table 1.4). These factors can be grouped into four areas: incentives, the transition between benefits and work, caring responsibilities and attitudes to working in general (see table 1.5). Policies have to address all four dimensions.

The social security and tax systems have a number of well known disincentives which discourage entry into paid work or increasing the hours and earnings once in work. First, the growth of part-time employment, insecure and casualised work and the rise in low wages has changed the balance of the equation between benefits and work. Beveridge's model of social security is ill-equipped to deal with these changes. The rapid expansion of in-work benefits is a response to the proliferation of low pay, but these benefits come with high MTRs. Inflexible earnings disregards cannot take account of erratic earnings patterns. Second, the polarisation between 'work rich' and 'work poor' households, exacerbated by the rise in means-testing, has made it more difficult for individuals in couples to make separate decisions about entering paid work. (As yet it is not clear what role social security benefits have on the way couples make decisions about work. Research from Australia suggests that other factors such as skills, education and gender roles all play an important part (Saunders, 1994).)

Table 1.4 Factors preventing claimants leaving income support (self-perceptions)

Worries about wages being too low	35%
Amount of council tax	32%
Losing housing benefit/help with mortgage	31%
Passported benefits	27%
Worries about job being temporary	26%
Managing till first pay day	23%
Worries about re-claiming IS after short time	23%
Paying extra costs (work clothes/travel)	21%
Not being fit enough	19%
Cost of childcare	18%
Worries about job not being right	17%
Paying back loans/debts	16%
Not knowing someone to look after children	14%
Not wanting someone else to look after children	12%
Hassle of sorting out benefits	11%
Employer discrimination	11%
Nervous about working	9%
Having enough time to care for elderly/disabled	6%
Waiting for family credit	5%
Waiting for other benefits	4%
Something else (includes no jobs available)	5%
None of these	19%

Source: Shaw et al (1996), Moving off Income Support: Barriers and Bridges, DSS Research Report No.53, London, HMSO.

Table 1.5 Types of barriers to paid work (self-perceptions)

Incentives	Transitions	Attitudes to Work	Caring
Wage levels	Managing to 1st pay day	Not being fit enough	Finding childcare
Council tax	Reclaiming IS	Job not being right	Not wanting childcare
Housing Benefit	Worry about job being temporary	Employer discrimination	Caring for disabled and elderly
Mortgage payments	Loans/debts	Nervous about job	
Passported benefits	Hassle of reclaiming		
Extra work costs	Waiting for FC		
Costs of childcare	Waiting for other benefits		

Source: analysed from Shaw et al (1996), Moving off Income Support: Barriers and Bridges, DSS Research Report No.53, London, HMSO.

Third, the previous government's policy of de-regulating rents and shifting subsidies from bricks and mortar in the public sector to housing benefit have resulted in sharply rising rents, a soaring benefits bill and major barriers to work. Tenants on income support are often unaware of the availability of housing benefit in low paid work and assume that they will have to meet their housing costs in full once in work (Ford et al, 1996). (The DSS no longer publishes statistics for the take-up of housing benefit for those in work.) The conjunction of the extension of owner occupation combined with high unemployment in the mid-eighties and early nineties and a formerly depressed housing market has trapped considerable numbers of home-owners on benefit (in 1995, 0.5m income support claimants received help with their mortgage interest). Some 38% of the unemployed are owner occupiers (Family Resources Survey, 1994/95). Home-owners in low paid work, unlike tenants, receive no help with their housing costs. Recent changes to mortgage interest payments for those on income support (making it much more difficult to re-claim) compound this problem. Table 1.6

shows the unemployment trap for hypothetical owner occupier families. It shows the very high replacement ratios for those on low earnings for both lone parents and couples. This suggests a strong case for a mortgage benefit for low income homebuyers which would target help with housing costs on the basis of need rather than housing tenure. However, this data needs to be qualified by other research which indicates that owner occupiers are most likely to take the risk of entering work as a result of a stronger 'commitment to work'(Ford et al, 1996). It is not clear how far the 'commitment to work' is an indicator of ownership *pe-rse* or a proxy for labour market experience and occupational history.

Table 1.6 Tax-benefit model tables showing replacement ratios for low income owner occupiers

Range of gross earnings per week	Lone parent, 1 child under 5 no childcare costs	Lone parent, 1 child under 5 childcare costs £40	Couple, 2 children under 5 no childcare costs
£50.00	120.4%	256.7%	162.9%
£70.00	99.9%	166.1%	137.8%
£90.00	89.3%	126.2%	125.1%
£110.00	84.8%	105.1%	120.4%
£130.00	81.3%	92.2%	116.7%
£150.00	78.2%	87.9%	113.3%
£170.00	75.3%	84.4%	110.1%
£230.00	60.5%	75.3%	97.3%

Assumptions are made about average mortgage and council tax payments.
Source: House of Commons Hansard, Parliamentary Answer to Malcolm Wicks MP, 29 July 1997.

Fourth, the UK has one of the lowest provisions of publicly-funded childcare in Europe. Public subsidy for childcare has stayed broadly constant throughout the period. Although the previous government introduced help with childcare for those on in-work benefits (now extended by Labour), the childcare disregard provides less help for those on the lowest earnings, especially for owner occupiers. Fifth, while changes to employee national insurance contributions at the bottom end have been positive for work incentives, the tax burden has grown for families with children on average and below average earnings. Other factors are important - the take up of in-work benefits, the loss of passported benefits (school meals and social fund payments can only be received by those on income support) and work and travel costs all act as obstacles to paid work.

The gap between incomes out of and in work is sometimes looked at in a static and oversimplified way. When looking at the benefit/work equation it is helpful to look at three dimensions identified by Millar (1994), the household context, mismatch between labour supply and demand and concepts of income. First, individuals make choices about paid work in the context of their families/households, in particular their caring responsibilities. These responsibilities are reinforced by rules for means-tested benefits, gender roles (which may be more entrenched in particular localities where young men might not even compete for jobs because they are considered 'women's work'), wages and employment conditions. Other members of the family may be a constraint (young children) or a resource - grandparents have been found to be an important source of help in enabling lone parents to get back into paid work (Bryson et al, 1997). Second, there may be a mismatch between labour demand and supply whether in the form of insufficient jobs, inadequate skills or unrealistic wage expectations. Clearly the first two are important and are addressed in Chapter 3. Research shows wage rigidity is not a major barrier to paid work: some groups of claimants take jobs which they know will make them worse off than on benefits. On the whole claimants are flexible both about the types of jobs and the wages they will accept (Shaw et al, 1996). Two additional factors are crucial - ineffective job search (the importance of informal job search/recruitment) and employer attitudes (discrimination against the long term unemployed) (Millar, 1994). Third, different types of income are valued differently both in terms of the kind of benefit and the distinction between wages and income. For example, claimants have more favourable attitudes to family credit than income support; this may be due to the fact that family credit is paid to those in work or it may be a result of the way in which it is assessed as an unchanging weekly payment over six months and is thus less intrusive.

As table 1.4 shows, transitions between benefit and work rank highly in claimants' concerns as they exchange the relative certainty of benefit for the uncertainty of work in today's labour market. Claimants identify the time gap between benefit payment and the first wage packet, the difficulty of re-claiming benefits, concern about the casual/temporary nature of jobs, the administration of in-work benefits and debt. Income support claimants are much more likely to have high levels of arrears; when they go back into paid work, direct deductions from benefit are no longer possible and creditors often change their expectations of repayment.

Caring responsibilities, not surprisingly, are major factors shaping decisions about work, ranging from access to childcare to perceptions about mothering/parenting roles. The way in which such responsibilities affect those decisions are complex - for example Ford (1997) found that while some groups of lone parents put a high premium on their role as mothers and the need for time with their children, this was not fixed and faced with better employment prospects some changed their views about the constraints of looking after children. There is a two-way process with caring responsibilities affecting views of paid work and vice versa. Finally attitudes and feelings about jobs are crucial in moulding decisions - health, the suitability of the job, confidence and issues of discrimination. This points to the important role of mentoring, in-work support and work trials in easing the path into paid work.

Strategies to tackle the barriers to paid work

This section is divided into two parts - the first deals with larger scale reforms to the tax/benefits system which are geared to both tackling disincentives and encouraging wider forms of participation. The second section considers other areas of policy such as easing the transition into work, childcare and the components of an active benefits system.

Large scale reforms to benefits/taxes

We have undertaken computer modelling of three different tax and benefit packages. This work has been carried out by Holly Sutherland at the Micro-simulation Unit, Department of Economics, Cambridge University, using POLIMOD (see Box 1.1 for assumptions used).

Box 1.1 POLIMOD modelling: general assumptions

POLIMOD is based on Family Expenditure Survey micro-data. Although this is a large survey designed to be representative of the UK population, results for small groups in the population may not be statistically reliable. All simulations assume the July 1997 tax-benefit system is in place, although the announced reduction in the rate of MIRAS to 10 per cent is also assumed. The calculations are first-round estimates of the impact of the policy changes that are modelled: no individual behaviour change is modelled.

Take-up assumptions
It is assumed, however, that the take-up of means-tested benefits is incomplete. The modelling assumes a rate (randomly applied) of 62% for family credit, 91% for housing benefit and council tax benefit and 80% for income support (based on DSS estimates). Take-up behaviour is not affected by the policy change. For the 'Wilcox' package take up of mortgage benefit is assumed to be the same as family credit (not only at the same rate - but the same households take-up). Note that Steve Wilcox's original model uses differential take-up according to tenure and assumes that either households take up all benefits or do not take up any. Doing it the way it is done here means that some households take up family credit and not housing benefit (and lose) and others take up housing benefit and not family credit - so the harmonisation does not work exactly.

Distributional assumptions
The distributional results are analysed according to changes in disposable incomes, measured after housing costs. Households are ranked by disposable income equivalised by a scale approximately related to benefit relativities (1 for a single person, 0.6 for additional adults, 0.4 for each dependent child).

Calculated incentives are derived as follows:
Replacement rates - for each individual not in full time education, employment or self-employment or on sickness, disability or invalidity benefit or aged 60+: out-of-work income is replaced by earnings at one of 3 (or 4) fixed levels. Household disposable income is re-calculated, taking account of changes for each such individual in the household.
RR=income out of work/income in work x 100
Marginal tax rates (MTRs) – for each individual with any earnings, re-calculate household income in the basis that earnings increase by £1 per week.

$$MTR= (1-(Y+1-Y)) \times 100$$

Box 1.2 Tax and Benefit Packages

The Wilcox/Simplifying in–work means–tested benefits package
- increase lone parent and couple earnings disregards in housing benefit and council tax benefit by £30. Total couple disregard can be split £20/£20 between a couple.
- mortgage benefit: 100% of first £80 of mortgage interest per week plus 50% of next £80, included on the same basis as rent
- harmonising family credit and housing benefit:

FC taper increased to		80%
FC starting point:		£62.00
FC allowances:	couple	£37.10
	couple (18)	£22.30
	lone parent	£36.55
	one parent (18)	£28.25
	child 0-10	£13.50
	child 11-15	£19.80
	child 16+	£23.70
HB additional earnings disregards:	household + 1 child	£21.75
	additional children	£ 9.00
FC extra needs for non-householders		£20.00

- two versions are run – a revenue neutral one when MIRAS is reduced from 10% to 2.9%; without the MIRAS changes, the package costs £1.23 billion.

Non means-tested benefits package
- minimum wage (£3.50 per hour) increases tax threshold by £185 per year (same threshold for everyone)
- Additional Personal Allowance/Married Couple's Allowance abolished and revenue for CB for 0-4s increase by £16.50 per week

- MIRAS reduced from 10-5% to fund reduction in social rents of 20%

Participation Income package
- £20 per week per adult to individuals who satisfy the following participation conditions:
- work as employee/self-employed minimum 8 hours (if they do not qualify on other grounds)
- pension age
- inability to work because of disability
- unemployment but available for work
- engaging in approved education/training course
- caring for young, elderly, disabled dependents
- approved forms of voluntary work
- 16-18 year olds at school get £11 education maintenance allowance (+ £9 child benefit)
- abolish personal tax allowances except residual age allowances
- count participation income for family credit, council tax benefit, housing benefit and income support
- abolish MIRAS
- remove national insurance ceiling on Class 1 and Class 4 contributions for self-employed

The first package is a simplification and integration of in-work means-tested benefits including a low income mortgage benefit. The second is a non means-tested approach which reduces social rents, increases child benefit, raises the tax threshold and introduces a minimum wage. The third models a participation income alongside the existing national insurance scheme (Box 1.2 describes each package in detail). Each package raises taxes (though not income tax rates) and/or national insurance to pay for the changes. The analysis shows the distributional effects of the packages and changes in MTRs and replacement ratios (see Appendix for relevant tables). However, the analysis does not show the behavioural effects of such changes, simply the broad direction of incentives. This is particularly limiting in relation to participation income which we discuss below. The components of each package are described in detail, the results analysed and the arguments for and against them explored. In addition, two other reforms are explored (although not modelled on the computer) - Earned Income Tax Credits and merging income support and family credit. All the packages are assessed with the goals of a welfare to work strategy in mind.

'Wilcox' or Simplifying in-work benefits packages
This package builds on work completed by Steven Wilcox for the Council of Mortgage Lenders (1997). It attempts to simplify and integrate in-work benefits by increasing earnings disregards, introducing individual disregards for men and women in couples, establishing a common threshold, allowances and taper for family credit and housing benefit and introducing a mortgage benefit for those on low incomes (the components are described in Box 1.2). The changes are financed by a reduction in MIRAS. This is a small scale change focused on the working poor unlike the other packages that are modelled. In the Appendix, table A shows gains of 5.7% of weekly equivalised income for the bottom decile and 2% in the second decile with small losses in the top five deciles from the reduction in MIRAS. Only 4% gain (highlighting that this is a small scale change), 56% experience no change and 40% lose, principally from the change to MIRAS (Appendix table B). The average replacement ratio falls by small amounts (between 1 and 3.5 percentage points) for all family types apart from couples with children and a full time employee (see Appendix table C). While overall MTRs rise very slightly from 30.8% to 31.9%) principally as a result of the introduction of a mortgage benefit) there is an average fall of 5.2 percentage points for those with marginal rates of more than 60% (Appendix table D). The changes result in an increase of 1.2 million people on means-tested benefits and a shift from those reliant on family credit to housing benefit (see Appendix table E). However, the intention is that family credit and housing benefit in effect become one benefit with the result that both the payment period of benefit (family credit is a fixed payment for six months, unlike housing benefit) and the administration would have to be entirely re-thought.

The measures by and large move incentives in the right direction at a relatively small cost - £1.23 bn - in spite of having to raise taxes.[2]

The cost would be smaller if people respond positively to the financial incentives. The introduction of a mortgage benefit for those on low income addresses the financial disincentive identified earlier. It would also allow greater experimentation with paid work without risking the loss of all help with mortgage payments and potentially possession of a home. These arguments have to be set alongside the evidence which suggests that some owner occupiers override better-off calculations and go into paid work. An important question is how far the merging of family credit and housing benefit would actually clarify decisions about paid work for claimants. Certainly, the higher disregards, the division of the disregard between men and women in couples and a unified benefit with a common taper should make the operation of the benefits more transparent and hence convey a clear message that people are better off in work. It should also increase the take-up of a single in-work benefit. However, the impact of small changes in MTRs on behaviour is less clear cut. Few people calculate their family credit with any accuracy, despite the fact that it has a single taper (Marsh and McKay, 1993). This may be partly due to the interaction with housing benefit and council tax benefit, which would be simplified by the Wilcox reform, or it may be that too many factors are at play when decisions about work are taken and that the taper is only a fairly minor barrier. The payment period of housing benefit would have to be considered - there is a strong case for a six month payment period as with family credit for administrative ease and providing a cushion for claimants.[3] However, six monthly payments also obscure the impact of changing hours/rates of pay as the benefit remains unchanged. The policy changes allow useful improvements within the confines of means-tested benefits. The disadvantage is that they increase the numbers on means-tested benefits, bringing more into a longer but shallower poverty trap.

The Non-means-tested package
This is a non-means-tested approach to welfare to work which introduces a minimum wage, a rise in tax thresholds, increases in child benefit for the under 5s (as this is a time of high costs, if childcare is included, and lower family earnings) and reduces social rents, financed by reductions in tax reliefs/allowances (the components are described

in Box 1.2). The package is progressive with gains of 9% of weekly equivalised household income for the bottom decile and around 3% for each of the second and third decile groups (see Appendix table G). There are small losses in the top two deciles of 0.3% of weekly household income. Appendix table H shows that overall 33% gain, 27% experience no change and 40% lose (by small amounts). A fourth assumption was added to the replacement ratios - which shows the effect of a minimum wage (assumption of in-work wage of £2.50 per hour for 30 hours before the policy change and £3.50 per hour for 30 hours after the policy change). Appendix table I shows small decreases in replacement ratios for all family types on the first three assumptions and more marked reductions on the fourth assumption (mean reductions of between 4.5 and 6.0 percentage points) capturing the critical importance of a minimum wage in a welfare to work package. While the overall average MTR rises very slightly from 30.8 to 31.0 there is an average fall for those with high MTRs (60% +) of 11.5 percentage points. The changes in MTRs show substantial improvements for couples with children (Appendix table J). This is reflected in the drop in the number of means-tested benefits of some 422,000. The numbers of family credit payments decreases by 12% because of the rise in child benefit (Appendix table K).

The changes highlight some important points of discussion; we pick out four issues: the changes in tax threshold, minimum wage, housing costs and child benefit reforms. First, the tax change modelled was a very modest rise in the tax threshold for all taxpayers of £185 per year. This measure has an almost insignificant impact on MTRs. The government's proposal for a starting rate of income tax of 10% was criticised as having little effect on those with the highest MTRs in the lower part of the income distribution. Increasing tax thresholds was proposed as an alternative (IFS, 1997). In fact, neither are particularly effective ways of dealing with the problem of high MTRs for low earners. Strategies to help this group either have to reduce the tapers for means-tested benefits, increase earnings disregards or lift claimants out of means-testing by increasing non-means-tested benefits or earnings. Second, the introduction of a minimum wage of £3.50 raises some £834m (this takes no account of possible employment reductions). Setting a minimum wage at the lower end of the range has the disadvantage of leaving those who are working only 16 hours below the lower earnings threshold for national insurance contributions (Sutherland, 1997). It would therefore have the long-term effect of excluding those people from entitlement to national insurance benefits and thereby increasing means-testing. Policy options should either raise the level of minimum wage slightly or look at ways of crediting in the low paid to the national insurance scheme.

Third, the reduction of MIRAS to finance lower social rents substantially reduces spending on housing benefit (by 20%) and has a modest effect on housing benefit claims (a drop of 6%) (see table K). The policy dilemma is whether to adopt this broad brush approach which benefits all (pensioners as well as the working age population) from a reduction in social rents or a more targeted one which either reduces tapers or raises earnings disregards (Giles et al, 1996). Fourth, child benefit has been consistently identified as an important tool in bridging the gap between welfare and work. The reform here concentrates all the resources on children under 5 (a rise of £16.50) as a time when earnings are likely to be lowest and costs high. The payment could be seen as either help with childcare or replacing lost earnings. Other options on child benefit might include a childcare payment for young children for those entering paid work, education, training, voluntary activity (this would particularly benefit lone parents as the age of youngest child is a key factor affecting lone parents' lower employment rates) or taxing it back from richer families (top third) to finance higher benefit for the less affluent two thirds (see p50 for discussion of child tax credits).

Participation Income
This third package builds on work by Atkinson and Sutherland (1995). It introduces a flat rate participation income of £20 a week for recognised activities alongside the national insurance scheme, financed by the abolition of personal tax allowances, MIRAS and rises in national insurance contributions (the details are described in Box 1.2). As can be seen from Table M the changes are highly progressive - the bottom decile group gaining 31% of average equivalised household income, the second decile group 9.5% and the third 5.4%. There are losses at the top of the income distribution - an average loss of 5.3% of weekly equivalised household income for the top decile group.

Overall, 36% lose from the changes, 6% experience no change and 58% gain (Appendix table N). The replacement ratios show small rises on all three assumptions by 0.8 percentage points for those working 16 hours, 2.0 percentage points for those working 30 hours and 2.1 for those working 40 hours (see Appendix table O). The reason for the rise is that the policy changes are not aimed at increasing the gap in incomes between in work and out of work as participation income is paid to those who are out of work (provided they are available for work) as well as to those who are in work. In addition, as an individually based benefit some members of households will get a benefit (for example, non-working spouses) they will not have received before the policy change. Whether participation income will in fact increase disincentives to work is discussed below. Table P shows that average MTRs go up by 4.7 percentage points as a result of the substantial tax changes, but for those with the highest MTRs (60% or more) they fall on average by 5.7 percentage points. The largest average falls in MTRs are for couples with children and for single people without children (a high proportion of these are pensioners). Appendix table Q shows substantially lower spending on means-tested benefits, in the region of £4.4 bn, and around 2.3 million fewer claims. The reduction in means-testing is in fact focused on income support fewer claims and particularly on pensioners. It would be possible to run a revised version of participation income which excluded pensioners from receiving a participation income (and retained the age allowances) and focused higher payments on those of working age. The package also introduces a payment of £11 (on top of £9 child benefit) for all 16 to 18 year olds who stay at school, building on Labour's proposals for reforming child benefit for this age group, though doing this on a non means-tested basis (one criticism of this approach is that there would be a large element of deadweight costs).

Participation income was proposed as a fall-back option by the Commission on Social Justice. It has recently been explored in more depth by Atkinson (1995). The case for a participation income to run alongside national insurance benefits has a number of strengths. First, in many respects it is much better suited to changing labour market patterns which have characterised the last decade and a half. It allows much greater choice about the hours of work. Flexibility about working fewer hours is an important factor in increasing the chances of moving into paid work (White *et al*, 1997). Part-time work remains an important way of allowing parents to combine childcare and paid work, to maintain contact with the labour market and provide a buffer for women in particular from divorce and separation. As a non-means-tested payment, it would bring illegitimate earnings into the formal economy as there will be much less incentive for people to hide their earnings. This regularising of the shadow economy should potentially generate more tax revenue. As an individually based benefit it allows more independent work choices for men and women helping to tackle the work rich/work poor divide. By dramatically reducing means-testing it allows people to take greater risks about entering paid work or adding hours as a substantial component of benefit income is not withdrawn. Participation income can be seen as providing the social underpinning for flexibility in today's labour market.

Second, participation income permits a broader definition of participation than paid work alone, endorsing a wider range of desirable activities. It builds upon aspects of the New Deal which pay 'benefits plus' while claimants undertake education or participate in the voluntary sector. By introducing conditions of entitlement - albeit much broader conditions than paid work alone – it is likely to carry greater legitimacy than proposals for an unconditional basic income. Participation income embodies a principle of reciprocity – the right to an income in return for the responsibility of contributing to society as a whole in a number of recognised ways. It thereby endorses a notion of active citizenship. It is of course possible to draw the boundaries of participation income more or less broadly than chosen in this particular version. For example, the definition of caring for a child full-time as participation could continue until the youngest child is at school full-time, thereafter the parent would have to participate in some other activity, or availability for work could be re-shaped along the lines of the New Deal. Third, the continuation of national insurance contributions and benefits maintains the contributory principle which still carries legitimacy and is an acceptable form of taxation. Proposals for participation income are consistent with improvements to national insurance benefits, such as crediting in the low paid and extending coverage to new risks such as residential care.

However, participation income does come with some important draw-backs. It is a substantial change to the tax and benefit system;

such large changes clearly carry more political dangers than fiddling around the edges of the tax/benefit system. One approach is to move to a participation income slowly by staging reforms that would move in that direction. The increase in replacement ratios raises the question of the impact of a more extensive flat rate payment on decisions to enter work. Participation income blurs the distinction between paying benefits largely for those outside employment and paid work (as does the more narrowly focused reform which proposes the merging of income support and family credit). While this distinction is not as clear cut as it once was, the behavioural impact is uncertain. As suggested above a participation income should encourage more people to experiment with paid work and declare earnings, however for some groups with caring responsibilities (particularly women) it might weigh in the other direction. While policies should support a variety of forms of participation, clearly enough people need to enter paid work. The rise in average MTRs (by five percentage points) also touches on a criticism frequently levelled at basic income - paying a much more extensive benefit comes with the cost of raising disincentives for the working population as a whole (Clinton et al, 1994). The question of what tax rise is acceptable for what level of participation income is clearly a political one, making decisions about redistribution highly transparent. This is in direct contrast to the proposals for Earned Income Tax Credits, where it is precisely *the lack of transparency* about payments to those on low incomes which is regarded as attractive in policy terms.

The measure also raise a number of tricky administrative issues: the taxing of small amounts of earnings, the definition, monitoring and enforcement of a broader range of activities. The job seeker's contract relies partly on a test of not undertaking certain activities - earnings and hours limits – and partly on a test of completing job search activities. A test of participation would move firmly in the direction of the latter, though more broadly defined - that is, it has to test whether people are actually undertaking a course, or looking after a sick/disabled person, for example. This is a more difficult test than the one currently in operation. Administrative costs would continue to be substantial despite the reduction of means-testing as three systems would continue to be in operation - participation income, means-tested benefits and the national insurance scheme. Finally, there remains the question of transparency - while the numbers on means-tested benefits decrease dramatically, many people remain on participation income with a smaller top-up of means-tested benefits or national insurance benefits. How clear will it be to claimants with combinations of benefit what they can earn and against which benefit it counts? The payment method becomes crucial: if paid like child benefit then it should be clear that this is a benefit that can be simply carried into paid work/education/voluntary work.

Earned Income Tax Credits

The Chancellor of the Exchequer's Pre-Budget Report has signalled the introduction of tax-credits for families. Earned Income Tax Credits (EITCs) were introduced in the US in 1975, and have been increased and extended under President Clinton's welfare to work programme, providing tax credits for the low waged. For a family with two or more children EITCs provide a credit of 40% of earnings up to $9,000, a flat rate credit for earnings between $9,000 and $11,000, it is then withdrawn at a rate of 21% up to a maximum of around $29,000. Tax credits thus increase as earnings rise to the $9,000 ceiling. In this sense they differ from a negative income tax or family credit which are withdrawn as earnings increase. The incentive to earn more, up to a given limit, is built into the scheme (the disadvantage of course is that it gives less help to the very lowest earners). Annual tax assessments have to be filled in by all taxpayers and the credits are usually received as a lump sum at the end of the tax year. However, there is an advance payment option where the credit can be received on a more regular basis through the pay packet.

Below we consider the advantages and disadvantages of EITCs, drawing on work by Meadows (1997) and Walker and Wiseman (1997). We go on to look briefly at proposals for introducing a child tax credit.

Advantages of EITCs

● Likely to have higher take-up rates among the low paid than family credit as the tax system doesn't carry the stigma of the benefit system. Automatic payment on a regular basis through the pay packet would also increase take-up;

- Increase the economic security of the low-paid while moving them largely out of the benefit system (housing benefit would continue);
- May encourage more people to enter paid work or increase their earnings/hours of work, depending on perceptions of scheme and withdrawal rates (in fact in the US in combination with food stamps, EITCs create a significant poverty trap at higher earnings (Walker and Wiseman, 1997);
- Carry the political advantage of being able to raise the incomes of the low paid through more popular tax cuts than less popular benefit rises, giving the government more room to improve the incomes of low earners (although if based on the US system, EITCs count almost entirely as benefit expenditure).

Disadvantages of EITCs

- Entail considerable administrative complexity in terms of the new information needed (rents, children, family circumstances) for tax purposes. It is likely to be more difficult to maintain the tax credit payment if the claimant moves employers, unlike the current family credit payment;
- Raise difficult issues about which body would administer the tax credits. Employers are unlikely to want to collect such detailed information; it may make relations between employer and employee strained and possibly increase the stigma if information is collected only for workers within certain earnings bands (there are difficulties currently in collecting evidence about earnings from some employers for family credit purposes). Inland Revenue or DSS could do the assessments and then employers act as agents as they do now, but both would involve some additional complexity for firms. A major source of opposition to the proposal to pay family credit through the wage packet as part of the Fowler reforms in the 1980s came from small employers (as well as from the poverty and women's lobby);
- Their role in subsidising wages and distorting recruitment decisions becomes more transparent than family credit if administered by employers, leaving open the possibility of employers taking unfair advantage of the scheme;

- Benefit a small minority of wage earners (especially those who are not currently claiming family credit), but would involve the tax system becoming more complicated for all tax payers;
- Would involve a return to joint taxation.[4] *One important advantage of joint taxation that is not specific to welfare to work issues is that it gives policy makers a non-stigmatising tool to relate benefits to income without means-testing.* However, this advantage has to be weighed against a number of disadvantages: i) the difficulty of dealing with cohabiting couples under joint taxation. Administering a cohabitation rule is difficult enough for the much smaller numbers of benefit claimants let alone for the population at large (though in Canada couples are counted as cohabiting if they were living together for one year previously); ii) a joint taxation system becomes more difficult to administer in the context of much greater fluidity in relationships; iii) one of the arguments for individual taxation was the question of autonomy for women in managing their own tax affairs. Joint taxation would clearly compromise this, though a system of a jointly signed tax return would at least imply some equality in how tax affairs were managed;
- Are primarily delivered through lump sum end of year payments in the US. This means that, unlike family credit, they are not geared to weekly needs and therefore are not an obvious incentive to enter paid work. In addition as the US tax system is not cumulative EITCs are even less transparent as they may be part of an end of year tax adjustment. This suggests that *they do not send a clear or specific signal about the benefits of working;*
- Reduce clarity for people contemplating entry into work. An unemployed person would have to think about their net earnings when doing a better-off in work calculation. (Similar difficulties apply to the topping up of earnings by family credit when claimants may fail to distinguish between their gross wage and their likely total income.) *While there are good political reasons for less visibility for payments to those on low income, there is a strong case for maximising visibility in relation to welfare to work;*
- Delivery through the wage packet would result in all probability in credits going directly to the main wage-earner who is more likely to be a man among couples.[5] In households where income

is not shared fairly, mothers and children would not benefit to the same extent from the credit. There might as a result be unintended detrimental effects on children, as women tend to spend a greater proportion of their own income on children than men. However this objection has be weighed against the likelihood that more families overall would be receiving the credit and that payment through the wage packet makes the work incentive element of the credit more obvious than if paid to another member of the household.[6] There is a tension between policy goals, as highlighted very clearly by Pamela Meadows:

> One issue that must be confronted is whether the objective is to improve the well-being of the worker (in which case the pay packet may be the appropriate vehicle) or to improve the well-being of the family (in which case payment directly to the mother is the answer). (Evidence submitted to the Social Security Committee *Tax and Benefits: an interim report, 1997*).

- May be more open to abuse. There is evidence from the US of considerable degree of fraudulent EITC payments (around 10%).

Alternative proposals for introducing a child tax credit rather than a US type model have also been floated. It would be possible to combine the element of support for children from income support/job seeker's allowance, family credit and child benefit into a uniform child tax credit for all those with families (along the lines of the Australian and Canadian schemes). The proposal has some advantages: it creates a uniform and coherent system of child support for those in and out of work; it allows the possibility of clawing back the tax credit from higher earners, without the disadvantage of a means-test, offering the possibility of higher levels of support for families on middle and lower incomes; and if paid to the main carer it would tend to direct resources to women in unemployed couples where the claimant is usually the man in the current system. (The proposal would require annual tax assessments which would be a significant additional administrative burden.) There are some important guarantees for any such scheme: the child tax credit should go to the main carer, be paid on a regular basis (at least monthly) and individual taxation should be compromised as little as possible (joint assessment only in relation to children's needs). This proposal represents one strategy for rationalising financial support for children and a way of re-directing resources from more affluent families with children to those on middle and lower incomes. As such it represents a general contribution to a welfare to work strategy by targeting extra resources to middle and lower income families, who find it more difficult to enter paid work. However, it is only one element of a welfare to work programme which would still need to address the coherence of in-work benefits, housing costs and the transitions between benefits and paid work.

Merging Income Support/Job Seeker's Allowance and Family Credit
An alternative reform proposed by the 1997 Liberal Democrat Manifesto, the Commission on Social Justice (in the context of a residual role for means-testing) and Loughborough's Centre for Research in Social Policy (Walker and Wiseman, 1997) is to merge income support/job seeker's allowance and family credit. This would follow the pattern of many European countries where in and out of work benefits are more unified (although the UK has a particularly extensive system of in-work benefits). The advantage of this measure is that it is focused on the transitional difficulties involved in taking the plunge into paid work pinpointed earlier. Claimants could enter paid work of different hours without endangering the security of their benefit. Earnings disregards and tapers could be smoothed to allow incentives to increase hours and earnings step by step. It would also have the advantage of unifying job search, placement, career development, wage supplementation and the safety-net in one place (Walker and Wiseman, 1997). If the proposal were linked to a broader conception of participation rather than paid work alone (as is proposed in the New Deal for specific groups) it becomes more attractive - thus the benefit becomes a platform for claimants to enhance their labour market skills, education, training, caring responsibilities and voluntary work. However, there are some difficulties with the proposal:

- The present six month fixed payment of family credit is an important strength in terms of administrative simplicity and reducing the intrusiveness to claimants (although there are some losers); it would be difficult to have a similar fixed period for the out-of-work component of the benefit - claimants on income support/job seeker's allowance are on such low levels of income that they cannot cope with falls in their benefit - hence the need for a benefit that is more immediately responsive. (A compromise payment period of three months would require higher benefit payments to cope with falls in income/changes of circumstances (see endnote 5)). If there was no fixed payment period it is not clear how much difference such a change would make to claimants on the ground as they would still need to inform the local benefits agency whenever there was a change of earnings/circumstances (though they would not have to actually come off the benefit).

- The danger is that by merging out-of-work and in-work benefits the signals about the advantages of paid work are less distinct (the same issue arises in relation to participation income).[7]
- The transitional difficulties of moving between income support and work can be tackled by administrative changes, for example income support extensions (see Box 1.3), but these are extremely complex.
- Income support/Job seeker's allowance are usually paid to the wage earner (more often the man) and family credit to the care (more often the woman). While dividing the means-tested payment between members of a couple is an attractive approach, in families where the woman has previously taken responsibility for budgeting, such a move could result in a reduction in the living standards for the family.
- It would lead to an extension of means-testing if there was an attempt to tackle the steep MTRs through raising earnings disregards and/or changing tapers.

An assessment of the five approaches to tax/benefit reform and welfare to work
The five approaches to reform are evaluated against the goals of a welfare to work programme (see table 1.7). The cost of the three computer-modelled packages is met by reducing or abolishing tax allowances/reliefs and in the case of participation income by raising

national insurance contributions. *There remains a strong case for redirecting fiscal welfare in a more progressive fashion whether through benefits or tax credits.* On their own, these measures would clearly raise the social security budget which the government is committed to reducing in the long term. However, if the changes encourage labour market participation then short term costs will eventually reap future savings. An alternative (though not painless) strategy is to find savings elsewhere in the social security budget. One possible route for consideration is the introduction of affluence tests via the taxation system to re-coup money from the top 25% for the majority. This allows some form of income-relation without means-testing.[8] Changes in replacement ratios and MTRs were looked at for the three computer-modelled packages. However, it is important to be wary of reading off changes in behaviour from those shifts in incentives; rather they suggest the potential for movement.

The Government has indicated that it favours some form of Earned Income Tax Credit. Its principal advantage would be its political appeal: it provides one useful tool of directing income to the low earners which may have greater public support than benefits. While it is possible to overcome some of the disadvantages in relation to joint taxation and payment to the carer, there is little convincing evidence that it is a particularly effective welfare to work strategy over and above the existing family credit. The disadvantages of administrative complexity, lack of transparency, uncertainty over who the credit should be paid to and fraud outweigh the advantages. However, a child tax credit (which is geared to broader policy aims than welfare to work alone) does offer useful possibilities and should be further considered.

The case for participation income has a strong theoretical appeal, particularly if the labour market continues to generate part-time, casual and temporary jobs. Such a reform represents a fundamental shift in how we define participation and the ways in which the tax/benefit system interact. It would be possible to model a participation income for the working age population which would be more focused than the one explored here or to draw the conditions for participation more tightly. Further work needs to be done on the impact of a participation income on employment behaviour, administration and implementation issues. However, in the context of apparent public tax resistance/ambiguity, the highly transparent form of redistribution

- increased child benefit/child tax credit for those on middle and low incomes
- lower social rents
- higher and separate earnings disregards for men and women in couples
- the integration of in-work benefits
- the merging of out-of work and in-work benefits
- entitlement to an integrated means-tested benefit resting on a broader definition of participation encompassing both full and part-time paid work, training, education, caring responsibilities for young children, elderly, sick and disabled people and volunteering.

Small-scale reforms to taxes/benefits

This section deals with a number of other welfare to work policy changes: easing the transition into paid work, childcare reforms and the ways in which benefit delivery can enhance labour market attachment.

Transitions

There are a number of other changes to the social security system recommended as short-term measures which cannot be modelled on POLIMOD. These changes are geared in particular to coping with the transitions between benefit and paid work. They are drawn from a number of sources : the Commission on Social Justice, the Rowntree Inquiry into Income and Wealth, Frank Field MP's work and in particular a recent report by the National Association of Citizens Advice Bureaux (Allbeson, 1997). Box 1.3 outlines the main proposals - they include more flexible earnings disregards for those in paid work, allowing members of a couple greater flexibility about independent choices about paid work, bridging payments between benefit and work, extending help for the costs of starting work, direct deductions from family credit for debts and developing low interest credit facilities, quicker re-entitlement to benefit to enable people to experiment with employment without risking all their security.

The issue of the level of benefits is now largely off the political agenda (with the exception of Peter Mandelson MP's recent mention of improving benefit levels in limited circumstances when resources allow). In fact meagre benefit levels do not help people into paid work (quite apart from considerations of social justice). Claimants who have some savings are more likely to be able to experiment with paid work without risking all (McLaughlin, 1994) and lone mothers who experience hardship are less likely to get jobs at a later stage (Bryson et al, 1997). An analysis of the level of benefits and how people use them as a springboard back into work should be part of any welfare to work programme.

Box 1.3 Short term improvements to social security to bridge gap between benefit and work

Earnings disregards	More flexible earnings disregards/roll ups for those in work
	Earnings disregards for in-work benefits to be indexed with rises in earnings
Separate decisions about work transitions	Earnings disregard for partners for in-work benefits
	Abolition of working hours rule for working partners of claimants getting income support/job seeker's allowance
	Income support for mortgage payers to be extended for 4 weeks once work is found
	Income support/job seeker's allowance paid to newly employed till first wage payment
	Re-entitlement to (contributory) job seeker's allowance after 12 weeks contributions
	Free school meals for family credit claimants
Starting work costs	Job start loan for initial expenses of starting work
	Job finders grant to be available to lone parents/spouses as well as long term unemployed
Maintenance	Child support guarantee for family credit
	Child support disregard for income support/job seeker's allowance with a higher disregard in family credit
Managing debt	Direct deductions from family credit
	The development of low interest credit facilities for those on low incomes
Administration	Six month assessments for housing benefit and council tax benefit
	Faster processing
	Improved take-up of benefit, in particular in-work benefits, using computer technology

Childcare proposals

The cost, accessibility and flexibility of childcare has been identified as an important barrier to paid work, especially for lone parents. The government is keen to address the childcare deficit and has proposed an extension of the childcare disregard, funding to provide a national network of after-school clubs and training for young people as nursery care workers. These are important starting points. *The aim of policy should be to increase both the level of informal and formal childcare.*

In the UK informal childcare arrangements predominate. In part this is an outcome of low levels of provision in the UK, but it is also likely to reflect some degree of parental preference for partners, relatives and friends to look after children. Currently only parents using registered childminders/childcare organisations can qualify for the childcare disregard. While regulating the quality of childcare is essential, payments should be more flexible. Nottingham City Challenge introduced a childcare voucher for low income families which could be paid to grandparents/close relatives in recognition of informal care, particularly among some ethnic minority communities. This strategy is also a way of transferring money to low paid female pensioners and a recognition of the importance of other family members in providing resources (financial and time) to enable parents to enter paid work. Careful monitoring of informal arrangements would have to be introduced alongside such a measure.

The childcare disregard is currently only available for people entering paid work. *There is a good case for providing some form of childcare payments for lone parents/spouses who are undertaking education and training courses as part of the New Deal for lone parents.* Finally, consideration should be given to proposals for childcare vouchers for those below nursery age (this would distinguish them from the former government's ill-judged scheme) with a generous affluence test along the lines suggested by the IFS (Duncan *et al*, 1996). The resources from the married couples allowance could be wholly or in part earmarked for such a measure. Such an initiative would be an important improvement on existing provision and would also allow flexibility about the choice of provider.

Policies which are geared to increasing flexibility of hours, work-sharing, parental leave, term-time contracts for men as well as women are an important accompaniment of a childcare strategy. The development of tax incentives, national insurance relief or business rates relief for employers who provide more flexible employment arrangements for parents should be explored as one means of encouraging such schemes. Another approach might include the development of employer consortia for small and medium enterprises to pool initiatives in this area.

How the benefit system can enhance labour market attachment

The New Deal is specifically geared to enhancing labour market attachment most directly through the employer subsidy, but also through the voluntary, environmental and educational options. Here additional initiatives are suggested. Finding ways of increasing the contact between the unemployed/economically inactive and those in paid work is an important way of widening job search and maintaining contact with the world of work. Recent work by Demos (Perri 6, 1997) illustrates the importance of 'weak' network links to extend contacts in the labour market. Recent research by PSI (White et al, 1997) found that the Work Trial programme, which places job-ready unemployed people (6 months duration) for three weeks with an employer increases the chances of securing employment by five times. The aim of the programme is to counter employer prejudice against the unemployed, decrease the costs and efforts of employer recruitment and increase confidence of the claimant who is placed directly in work without the barrier of an interview. *We recommend the extension of Work Trials to larger numbers and that they should also include lone parents/spouses.* The same research found that Job Clubs and the Job Interview Guarantee increased employment chances for women by two and two and half times respectively, though these jobs were temporary. Interestingly, it had no significant improvement on male participation apart from men without a qualification whose chances were improved by 1.7 times. *Job Clubs and Job Interview Guarantee schemes should be more focused on men without or with low qualifications and extended to lone parents and spouses given the evidence about the impact on women's employment chances.*

Denmark introduced far-reaching active labour market policies in the early 1990s which contained an element of job rotation placing long term unemployed in jobs vacated by those taking parental/educational/sabbatical leave (Bewick, 1996). While the Danish scheme is expensive, paying the 'rate for the job', it does provide us with some clues for policy. Consideration should be given to exploring the possibility of combining the encouragement of parental/educational leave with increasing the work experience of the economically inactive. Such employment does not necessarily have to be paid at the going rate – 'benefits plus' options are worth consideration (see below). The challenge would be to find people with relevant skills and a cost-effective way of administering such a scheme; and to ensure that employers have a choice of job-ready candidates whose skills have been assessed and matched.

The question of compulsion plagues this area of policy. It is important to distinguish between compulsory participation in a variety of programmes (such the New Deal) and a harder model of workfare (working for benefit). Government sanctions for the New Deal are based on existing job seeker's allowance sanctions. The idea behind compulsion is that it removes the leisure bonus and can enhance employability (IFS, 1997). The evidence from the US suggests that for some groups (though not for lone parents) it can provide modest help to move people into work and increase earnings. However, in assessing the impact of compulsion, important questions remain about the duration and value of such employment.

There are dangers if the sanction regime is too tough. First, claimants who are most difficult to place and often the most disadvantaged may disappear into the twilight world of the shadow economy and crime. Others may become pregnant if all alternatives are shut off.[9] We need to find ways of pulling young people into rather than pushing them out of the programme. Second, compulsion is off-putting for employers, if a placement is going to be successful employers need to know that participants are willing rather than being press-ganged into employment. Third, it sends out the wrong signals about the New Deal to participants, which is primarily about enabling and re-skilling and only secondarily about policing. If policing becomes over-riding then it becomes hard to distinguish active labour market policies from workfare schemes (Robinson, 1997). There are a number of ways in which the role of sanctions can be minimised:

● high investment in Gateway programmes which prepare young

people for the New Deal options should reduce the number of sanctions. (We welcome the proposal to combine New Deal advice on labour market choices with help from specialist agencies to support people with exceptional difficulties such as those who have been homeless or are drug dependent.)

- the four options need to be of high quality and perceived as such by the participants;
- boosting the 'plus' element of 'benefit plus' (see below);
- clear procedures for appeal;
- continuation of hardship payments despite refusal. Governments continue to have responsibilities for mitigating hardship even if people do not carry out their responsibilities. The lower rate of hardship payment would thus embody a sanction for non-participation, but would protect people's livelihood, albeit minimally.

There is the related question of payment when claimants are involved in work experience placements. As discussed earlier the source and the perception of different types of income is significant in welfare to work decisions. For example, the Wise Group has argued strongly that paying 'the rate for the job' is an essential component of the success of the scheme. In fact, a considerable minority of its participants are receiving 'benefits plus' as they are better-off under this arrangement (this particularly affects those with children). This suggests that it is the quality of the scheme and the way in which people are paid which may be crucial rather than whether it is a wage or top-up for benefits. *The 'plus' element of 'benefits plus' is worth further exploration; it is in some sense a recognition of the importance of participation and a useful way of encouraging involvement without going down the route of sanctions.* A recent IPPR submission on the design of the New Deal (McCormick, et al 1997) proposes paying the 'plus' element in a way which increases with the length of time on the scheme or as a bonus at the end. Research on unemployed people in Germany and Sweden found that the earning-related component attached to training for the unemployed was valued. *Thus, both the amount and the way in which payment is made (for example, not delivered through the benefit system) is an important aspect of recognising and valuing participation in work/education/voluntary work.*

Policy is now increasingly focused on the mediators between labour demand and supply recognising the isolation of the unemployed and therefore the importance of effective job search. The quality and effectiveness of the mediator, whether the Employment Service, the voluntary sector or private sector, is crucial. The government has inherited an Employment Service which, in the eyes of some, is mistrusted, strongly associated with policing and is seen as providing no-hope schemes (Finn, 1997b). In areas with high unemployment where there is strong mistrust of mainstream bureaucracy it is particularly important to look at alternative mediators or 'brokers', as developed in Chapter 2. The local community/voluntary sector may be much better placed to recruit and prepare people for work than the Benefits Agency or Job Centre. An effective, highly localised and trusted service will mean that sanctions become the last resort rather than the main tool of policy (McCormick et al, 1997). The importance of mentoring for people once in work, providing continuing support for the formerly unemployed is now widely recognised. Getting a job is only the beginning of the process of returning to work. This approach is borne out by the experience of the Lone Parent Employment Programme in the UK which used mentors (often lone parents themselves) to support lone parents back into work, education and training and has been built into the New Deal for young people.

Our current social security system is highly centralised with little scope for local discretion (with the exception of the Social Fund). Yet we know that the operation of local labour markets and local rates of unemployment are important elements affecting the success of active labour market policies. One of the challenges for welfare to work is to find ways of dovetailing the local Benefits Agency Office, the Job Centre, voluntary sector networks, local authority economic development units and the private sector to create work experience and job opportunities. At the moment it is not possible for local Benefit Agencies to use Job Seeker's Allowance or other benefits for other forms of support such as training. If we are to move to a greater degree of discretion for both local Benefits Agencies and Job Centres, we need at the same time to ensure that claimants are protected by minimum standards. In Northern Europe it is much more common for local authorities to play a major role in social security provision. For example, in Germany and Sweden local authorities are responsible for social assistance and so have a strong interest in providing schemes for the long term unemployed (Clasen and Gould, 1997). If the UK were to go down a similar route this would mark a sharp change in social security policy and it is not clear whether the centre will tolerate a sufficient degree of local autonomy.

Welfare to work tends to be conceived primarily in relation to labour market attachment yet other networks of family and friends are important for financial and moral support for the unemployed. If welfare to work is to be about inclusion then policy needs to look not only at local employment networks but at community, and volunteering/be-friending networks to counter some of the isolation of unemployment.

Lone parents

The UK has a particularly low proportion of lone parents in paid employment in comparison with other industrialised nations. This has been attributed in particular to lack of childcare and a low expectation that lone parents will be in work, embodied by the availability for work rules. Given the high cost of lone parent's reliance on out-of-work benefits, government policy past and present has been geared to increasing work incentives. We briefly discuss the particular issues that affect lone parents' interaction with the labour market, drawing on two studies completed by the Policy Studies Institute (Ford, 1996 and Bryson *et al*, 1997).

> Lone mothers assessed incentives in financial and non-financial ways. The rewards of working had to compensate for the inconveniences of employment, of using child care and of being apart from the children. (Ford, 1996, pxii).

● The barriers which prevent lone parents from taking up paid work are more complex than those which affect other groups. In the medium term Family Credit has the advantage of allowing lone parents to top-up low wages and work a limited numbers of hours, however, in the long term it traps lone parents in low paid sectors of the labour market, preventing them from moving beyond means-tested benefits.

- Lone parents' decisions about work are strongly influenced by the going rate for job, rather than taking into account in-work benefits.
- The cost and availability of childcare are identified as barriers to paid work by 16% and 13% of lone parents respectively.
- A large proportion of lone parents have no academic qualifications whatsoever - in the PSI sample it was half. For many lone parents in low paid work, supplemented by Family Credit, there is little chance of on-the-job training.
- In the period following divorce or separation, the search for paid work ranks low on lone mothers' list of priorities which are focused on settling children, home and finances.
- Lone parents also have fewer opportunities for job search and are less likely to be linked into informal job networks. For some who have either had little employment experience or who have been out of employment for some time, there was low confidence about moving from a private caring to public employment role.
- The Employment Service is poorly geared to assisting this client group, at least until the recent New Deal for lone parents was established. It is now using trained counsellors with the advice of groups like the National Council for One Parent Families and Gingerbread.
- There appears to be a spatial relationship between high levels of unemployment and high rates of lone parenthood (Webster, 1997). This suggests that it will be particularly important to generate job opportunities in areas of high unemployment not only to improve living standards but also to help reduce the incidence of lone parenthood.

Policy

Benefit reforms have to take into account the trade-off lone parents make in balancing the employment, time and needs of their children. That trade-off is not static but changes over time and depends on the earning capacities of lone parents and the age of their children. Policies need to strike a balance between supporting part-time opportunities for work, education and volunteering and encouraging lone parents to move out of the marginalised sectors of the labour market. For example, a part–time set of New Deal options for lone parents backed up by help with childcare would encourage involvement in a wider range of activities. These should not be restricted to those with a child over the age of five once the pilots have been completed. At the same time policy–makers need to address the education and skills deficit of many lone parents who are in low paid work to enable them to climb up the earning ladder as children get older. One option is to provide a training top-up for all Family Credit recipients. This could be paid to the claimant directly (for example into an individual learning account) and then combined with an employer obligation to provide time off for learning. This option has the advantage that childcare is already built in through the childcare disregard.

The issue of the visibility of in-work benefits can be addressed in the short-term by the Benefit Agency and the Employment Service providing more information about likely income. It is possible that with a simplification of means-tested benefits as under the Wilcox/merging packages explored earlier that clarity, take-up and understanding of means-tested benefits would improve. However, to a certain extent complexity is an intrinsic problem of means-testing.

Childcare reforms have been discussed in an earlier section. The main reason for lone parents not being in paid work is the age of the youngest child. *Increasing the childcare for this group whether through a childcare payment or higher Child Benefit for young children should begin to address this issue. Making childcare available for people on Income Support who are undertaking work experience, education and training (as the Australian JET scheme did) should increase the incentive to participate.*

The way in which employment schemes are delivered is particularly important for lone parents. It is here that the voluntary sector may have an important role to play as employment brokers. *Voluntary groups may be more flexible and gain greater trust among lone parents who are new to the world of work.* The mentoring scheme, developed as part of the Lone Parent Employment Initiative (NCOPF, 1997), was found to be important in providing support, building confidence and role models for lone parents planning on entering paid work or training or education. This should be built upon as part of the New Deal for Lone Parents.

The question of compulsory attendance for lone parents has been raised in relation to recent government initiatives. There are good grounds to be very cautious about compulsion for lone parents:

- The evidence from the USA suggests that compulsion might be counterproductive, failing to increase earnings of lone parents and further impoverishing them; the voluntary JET scheme in Australia found no difficulty in recruiting sufficient participants
- Compulsion is costly
- The application of sanctions to those with children punishes those who have no power to control the actions of their parents.

The UK approach – voluntary participation with encouragement – is the right one.

Conclusion

We have looked at a wide range of policies which are geared to increasing opportunities for paid work and other activities. One promising approach to tax/benefit reform is to simplify means-tested benefits alongside reductions in social rents, improvements to Child Benefit and the introduction of a minimum wage. The practicalities and incentive effects of participation income should be explored further. We are not convinced that the introduction of Earned Income Tax Credits offers the best approach to tackling the barriers to work. Other reforms which deal with the transitions between benefit and work, developing greater access and flexibility for childcare and enhancing the way in which the social security system interlocks with the labour market, training and education are vital components of welfare to work. A common form of evaluation of different welfare to work initiatives is crucial. *Evaluation should focus on movement towards participation, job-entry rates, earnings, retention levels and movement beyond means-tested benefits.* We need to look at why people manage to remain active (or not) over time. This broader form of evaluation, which is not solely premised on job entry, would ensure that welfare to work has a broad remit to encourage social inclusion.

Appendix
Table A
Average gains and losses of household income by decile group for 'Wilcox'/means-tested package (including MIRAS rate reduction)

Decile	Average Gain/Loss (non equivalised)	%change in income (equivalised)
First (bottom)	£2.51	5.7%
Second	£2.34	1.7%
Third	£1.93	1.3%
Fourth	£0.97	0.5%
Fifth	-£0.30	-0.1%
Sixth	-£0.76	-0.3%
Seventh	-£1.22	-0.5%
Eighth	-£1.63	-0.5%
Ninth	-£1.79	-0.5%
Tenth (top)	-£1.94	-0.3%
Average totals	0	0.7%

Table B
Percentage of gainers and losers in each decile group for 'Wilcox'/means-tested package

	Losers				Gainers		
Decile	-£20+	-£20 to -£10	-£10 to 0	no change	£0 to £10	£10 to £20	£20+
1	0.1%	0.6%	10.4%	79.0%	2.9%	1.1%	6.0%
2	0.7%	0.3%	7.4%	78.1%	5.7%	2.6%	5.4%
3	0.3%	0.4%	12.1%	73.7%	6.2%	2.7%	4.7%
4	0.2%	0.2%	19.5%	73.7%	6.2%	2.7%	4.7%
5	0.2%	0.2%	33.5%	62.1%	2.0%	1.1%	1.1%
6	0.4%	0.1%	47.7%	49.5%	1.2%	0.3%	0.8%
7	0	0	53.6%	45.3%	0.6%	0.3%	0.8%
8	0	0	61.7%	37.8%	0.4%	0	0.1%
9	0	0	68.9%	31.0%	0	0	0.2%
10	0	0	70.9%	28.8%	0	0	0.3%
Overall	0.2%	0.2%	38.6%	55.9%	2.1%	1.0%	2.2%
		40%		56%		4%	

Table C
Replacement Ratios for 'Wilcox'/means-tested package

	Total no. (000s)	Current mean RR	Mean change in RR	% with increase with RR	% with decrease in RR
Single no children	2,360	i) 85.8	-0.9	6	25
		ii) 75.1	-0.2	6	24
		iii) 69.2	neg	6	24
Single parent	740	i) 83.0	-2.7	12	60
		ii) 71.1	-2.7	16	66
		iii) 68.3	-3.5	15	76
Non-employed people in couples with children, partner not employed	1,330	i) 96.7	-3.0	18	54
		ii) 81.9	-2.3	19	54
		iii) 78.6	-2.8	19	54
Non-employed	1,420	i) 86.7	+0.8	23	63
		ii) 79.1	+1.1	24	62
		iii) 74.7	+1.2	25	61

Assumptions:
In-work wage of £3.50 an hour on assumption of
i)   16 hours (£56 per week)
ii) 30 hours (£105 per week)
iii) 40 hours (140 per week)

People on sickness, disability, carers' or invalidity benefits are excluded as are people aged 60+

Average replacement ratios:
i)   89.09 to 88.68
ii) 78.93 to 77.08
iii) 73.16 to 72.18

Table D
Changes in Marginal Tax Rates (MTRs) for 'Wilcox'/means-tested package

	Total no. (000s)	With MTR >60% (000s)	Mean change (% points)	% with fall in MTR	mean decrease (% points)
Single no children	5,690	137	0	0	0
Single parent	470	211	-8.5	25	48
Employees in couples with children, partner not working	2,190	265	-9.3	40	33
Employees in couples with children, both working	4,860	71	+7.1	neg	neg
Employees in couples without children	7,660	45	-0.5	neg	neg

[Note: some figures are based on very small numbers of FES cases so are not statistically significant (lone parent category)
Average MTR rises slightly from 30.8 to 31.9 per cent. There is an average fall however for those with high MTRs (60 or more) of 5.2 percentage points.

Table E
Changes in cost and numbers claiming means-tested benefits for 'Wilcox'/means-tested package

	£s (000s)	%	Nos (000s)	%
Income support	+£41	+1%	+9	+0.3%
Family credit	– £423	– 48%	–154	–36.0%
In-work housing benefit	+£1,459	+54%	+767	+42.0%
Housing benefit (IS)	no change		no change	
Council tax benefit	+£264	+12%	£569	+10%

Table L
Revenue changes for non-means-tested package

	Gains £m	Costs £m
Increases in child benefit		£3,554
Reductions in social rents		£2,266
Decreases in means-tested benefits	£2,276	
Changes in taxation	£3,295	
Changes in national insurance	£234	
Total	+£5,805	−£5,820

Table M
Average gains and losses of household income by decile group
for participation income package

Decile Group	Average Gain/Loss (non equivalised) £ per week	% change in income (equivalised)
First (bottom)	£12.84	31.2%
Second	£8.96	9.5%
Third	£6.35	5.4%
Fourth	£5.88	3.8%
Fifth	£6.30	3.4%
Sixth	£3.10	1.4%
Seventh	£1.44	0.6%
Eighth	-£3.64	-0.9%
Ninth	-£8.74	-1.9%
Tenth (top)	-£35.49	-5.3%
Average totals	-£0.30	4.7%

Table N: Percentage of gainers and losers in each decile group for participation income package

Losers		Gainers					
Decile	-£20+	£20 to -£10	£10 to 0	no change	£0 to £10	£10 to £20	£20+
1	1.0%	0.6%	6.2%	18.6%	20.7%	23.4%	29.6%
2	0.2%	0.4%	7.3%	18.4%	40.8%	16.0%	17.0%
3	1.0%	0.5%	10.3%	9.9%	50.0%	18.9%	9.5%
4	1.8%	1.1%	11.6%	6.6%	48.6%	22.3%	8.0%
5	0.4%	1.6%	19.2%	3.6%	44.2%	21.9%	9.1%
6	2.0%	3.2%	26.7%	2.9%	45.9%	14.9%	4.5%
7	2.4%	4.6%	35.3%	2.1%	41.6%	11.1%	3.0%
8	9.3%	8.7%	41.6%	0.4%	31.6%	6.8%	1.5%
9	17.7%	8.0%	48.6%	0.3%	22.1%	2.7%	0.6%
10	56.5%	11.6%	22.6%	0	9.2%	0.3%	0
Overall	9.2%	4.0%	22.9%	6.3%	35.5%	13.8%	8.3%
		36%		6%		58%	

Table O
Replacement Ratios for participation income

	(000s)	mean RR (000s)	change in RR	increase inRR	decrease in RR
Single no children	2,360	i) 85.8	1.3	56	44
		ii) 75.1	2.7	68	32
		iii) 69.2	2.9	69	31
Single parent	740	i) 83.0	0.35	29	71
		ii) 71.2	2.53	91	9
		iii) 68.3	2.45	93	8
Non-employed people in couples with children, partner not employed	1,330	i) 96.7	-2.3	46	54
		ii) 83.1	2.0	55	45
		iii) 78.6	2.5	55	45
Non-employed people in couples with children, partner full-time employee	1,420	i) 86.7	2.3	91	10
		ii) 79.2	3.0	94	6
		iii) 74.7	3.0	95	5

Assumptions:
In work wage of £3.50 an hour on assumtion of
i) 16 hours (£56 per week)
ii) 30 hours (£105 per week)
iii) 40 hours (£140 per week)

People on sickness, disability, carers' or invalidity benefits are excluded as are people aged 60+

The average change in RR is i)88.1 to 88.8, ii) 78.1 to 80.1, iii) 73.13 to 75.3

Table P
Changes in MTRs for participation income

	Total no. (000s)	With mtr > 60% MTR (000s)	Mean change in MTR (% points)	% with fall in MTR	Mean decrease (% points)
Single, no children	5,690	137	-6.2	20	40
Single parent	470	218	- 0.2	6	51
Employees in couples with children, partner not working	2,190	265	-9.5	32	38
Employees in couples with children, both working	4,860	71	-6.1	26	49
Employees in couples without children	7,660	45	2.5	15	53

Average MTR rises from 30.8 to 35.5 per cent. There is an average fall however for those with high MTRs (60 or more) of 5.7 percentage points.

Note that some of thse figurse are based on very small numbers of FES cases and so are not statistically significant.

Table Q
Changes in cost and numbers claiming means-tested benefits for participation income

	£s		Nos	
	(000s)	%	(000s)	%
Income support	-£2,757	-32%	-1,281	-35%
Family credit	-£158	-18%	-57	-13%
Housing benefit	-£1,043	-14%	-370	-9%
Council tax benefit	- £460	-21%	-619	-11%

Table R
Revenue changes for participation income

	Gains £m	Costs £m
Participation Income		£43,593.0
Decreases in means-tested benefits	£4,417	
Tax	£35,311	
National insurance	£4,225	
Total	**+£43,953**	**-£43,593**

Small revenue gain of £360m

Bibliography

Allbeson, J (1997), *Benefits and work: a CAB perspective on the welfare to work debate,* London, NACAB.

Atkinson AB (1995), "Beveridge, the national minimum and its future in a European context", in Atkinson AB, *Incomes and the Welfare State,* Cambridge, Cambridge University Press.

Brown, J C (1994), *Escaping from Dependence, Part-time workers and the self-employed: the role of social security,* London, IPPR.

Bryson A and McKay S (eds) (1994), *Is It Worth Working? Factors affecting labour supply,* London, PSI.

Bryson A, Ford R and White M (1997), *Making Work Pay: Lone mothers, employment and well-being,* London, PSI.

Clasen J and Gould A (1997), *Long Term Unemployment and the threat of social exclusion,* Bristol, Policy Press.

Clinton D, Yates M and Kang D (1994), *Integrating Taxes and Benefits,* Commission on Social Justice, IPPR.

Commission on Social Justice (1994), *Social Justice, Strategies for National Renewal,* London, IPPR, Vintage.

DfEE (1997), *Design of the New Deal for 18-24 year olds.*

DSS (1996), *Households below average income, a statistical analysis, 1979-1993/94,* London, HMSO.

Duncan A, Giles C and Webb S (1995), *The impact of subsidising childcare,* Manchester, Equal Opportunities Commission.

Evans M, Paugam S and Prelis J (1995), *Chunnel Vision: Poverty, social exclusion and the debate on social welfare in France and Britain,* WSP/115, London, LSE Sticerd.

Finn D (1997a), *Working Nation, Welfare reform and the Australian Job Compact for the long term unemployed,* London, Unemployment Unit.

Finn D (1997b), 'The Stricter Benefit Regime and the New Deal for the Unemployed', paper for the Social Policy Association, 15-17th July, Lincoln.

Ford R (1996), *Childcare in the Balance, How lone parents make decisions about work,* London, PSI.

Gardiner, K (1997), *Bridges from Benefit to Work,: a review,* York, Joseph Rowntree Foundation.

Gosling A, Johnson P, McCrae and Paull, G (1997), *The dynamics of low pay and unemployment in early 1990s Britain*, London, Institute for Fiscal Studies.

Jackson P R (1994), "Influences on commitment to employment and commitment to work" in Bryson A and McKay S (eds) *Is It Worth Working? Factors affecting labour supply*, Policy Studies Institute.

Institute for Fiscal Studies (1997), *Green Budget 1997*, London, IFS.

Marsh A and McKay S (1993), *Families, Work and Benefits*, London, PSI.

McGregor, Ferguson, Fitzpatrick (1997), *Bridging the Jobs Gap, an evaluation of the Wise Group and the intermediate labour market*, York, Joseph Rowntree Foundation.

McCormick J et al (1997), *Designing the New Deal*, IPPR Memorandum to the DfEE/Employment Service Consultation.

Jarvis S and Jenkins S (1997), 'Low income dynamics in 1990s Britain', *Fiscal Studies*, Vol. 81 (2) May 1997, pp123-143.

McLaughlin, E (1994), *Flexibility in Work and Benefits*, Commission on Social Justice, London, IPPR.

Meadows, P (1997), *The integration of taxes and benefits for working families with children*, York, Joseph Rowntree Foundation.

Millar J (1994), "Understanding labour supply in context: households and incomes" in Bryson A and McKay S (eds) (1994), I*s It Worth Working? Factors affecting labour supply*, Policy Studies Institute.

National Council for One Parent Families (1997), *Lone Parents into employment - good practice, sound policy*.

Nye, R (1997), Welfare to Work, *The America Works Experience*, London, Social Market Foundation.

Ritchie J and Morris L (1994), *Income Maintenance and Living Standards*, SCPR.

Robinson P (1997), "Beyond Workfare: Active labour market policies", Paper for Poverty and Social Exclusion in the North and South, April 1997.

Saunders, P (1995), Improving Work Incentives in a means-tested welfare system, 1994 Australian Social Security Reforms, *Fiscal Studies*, May 1995, May 1995, No.2, vol.16, pp45-70.

Shaw A, Walker R, Ashworth K, Jenkins S and Middleton S (1996), *Moving off Income Support: Barriers and Bridges*, DSS Research Report, No 53, London, HMSO.

Sutherland H (1997), "Submission to the Low Pay Commission", Micro-simulation Unit, Cambridge University.

Walker R and Wiseman M (1997), *An Earned Income Tax Credit, possibilities and alternatives,* Centre for Research in Social Policy, Loughborough.

Webb, S, Kemp M and Millar J (1996), *The Changing Face of Low Pay in Britain,* Bath Social Policy Papers, No 25, Bath University.

Webster, D (1997), Promoting Jobs could reduce lone parenthood, *Working Brief,* Issue 88, October 1997, London, Unemployment Unit.

White, M, Lissenburgh S and Bryson A (1997), *The Impact of Public Job Placing Programmes,* London, Policy Studies Institute.

Wilcox, S (1997), *Replacing housing benefit with housing credit, a better way to help people with their housing costs,* Chartered Institute of Housing.

Endnotes

1. Sanctions are to be set as follows: a 2 week benefit disqualification for a first refusal, a 4 weeks penalty for any further refusal. Sanctions will not be imposed if 'good cause' can be proved. Hardship payments available for people who fall into the category of 'vulnerable group'.

2. More recent work by Steve Wilcox and Holly Sutherland suggests the reform could be implemented at a lower cost of around £800m.

3. In Germany, help with housing costs is based on the previous year's rent (Walker and Wiseman, 1997). There remains the problem of rough justice, different responses are possible: a three month review process to allow for sudden changes in circumstances (see Allbeson, 1997), raising benefit levels to allow for coping with falls in income/changes in circumstances and greater access to low interest credit (see Box 1.4).

4. In fact in Canada where there has been a Working Income Supplement (currently being phased out), there is independent taxation, but joint taxation for this purpose.

5. One indicator of the gender of recipients of an EITC would be the current pattern under family credit - recent figures show that 45% of family credit claimants are lone parents, 40% are couples where the main wage earner is male and 15% are couples where the main wage earner is female. The question of who might receive an EITC is clearly not an issue for lone parents and it is possibly less of an issue where the main earner is female. However, for the remaining 40% a shift from family credit being paid to the carer to the main earner through the wage packet in the form of a tax credit would represent a significant and possibly worrying change in how money is distributed within households.

6. In Canada payment of Working Income Supplement is to women rather than through the wage packet.

7. This depends on the reading of the labour market – if the distinction between working part-time/temporary/casual and full-time/permanent/standard work becomes ever more blurred the case for a merged payment becomes stronger, as does the case for a participation income.

8. The importance here is to maintain the principle of inclusion, ie the benefit serves the bulk of people. This approach has some disadvantages: it would involve changes to the taxation system (allowing some joint taxation); it compromises the contributory

principle if applied to contributory benefits; and the 'thin end of the wedge' argument – the benefit could gradually be eroded, losing inclusivity.

9.   While this may only be a tiny minority it is based on a case of a highly vulnerable young girl (though not assessed with special needs) who, when faced with the withdrawal of her income support, became pregnant shortly afterwards.

2. BROKERING A NEW DEAL

The design and delivery of welfare-to-work

by James McCormick

Introduction

In much of the OECD, concern about the changing composition as well as the numbers of long-term benefit recipients has been growing. Whereas most claimants twenty years ago were considered unavailable for work due to disability and illness for example, approaching three-quarters of working age claimants are now available for work but not employed. The weight attached to different explanations has changed over time. Structural change in the labour market has been considered a more effective explanation at some points in the economic cycle than others. In recent years politicians and policy makers have attached growing importance to the problems faced by particular claimant groups. As the average duration of unemployment reached unprecedented levels in Europe, a focus on the long-term unemployed sharpened. As expectations of who should be available for work have changed, lone parents have been brought further into welfare-to-work programmes.

Such programmes are not new. A wide range of policy instruments has been used to reduce the barriers into paid work. The mix of voluntary incentives and mandatory requirements is in flux. Although international approaches are without clear and consistent guidelines over time, two broad approaches are identified by Peck (1997).

The **Labour Force Attachment** model (LFA) has been dominant in North America in recent years. Under this heading, interventions are designed to be short-term and have as little impact on the labour market as possible. The priority is instead to achieve a more effective attachment to paid work for unemployed clients by addressing the barriers they are assumed to face: primarily disaffection, demotivation, erosion of specific and generic job skills, with a secondary emphasis on gaps in service provision such as affordable childcare and transport, and financial barriers due to the social security system. It is variously described as a 'labour market clearing' model. Ontario's recently-established programme *Ontario Works* is driven by the provincial government's belief that 'work must come first' and that 'any job is better than none.' Key indicators of success are related to reductions in the benefits caseload.

The **Human Capital Development** model (HCD) has been more common in Europe (and in some of the other Canadian provinces). While this, too, is focused on moving claimants into work, it is usually informed by an understanding of weaknesses in the labour market as well as problems which prevent long-term claimants from competing successfully for whatever jobs are available. The range of policies typically used under this heading is wider, including adult basic education to improve job readiness, pre-vocational training, in-work training and other forms of in-work support. While programmes are expected to move people off benefit as quickly as possible, they are also judged by participants' success in retaining jobs and moving up the earnings ladder: 'Get them off faster and keep them off longer' according to advocates of British Columbia's *BC Benefits* programme. The HCD could be judged by how far it succeeds in moving people out of poverty, whereas a more limited LFA model might be considered to have done its job by assisting the non-working poor into jobs (not necessarily by helping them out of working poverty).

Britain's New Deal programmes borrow heavily from accumulated international experience of welfare reform, especially from Australia and the USA. There is already considerable experience in the UK of using the tax and benefit systems to improve incentives for both the employer and the benefit claimant. In the previous chapter, Carey Oppenheim reviews different models which could be used to underpin both the New Deal and create better bridges into work for non-target groups. Until now, however, there has been no dedicated welfare-to-work initiative. Labour's programme represents the most ambitious attempt to change that. It has a number of crucial advantages which, on paper at least, may provide an unprecedented chance of success:

- It carries a significant new budget. Elsewhere, programmes which have been carefully designed have been limited in their capacity to tackle long-term unemployment by inadequate budgets. British Columbia's Youth Works/Welfare to Work programme has provided in-work credits for the long-term unemployed to get jobs with training. Because it is revenue-neutral (funded by cutting benefit rates), a model which appears to be working cannot be offered on the scale that is clearly needed. The New Deal begins from the belief that high quality welfare-to-work programmes do not come cheap.
- It is being implemented against the background of falling levels of registered unemployment. Welfare-to-work programmes

which focus only on supply-side improvements cannot succeed when an economy is in recession. Not even the best designed job search measures can assist people into jobs that do not exist. High and sustained levels of demand are necessary - though insufficient - to ensure that an adequate stock of jobs exists and are accessible to long-term claimants.

● It is invested with a strong degree of political capital. The New Deal is one of the Government's key manifesto commitments. There is at least the possibility that competition between the parties will come to focus on how to improve welfare-to-work programmes, rather than whether government should be involved with them in the first place.

None of these conditions can be taken for granted. Their absence explains why programmes in other jurisdictions have failed to deliver the outcomes expected of them. Making the New Deal succeed, however, will require an ongoing process of evaluation, comparison and adjustment. The problems it seeks to address are too dynamic for any programme to be carved in stone. Our argument in this chapter is that at least as much attention must be paid to the delivery infrastructure as to the substance of the programme itself. And in this respect it is less clear that Britain's New Deal can be effectively delivered to target groups throughout the country.

Even if we assume that sufficient jobs are available in the first place and that the tax and benefit systems are reformed to improve work incentives, the New Deal still has to be 'sold' to sceptical employers as well as claimants. Lower benefit tapers will not be enough to attract people into jobs if they are unsure of how working will affect their household income. A guiding philosophy for the New Deal should be to keep *it simple and sell it well.*

As well as the financial strategies which make working worthwhile, other elements of the HCD model should be in place. There is some evidence from Australia to suggest that neither the extent of means-testing in the benefits system nor traditional gender barriers explain as much of the growth in the number of 'work poor' households as expected. Other personal factors are at least as important: lack of self-confidence, low levels of educational attainment, uncertainty about what employers are looking for. If the policy objective is to enhance employability in the long-term, rather than simply to get people off benefit, a broader focus on job preparation will be essential. Is the infrastructure in place to maximise the chances of the most excluded getting jobs and keeping them? Based on what we already know about welfare-to-work in other countries, and drawing upon fieldwork conducted for this book in the UK and Canada, this chapter argues that the way the New Deal is delivered will be central to whether it is judged a success.

Active Labour Market Policies: Designing the New Deal

Active Labour Market Policies (ALMPs) command widespread support throughout much of the OECD. Increasingly conditions have been attached to the receipt of unemployment benefits to encourage or require claimants to look for jobs, to participate in education or training, to accept job offers and to perform unpaid work in return for benefit. (The last of these is usually understood as workfare, Walker 1989). Depending on the prevailing political mood and the mix between incentives, requirements and penalties for non-compliance will vary according to age group, household type and duration of claim.

Some form of reciprocal agreement between the state and the individual is usually required if ALMPs are to be put into practice. In some American states, lone parents have been exempted from workfare schemes because the states did not provide a guarantee of adequate childcare. Until they did so, the courts ruled that mandatory participation could not be enforced. ALMPs carry responsibilities for the state to be active in reducing the barriers to work, not just the claimant. However some ALMPs are more active than others. The LFA model is likely to place more of the activity requirement on the individual than on government and employers.

For example, *Ontario Works* is a mandatory programme offering three streams of Employment Support, Community Placement and Employment Placement. The second of these has been widely described as workfare. The programme's mission is to secure 'the shortest route possible to a job.' According to those who have designed the programme, if an employer offered a job which did not actually require basic literacy and numeracy skills, the Province does not consider it has a responsibility to provide training to those who lack such skills. While it is doubtful that many such jobs paying minimum wage and meeting minimum standards will be available, this approach is revealing. *It shows a laying off of risk onto the individual where neither the employer nor the state considers it their responsibility to invest in a second chance of basic education.* Although it may be possible to get a job without these skills, the odds are against keeping it and moving into a better job. The client is likely to be back on income assistance quickly and will continue, at best, to cycle on and off benefits in the long-term. If this risk is to be reduced, publicly-funded investment in job preparation is essential.

Welfare-to-work: Supply side programmes

To place Britain's New Deal in an international context, we ask the following questions:

- When should governments intervene?
- When a limited amount of money is available, who should take priority?
- What should welfare-to-work budgets be spent on?
- How long should dedicated support last?

In Britain as elsewhere, the major welfare-to-work programmes are to be targeted according to the duration of registered unemployment.

This form of rationing is justified by a concern to avoid deadweight - spending public money too early on people who are job-ready and require no more than a short period of job search before coming off benefit. Rationing may be an effective screening device. It decides who should be assisted. But waiting could mean that the intervention is far less successful and rather more expensive than if participants had been identified early. Here we should also note that the UK's approach to unemployment cannot adequately be described as 'passive.' In fact as Robinson (1996) argues, stricter tests of work-seeking activity and tighter eligibility rules have gone alongside a 'battery of measures run by the Employment Service designed to improve placement services, assist job search and provide enhanced counselling for the unemployed.... all aimed at catching the unemployed as they approach different durations of unemployment.' In this chapter we concentrate on the particular rules that will apply to dedicated welfare-to-work programmes rather than the rules that apply to unemployed claimants in general.

Box 2.1 Queuing times before access to major welfare-to-work programmes

Programme	Queuing Time
New Deal for under-25s UK, 1998	Six months
Ontario Works Canada, 1997/8	Four months
YouthWorks/ Welfare to Work British Columbia, Canada 1996	Nine months*
Jobs Compact (Original version) Australia, 1994	Eighteen months
New Deal for Over-25s UK, 1997	Two years

* Participants enter the Employment Programmes phase at this stage.
Those aged 19-24 are required to complete nine months of job search before this.

Early preparation: Britain's Gateway

Finding the shortest route to paid employment may not be a sustainable approach for all participants. Some will need to move through a number of stages before they will be in a position to hold down a job. Research evidence from the UK and Australia suggests that 10-15 per cent of the long-term unemployed face particularly strong labour market barriers which are not related to disability or care responsibilities for example. It may be in no-one's interest if the first destination for this group of the most disaffected is a full-time job. Some will face numerous hurdles in their lives which mean work, training and learning are simply unrealistic first options. Care leavers, the homeless, those with drug and alcohol problems and young offenders are among those most at risk of being unable to hold down one of the options without co-ordinated effort to address the other barriers.

Added at a late stage to plans for the New Deal, the Gateway period offers up to four months of job preparation before the core options begin. It has the potential to make the New Deal work for some of the most 'difficult to reach' target groups. As discussed below, a wage subsidy is little compensation to the employer who recruits someone lacking in the basic skills required in the labour market. Without these as the building block, many employers will be reluctant to invest in job-specific skills even if a training allowance covers their costs. If unemployed under-25s are to be offered the guarantee of a job with training or further learning opportunities, employers will also seek a guarantee of employability. It is therefore vital that Gateway is appropriately resourced and tailored. As the unemployment caseload falls, the New Deal will quickly reach the hardest to employ. This should be taken as an opportunity to target more resources on these individuals.

The UK Government has adopted a flexible approach by allowing certain groups early access to Gateway (such as those noted above). It is particularly important that those individuals who are known to be at high risk of spending long periods out of work should not have to queue for six months before gaining access. Given what we know about the link between poor educational attainment and long-term benefit reliance, the most poorly qualified should be encouraged to join early. Longitudinal panel analysis in British Columbia has influenced the Province's decision to open its YouthWorks programme to 16 to 18 year olds where appropriate, even though they fall outside the original target group. There is a growing belief that those who have dropped out of school early should not be forced to complete their education before being allowed to work. A period of work experience may act as a route back into learning. As one community training manager told us:

> If the Careers Officer or Job Centre advises you to go
> back to school, you probably won't take any notice. But
> if you have gained some work experience and your
> employer advises you to complete your education - and
> then come back for a job – the incentive may be
> completely different.

It should be possible to offer mixed packages of work experience, education and assisted job search for under-18s who are at any rate likely to have to join the New Deal in the coming years. Early intervention should be the guiding rule, with Gateway offering a range of options to test job readiness including employment 'tasters'.

Gateway should build upon the best practice examples of the 1996-97 Pre-Vocational pilots undertaken in 60 areas of Britain. These offered a range of basic skills, job preparation and team-work activities to people of all ages unemployed for more than six months. The methods used by one training and work project in Edinburgh have been described as 'a world away from the job-specific training found in output-driven funding regimes' (Crighton, 1997). The success of diverse activities from creative writing to community volunteering should inform the design of Gateway.

Pre-vocational training is likely to work best where it is related to the workplace. Drawing on the experience of Work Trials would have the advantage of bringing employers into contact with the New Deal without either side having to commit too early. This programme places job-ready people who have been registered unemployed for at least six months with an employer for three weeks. Recent research by White et al (1997) found that the chances of securing employment at the end of the period increased fivefold. As part of Gateway (or indeed the New Deal for Lone Parents) the participant would remain on benefit and be eligible for work-related expenses from the discretionary fund of £20 million outlined by the government in July 1997. At the end of the period, the trial could be ended by either party. Since participation in *particular* Gateway activities should be chosen rather than enforced, no benefit sanction would be imposed if the trial went wrong. The same research found that the Job Interview Guarantee scheme and Job Clubs at least doubled the chances of getting a job for unemployed women (though less so for men). Further effort is needed to include these services in the New Deal.

Gateway should be tailored to fit the lives of its participants. The under-25s client group is composed mainly of young men (70 per cent), Half have not attained the equivalent of NVQ Level 2. From what we know about the geography of long-term youth unemployment and teenage pregnancy, a disproportionate number are likely to be parents already. They have an important resource: the motivation to do better for their children than they have done themselves. Gateway should be able to serve as a signpost for young fathers who need help with literacy and numeracy towards family learning initiatives which encourage parents and children to learn together. These could begin to tackle the barriers that lead fathers and their sons to see reading as 'not for them' and could widen the impact of Gateway considerably (although the amount of effort required to tackle this issue in a sensitive way should not be under-estimated).

A more promising route in the short-term may be through the voluntary New Deal for Lone Parents, where mothers could be encouraged to become involved in pioneering initiatives like Liverpool's ReachOut to Parents (building on the city's long-established Parent-School Partnerships). Local primary schools could serve as access points for parents who had a poor educational experience themselves, providing a familiar environment in which they can learn with their children. Although many parents will go on to training and jobs, a flexible model would include *welfare to learning* rather than simply welfare to work.

Elements of welfare-to-work

Although Britain has not pursued a dedicated welfare-to-work programme in the past, it has tried a succession of initiatives designed to make the benefits system more active. In this section we compare past initiatives with some of the strands of the New Deal. They range from the less to the more active, and from those designed to reduce frictional unemployment to those aiming to tackle job-specific skill deficits.

Gardiner (1997) has assessed more than 40 welfare to work initiatives in the UK which pre-date the New Deal. These are a combination of job search, in-work benefits, training programmes and tax breaks for employers. On a straightforward measure of additionality (how many people got jobs as a result of the intervention), the most effective initiatives were grants and benefit top-ups for those moving into part-time jobs. Up to 28 per cent of participants were directly helped into work. These were also among the least expensive parts of the welfare-to-work toolkit. Other interventions were less effective on this measure, although questions of eligibility, take-up and how actively (and accurately) these benefits were sold would have to be considered before drawing firm conclusions on what works for whom. How do other employment programmes compare, both in the UK and abroad?

Job Search Assistance

Active job search is a condition of benefit receipt in most OECD countries, although the balance between independent and assisted job search varies, as does the requirement to provide evidence of employers approached. In the UK, unemployed claimants are eligible to participate in job search activities after three months, and for a Restart interview after six months (which might lead to assisted group job search, a skills training programme or qualification for a wage subsidy through the limited number of places available through Workstart). After two years of unemployment, Restart is mandatory.

Gardiner (1997) has studied thirteen job search measures in the UK. While these provided average levels of value for money, their success in moving participants into jobs was modest - around 3-4 per cent additionality. However, we cannot conclude that job search as a strategy is ineffective. It may be rather more successful among the short-term unemployed and in localities where the labour market is more dynamic. The *techniques* of job search are also changing. On-line 'Job Banks' are being developed in Australia and Canada, providing clients with the opportunity to search for jobs more quickly. The common problem there, as in Britain, is the falling share of vacancies notified through the public employment service. Canada's Employment Centres now place less emphasis on screening and matching clients with employers' needs. In an effort to boost the share of jobs notified, they have instead developed the *Electronic Labour Exchange* where clients can post a record of their own skills and work experience on the internet and seek direct matches with a wider bank of employers. Given that about half of the UK's Job Centres do not even have their clients' records on-line, it may be a considerable time before similar methods will be harnessed for more efficient job search. In the meantime, Britain could learn from a number of low cost but highly effective community-based approaches to job search, including the Information Interview pioneered in British Columbia's welfare-to-work programme (see below).

International evaluations show variable results for job search. One assessment concluded that assisted search delivered through Job Clubs had been relatively successful in helping clients find jobs and that, on a cost per outcome basis, it performed at least as well as more intensive measures such as occupational training (Government of BC, 1992). However, job search measures were found to have 'a very limited impact on employment rates and earnings in the long-term'. A more comprehensive analysis by the US Department of Labor *(What's Working (And What Is Not, 1995)* found significant short-term gains through job search assistance, although even on this measure results were less impressive among young people.

In an international survey of ALMPs Bernstein and Trebilcock (1995) concluded that job search produces gains more quickly and more cheaply (explaining why it is the most favoured measure of LFA programmes). However underlying productivity constraints inevitably emerge. When the unemployed caseload is falling, as it is among under-25s in the UK, those constraints will be reached more quickly. In all probability, the long-term unemployed will be searching for relatively low-skilled and poorly-paying jobs. The main problem is not that such jobs are the only option available for some claimants. A national minimum wage and better in-work benefits should provide a bridge to ensure that even families with children are better off in work. Britain probably needs to create more rather than less entry-level jobs for lower-skilled and younger workers. The real risk is that these jobs are insecure even when they are not advertised as temporary and tend to offer an early return to unemployment.

Employment Training
While there is considerable scope to design better job search measures in the UK, they are unlikely to secure long-term gains without employment training. Unlike job search assistance, training can strike at the heart of the skills mismatch and have an effect on structural unemployment. While it will certainly be more expensive in the short-term, it has the potential to pay for itself by improving job retention rates.

Britain's New Deal for the under-25s offers a training guarantee of one day per week for six months. The training subsidy amounts to around one-third of the total public investment per participant, with two-thirds being spent on wage subsidies (see below). Whether this combination of flat-rate training and wage subsidies will prove flexible enough to attract a large pool of employers and accommodate the diverse client group moving through the New Deal should be carefully monitored.

The case for in-work training has been challenged by the recent wave of LFA programmes in the USA, following the lead of California's Riverside-GAIN programme (Peck, 1997). By concentrating on intensive job search support, Riverside achieved a high rate of job placement. Spending more on education and training was considered expensive and not necessarily more effective in getting people 'off welfare'. Whether training is a sound long-term investment in practice depends on how well tailored the options are. From the limited international evidence on what type of training works best, it appears that on-the-job training (OJT) has a more significant effect on post-programme employment and earnings than classroom training (CT), although even here significant gains have been achieved for women returners for example (Bernstein and Trebilcock, 1995). By itself, CT can be expected to have little short-term impact for participants with the lowest attainment, largely because an extended period of basic skills upgrading and work experience is needed before they can expect to secure employment with a reasonable chance of keeping it.

One criticism of North American training programmes, which Britain appears to have learned from, is that they rarely combine classroom-based with work-based training in appropriate measure. An exception is California's Employment Training Panel (ETP) described by Bernstein and Trebilcock as perhaps the most effective US example of employer-centred training in boosting earnings. Employers propose training plans to the Panel, offering work placements for around three months. The main criticism is one of cream-skimming - placing the most job ready with the best employers. Based on an assessment of good practice the authors conclude that a standardised approach to training is likely to fail; that the effectiveness of training programmes depends on a good match between workers and trainers/employers; that creaming can be reduced by locating decision-making with local/regional partnerships drawing on trade unions as well as employers (in order to promote a range of interests beyond those of the individual private employer); and that we should have realistic expectations of training. In evaluating the effect of training programmes, Gunderson and Riddell (1995) state that value-added rather than strictly final outcomes should be assessed:

> It is distinctly possible that the value-added is greater for more disadvantaged workers even if they do not emerge as high-productivity workers. Going from (close to) zero productivity to low productivity can involve greater gains than moving from high to marginally higher productivity.

The evaluation strategy for Britain's New Deal should adopt a similar approach.

Wage subsidies
The use of wage subsidies in an attempt to level the pitch in favour of excluded groups is not without controversy. The New Deal for Under-25s includes one option which will pay a flat-rate wage subsidy of £60 a week for six months to participating employers provided the job is for at least 30 hours a week. The subsidy must be no more than half the total labour cost for each participant (DfEE,1997). Those aged over 25 and unemployed more than two years will qualify for a subsidy of £75 a week.

The case for offering variable rather than flat-rate wage subsidies in Britain has been made by Professor Dennis Snower (1994). He argues that the level of wage subsidy should be related to *the duration of registered unemployment*, so that someone out of work for five years would attract a larger subsidy than someone out of work for two years. This is similar to the model adopted in Australia's expanded *JobStart* programme (Finn, 1997). This might help to tilt the labour market in favour of those who need most assistance. However, faced with a complicated system of payment, many Australian employers decided it was simply not worth participating. There is no reason to believe that Britain's employers would take a different approach. In the UK, variable wage subsidies have been used in the construction industry for those unemployed at least three years. The training co-ordinators and employers involved described it as 'a bureaucratic nightmare'. During the consultation period around the New Deal in summer 1997, one employer intending to recruit young participants expressed a view about wage subsidies that may prove to be typical, calling for '£60 a week and no hassle please' (McCormick et al, 1997).

More important in determining whether the take-up rate among employers will match government expectations will be perceptions of job readiness. A complicated subsidy system clearly did not help in Australia, but the fact that many employers were not persuaded that employment service caseworkers had assessed and matched candidates effectively was a determining factor. Despite increasingly generous wage subsidies, with eligibility widened over time to short-term unemployed and employers offering part-time work, the proportion of employers willing to recruit continued to fall due to the fear that candidates were being 'indiscriminately pushed at them' :

> Employers would prefer to recruit people who are job-ready and their reluctance to recruit the very long-term unemployed could not be overcome by simple wage subsidies..... (Finn, 1997).

The evidence from Australia and pilot schemes in the UK suggests:

- Wage subsidies can work. In one evaluation of Australia's *JobStart*, participants helped by a wage subsidy were twice as likely to be in employment six months after it ended as the matched control sample that did not participate. In the year to spring 1996, 40 per cent of participants were employed in unsubsidised jobs three months after the wage subsidy ran out (10 to 20 per cent higher than the employment rates among participants in some of the other streams of the Job Compact).

Limited UK experience also shows that wage subsidies can be effective in helping those out of the labour market for the longest to compete more effectively. The UK's experience with the WorkStart pilots is also instructive. The Employment Service was given the responsibility of finding 1,500 new job opportunities in four pilot areas in a year. The outcomes were encouraging: one study showed that 55 per cent of participants were still in employment three months after the subsidy ran out, the majority remaining with the original employer (Sheppard 1997). Yet the amount of effort required to identify the jobs, overwhelmingly with very small enterprises, suggests that it will not be easy to apply wage subsidies across the client group and across the UK. If there are limits to how far this model can be taken, certainly in the space of three of four years, Robinson (1996) argues that wage subsidies should be applied selectively to the most disadvantaged job-seekers.

● Wage subsidies are a useful part of the welfare-to-work toolkit but should be used following other interventions rather than applied to an entire client group. Proposals for wage subsidies have usually been met with concerns about employers dipping into the pool of those eligible for the subsidy and dropping them once it runs out. The New Deal aims to reduce the risk through Employer Agreements, where government expects participants to remain in work after the six months placement unless there are particular reasons related to the performance of the company or the worker.

Similar concerns in British Columbia have led the province to focus its welfare-to-work programme on training credits instead of wage subsidies, which employers had found to be unwieldy in the past. The New Deal will place relatively more weight on getting participants 'through the frontdoor' than on improving their skills once inside. British Columbia relies upon an efficient matching and screening system to achieve job entry and spends money on trying to keep them in work by raising their human capital. Many observers there believe that training credits are more effective if job retention is the key objective. Wage subsidies may get people working sooner. Training credits may keep them working longer. Britain is in the unusual position of offering both and being able to monitor whether the balance is right.

● Evaluations of the New Deal should take into account the job-readiness of participants and any evidence of selection bias before a judgement on the relative impact of the four options can be made. Given that under-25s in the UK will be able to enter the employment/wage subsidy option earlier than the Voluntary Sector/Environmental Task Force options, the less job-prepared may find themselves disproportionately 'streamed' away from wage subsidies. All of this confirms that the Gateway period will be pivotal in preparing people for jobs, screening and matching participants for the appropriate vacancies, and in persuading employers they will not have to take on people who are not job ready. If the wage subsidy delivers fewer jobs than anticipated in the early period, government should not respond by raising the wage subsidy. It should instead consider how to improve the capacity of Gateway to promote human capital development among those who have furthest to go before they are considered job ready by employers as well as the Employment Service. Investment at this stage is likely to have a greater impact on job prospects than carrying an even larger wage subsidy (which may well be more of a badge of stigma than a passport to a better job).

How long should government support last?
It is proposed that the New Deal options for under-25s should last for six months, and that the full-time education option could last for anything up to twelve months. Many of those who enter the New Deal will get a job for six months. Providing they receive appropriate training, their productivity should rise during that time to a level where unsubsidised work is feasible. But we cannot assume that will be true across the board. There will certainly be some young people whose productivity will be slower to rise. By the end of six months they may have been unable to demonstrate their true potential, and so be unlikely to retain their jobs. If jobs and training could last longer - up to twelve months - levels of retention may be improved.

Recent evaluation of the Citizens' Service pilots on volunteering (Moens, 1997) shows that a significant minority of young unemployed people need to adjust progressively to moving back towards structured activity, starting with a commitment of two or three days a week. Gateway provides an opportunity to take young people through this transitional period and should mean that more are prepared for full-time work. Nevertheless, as the Government recognised following the initial consultation round on the New Deal, part-time work attracting a proportional wage subsidy is an appropriate option. If greater flexibility can be achieved without added complexity, there is also a strong case for allowing part-time work to last for up to twelve months, perhaps with a declining wage subsidy during the second six months. This would widen the pool of prospective employers where opportunities for additional full-time work are limited. It would also provide a chance to test the proposition that the duration of the work experience is more important for some participants than working full-time.

Government should test for any negative effects of a part-time option. Where young people are required to be available for work on a part-time basis only (such as disabled jobseekers and those with care responsibilities), there is the option to work up to 24 hours a week (DfEE 1997). The lower wages applying at this level may be less than the Lower Earnings Level (LEL) of £62 a week. While the employer and employee would not have to pay National Insurance Contributions, insurance entitlements received while on full-time benefit (such as credits towards the basic state pension) would be lost. When under-25s do earn above the lower threshold, they pay the same rate of income tax and national insurance as over-25s but they qualify for lower rates of Job Seekers Allowance and Housing Benefit. The New Deal should send out a signal about the future balance between work and welfare. One way to address this anomaly as part of the government's overall review of national insurance would be to ensure that all New Deal participants are eligible for 'starter credits'.

Based on our brief review of international evidence, there is good reason to believe that the balance of Britain's New Deal programme is broadly right. It includes the key components of a period of preparation and assisted job search, a significant period of employment experience with a guarantee of in-work training, and a large additional budget to drive the programme forward. The discussion now turns to questions of implementation.

How should the New Deal be delivered?

Taking a welfare-to-work blueprint off the page requires a delivery infrastructure capable of meeting government targets, and ensuring that the least job-ready are given opportunities to reach the starting line of the labour market. Given the geographically uneven nature of the problem, a 'one size fits all' infrastructure will be inappropriate. The UK's public Employment Service works through a national network of Job Centres. In most cases these will be the immediate point of entry to the New Deal. While there are obvious advantages in not having to invent a new infrastructure, there is a risk of standardised models being applied throughout the country (even when there is a genuine willingness to form local partnerships). In this section we set out why the Employment Service cannot be expected to perform the essential tasks of orientation, assessment and matching by itself. We consider options for localised 'brokering' to help the New Deal reach communities and individuals who might otherwise fail to participate.

Why the ES cannot do it alone: employers' views

For all your recruitment needs – call the Job Centre
(Local Radio broadcast, Autumn 1997)

That the public Employment Service launched an advertising campaign to persuade employers to use it to fill their vacancies might be taken as a welcome sign of its commitment to serve many kinds of employer under one roof. Unlike most private employment agencies it does not specialise in sectoral niches. However it also reveals something about the perception of employers.

There is firstly a problem of notifying vacancies. While estimates vary, a significant proportion of job vacancies are never officially advertised. They are filled through internal appointment or through word-of-mouth recommendation. Some employers will have a stronger preference for recruiting those who are already in work than Job Centre clients. There is a hidden labour market to be tapped if job search is to be effective. Second there is the problem of employer reluctance to use the Job Centre to notify those vacancies which are advertised. The Employment Service estimates that around one-third of jobs are advertised in Job Centres, higher than the 16% estimate for the CES in

Australia (Finn, 1997) or the 12% share estimated through Canada Employment Centres, but a low proportion considering the more comprehensive public infrastructure that exists in the UK.

Where jobs are advertised, many employers would rather use other channels to recruit staff even at considerable cost. This reflects doubt about the ability of hard-pressed ES staff to screen and match clients to their vacancies. Employers are likely to use Job Centres as long as they believe the candidates referred to them are appropriate. Whether or not these concerns are misplaced, there is little doubt that the capacity of the ES is geographically uneven, even within the same locality. In one low-income housing estate in the North-West of England, two Job Centres face each other across a busy road. The caseload is shared according to family name. One provides claimants with advice on in-work benefits, adult education and training courses in the area, as well as standard job advertisements. It is modern and welcoming. The other provides a minimal service in cramped conditions. Neighbours as well as employers receive very different services from their Job Centres. While research evidence on this problem is lacking, we might assume that where the labour market is failing, the formal employment services infrastructure is weakest.

In other countries, the weakness of the public employment service is partly overcome through alternative referral networks. Institutions like trade unions and community associations provide employment services and act as unofficial job centres for some sectors. In the UK, it is not obvious that an alternative infrastructure exists to help the most excluded get jobs. Two controversial options are used in other countries to improve public employment services. The first is to require employers by law to notify all vacancies through Job Centres (or their equivalent). The second is to ban private employment agencies from competing with the public service. These elements of regulation might improve the reputation of the Employment Service and make for a more efficient flow of information. Moving in this direction would require a significant compliance effort however. It is not at all clear that the practical benefits would outweigh the costs. Instead we would prefer to explore ways of improving the performance of the Employment Service where it is considered to be failing employers' needs.

Claimants' views

The real test of the New Deal will not come where the labour market is dynamic, the client group small and assistance with job search the main priority. It is in those areas containing a disproportionate number of the long-term unemployed that success will be measured. Often such neighbourhoods will be suspicious of mainstream bureaucracy: the police and legal system, social services, the council and perhaps the education system. The Benefits Agency and the Job Centre will certainly be considered part of the problem rather than part of the solution. They are likely to be viewed simply as benefit surveillance agencies. In these areas, attempts to integrate income assistance and employment services under one roof may prove mistaken. It may instead be wise to separate the two functions as far as possible in order to improve the prospects of active labour market policies succeeding.

The first point of contact with those bodies charged with delivering welfare-to-work will be vital in setting the tenor of ongoing relations. Organisations which are in a position to build the confidence of the most disadvantaged communities – becoming points of trust in otherwise suspicious communities – should be given a central role in delivering the New Deal. In particular the Employment Service cannot assume that because a programme is mandatory, there is no scope for experimenting with different recruitment methods.

In order to reduce the risk of non-compliance, the Employment Service should form agreements with a network of Employment Brokers. A fledgling network exists to deliver assessment, job search and job placements tasks. Some of these organisations already have Service-Level Agreements with the Employment Service to prepare people for the mainstream labour market. Others have less formal links. Many more community and voluntary organisations have the potential to become brokers. Drawing on existing UK and international experience, effective brokers are likely to share common features:

● A commitment to earning the trust of local people and a high reputation with local employers (as an organisation with the capacity to refer people who are prepared for work) and with the ES. Small-scale, resource-intensive projects delivered in familiar surroundings are typical elements of success (Campbell, 1997; Crighton, 1997). In some neighbourhoods, very localised delivery may be necessary.

- The flexibility to bend the rules without breaking them. In the Speke-Garston area of south Liverpool, unemployed residents are encouraged to register their skills with the local Partnership agency, irrespective of how those skills were attained. Implicitly this recognises some of the work which has occurred in the shadow economy, often for small amounts of money. Without legitimising such activity, the broker asks no questions about the claimant status of individuals in the past. It represents a retrospective 'skillseekers amnesty' (McCormick et al, 1997). In this case, the success of the Partnership in assisting the transition from informal to marketable skills clearly reflects the fact that it is not and is not perceived to be involved with the benefit policing function. Such a localised approach may be underpinned in the longer-term by moves to raise the earnings disregard for benefit claimants.

- A willingness to experiment with different recruitment methods is a hallmark of some of the most successful initiatives. Some companies by-pass the formal Employment Service and conduct their own outreach work on estates where regeneration projects are about to begin. Pubs, betting shops, churches, mosques and residents' committees/tenants' groups are identified, with the offer of a presentation on how residents can be equipped to get local jobs.

- In central Manchester, a Community Development Trust responded to the closure of the local Job Centre by creating an on-line jobsearch and job preparation service, run by and for residents. Through the persistence of the Trust, employers in the region came to value its employment referral service. It earned the kind of reputation that will be vital in making the New Deal work.

- A community-based vocational training and work initiative on one estate in Edinburgh worked with a client group of the very long-term unemployed, on average out of work for seven years. Its success in moving two-thirds of participants into stable work and higher-level training reflected its innovative mix of pre-vocational learning and guidance methods. Perhaps most importantly it addressed participants as individuals while also developing a powerful sense of group purpose and loyalty (Crighton, 1997).

The New Deal programmes should experiment with some of these methods on a local basis.

Mandatory and voluntary programmes

The Employment Service will be the first point of contact for mandatory programmes like the New Deal for Under-25s, but there is no reason why referral on to Gateway delivery agents - to design the most appropriate assessment, services and signposting towards the New Deal options - cannot be done quickly. Mandatory participation raises a series of concerns, quite apart from judgements about whether it is necessary or effective. Government agencies will continue to rely upon a range of education and training providers to deliver key parts of their welfare-to-work programmes. They will also rely upon private sector employers to recruit participants. Yet there is little enthusiasm for compulsion. Neither the community agencies nor private employers will wish to work with someone who is simply going through the motions to avoid being cut off benefit. While much of the policy debate has focused on how target groups participate in welfare-to-work programmes (through persuasion or requirement), the risk is that mandatory programmes may fail to achieve their targets because some of the key partners in the delivery infrastructure are wary of co-operating.

The experience of British Columbia's *YouthWorks* initiative for 19 to 24-year-olds suggests that mandatory programmes may succeed if they are handled with care. One community training manager delivering assisted job search argued:

> We didn't make the policy. We haven't forced them to turn up. But once they come through the door, its our job to persuade them that we are on their side and that we believe they can get a job. *(Assisted Job Search Project, YouthWorks, British Columbia).*

A not-for-profit broker who canvasses employers for six month training placements insists that the nature of the first contact is crucial:

> We don't say 'do this or you lose your benefit'. We say 'here is an employer interested in someone like you.

(Community Broker, Workplace Based Training Programme, British Columbia).

This is not the place to re-open the debate about whether compulsion was necessary in Britain for the under-25s in order to reduce the risk of falling into long-term unemployment for the first time. A number of the Pathfinder pilots launched in January 1998 could have offered the New Deal options on a voluntary basis, to provide comparative data with the mandatory pilots. We simply conclude that the evaluation strategies for the mandatory and voluntary elements of the New Deal will have to be designed with caution.

Employment brokers must have the capacity to engage client groups from their different levels of job-readiness. For the voluntary New Deal for Lone Parents for example, it is not self-evident that the Job Centre is the most appropriate first point of contact for participants who have never worked or been out of the labour market for a long time - both because it is an unfamiliar environment and because the Employment Service itself faces the considerable task of equipping itself to deliver appropriate services to a client group it has traditionally had little contact with. The series of pilots establishing this programme in summer 1997 have drawn on the expertise of lone parent organisations. The proposal to invite lone parents for a voluntary interview at a Job Centre once their youngest child is at school is a step forward, but it may be a daunting first step. Some may simply fear that their benefit eligibility is at risk.

One way to reduce the barriers in some communities would be to identify *affinity groups*. Across the UK, self-help groups for lone parents and others could serve as the first point of contact for the New Deal, buying in the appropriate training advice and job preparation for those wishing to go to work. The Employment Service could advise these organisations on which of its clients were eligible for assistance, and they would make the first invitation. Access on a group basis, through primary schools for example, may provide a key ingredient for success. Unemployed Workers Centres or Community Centres could provide a more effective job centre function than the Job Centre alone. There is one proviso however: affinity groups bring together people from similar backgrounds and often with similar expectations, when what may be needed is interaction with role models who have already succeeded (especially when they have come from a similar background).

Local initiatives

There is a strong case for a mixed economy in employment services simply to find out which partnership arrangements work best. We can learn from a range of local methods which have helped some of the most excluded groups get jobs.

- As discussed above, employment brokers may come to be trusted enough for people to register the skills they have gained through small amounts of working on a cash-in-hand basis. Currently there are few incentives for claimants to report additional income. Following Carey Oppenheim's analysis, raising the amount of income that either partner in a household may earn before their benefits are reduced could increase reported earnings. Alongside this, a time-limited amnesty for skills registration might bring forward a number of viable activities that could lead into formal employment. Alternatively, the fifth strand of the New Deal for under-25s – small business start-ups – might be appropriate here. Forced by the Benefits Agency to choose between giving up benefits or giving up informal earnings, most opt to continue claiming. This is not because life on Income Support is comfortable but because casual earnings are typically much less *secure* than benefits. If the New Deal can bring resources to bear on this problem, there may be new ways to tap into the entrepreneurialism that often exists in 'work-poor' neighbourhoods instead of ignoring it.
- The same Partnership in Liverpool referred to above has taken an active approach to tackling some of the benefit hurdles that slow down the move into work. Anecdotal evidence there and elsewhere suggests that even the existing advantages for the long-term unemployed are not understood well enough by those responsible for implementing them. Of the numerous grants, bridging benefits, deferred earnings and tax reductions available to claimants and employers, none of the key agencies could name more than half. While there is certainly a job of awareness-raising and promotion to be done by the Benefits Agency and Employment Service, the Partnership has taken a more direct approach to self-marketing. *Residents who stand to bring benefit and tax advantages with them into work are now encouraged to*

say so in their job applications.

- A neighbourhood centre based in a low-income community of Victoria in British Columbia delivers assisted job search to unemployed residents. Every morning, a volunteer extracts the latest job vacancies from the Internet and Canada's on-line 'Jobs Bank'. According to the programme staff, 'If a job appears in the evening paper, it's already been filled.' Searches of the hidden jobs market are also required. The centre has therefore developed a simple technique called the *Information Interview*. Participants are trained to approach employers by telephone, requesting a fifteen minute meeting simply to find out more about their company and the skills they look for when recruiting. The impact on self-esteem is striking. After meetings that are more likely to last for an hour, participants bring back the most accurate and up-to-date jobs information in the area, sharing their knowledge with the other members of their group. Job entry levels have improved as a result. By learning a technique more typically used by the most confident graduates, some of the long-term unemployed can improve their job prospects. It is a low-cost, effective training tool which could be used by the community-based agencies involved in Britain's New Deal. It may also be effective in reducing some of the barriers associated with the concentrated 'network poverty' (Perri 6, 1997) which means for example that only one in five men who are long-term unemployed say that most of their friends have jobs.

A market in brokering?

One response to the performance of the public employment services is to introduce alternative providers, either in partnership agreements with the public service or through contract and competition. Markets in employment services - from casework through to placement work with private employers - are developing in North America and Australia. Different models for splitting the purchasing and provision roles are being put into practice. What might this mean for Britain?

According to Finn (1997), the most radical element of the way Australia's Jobs Compact was delivered was its case management contracting process. The Labor Government established an Employment

Service Regulatory Authority (ESRA) with the power to call for tenders from the not-for-profit sector and private agencies, in direct competition with the public service. Within the space of eighteen months, over 400 community and private sector providers were delivering a mixture of generic and specific case management services (to young offenders and immigrant communities for example). If this was an exercise in benchmarking the public sector's performance, the results were inconclusive. Recent evaluation has shown a striking similarity in the capacity of public and external agencies to assist clients into jobs, even though public service staff typically had larger caseloads. *Based on this evidence, there is no reason to believe that Britain should embark on a course of contracting out large parts of the Employment Service.* Yet, however, where there are localised weaknesses in the service, there is no reason to rule out arrangements with alternative service providers. On what terms might these be based?

Performance and outcomes

Different countries have adopted very different approaches to competition in employment services. However, a common theme throughout is the belief that in the past public investment in this area was not scrutinised closely enough and that a range of more clearly-defined performance standards should be in place. The British government is likely to place increasing emphasis on performance indicators in the Employment Service.

Where competition has developed, various models of judging performance are used. In some American states the impulse is towards privatisation rather than competition with public providers. Many welfare-to-work programmes are driven overwhelmingly by the desire to reduce the caseload – typically meaning to get single mothers 'off welfare'. Those administrations which are most successful in reducing the number of claimants stand to gain by retaining the savings. Moving people off benefit is considered more important than moving people on to the earnings ladder. While evaluation studies have looked in great detail at the employment rates and earnings of participants, there is virtually no evidence about what happens to those who exit the system without finding a job, or those who decide not to claim in the first place ('application dissuasion'). Where a claimant drops out without getting a job, training or some other productive activity, there can be no claim to have achieved a successful outcome and there should certainly be no question of a performance fee being paid to an employment agency.

Employment agencies may receive funding according to various *pay by placement or pay by performance models.* The first typically provides a fee for assisting clients into a job or training place. In Canada, two streams of *Ontario Works* delivering job preparation and unpaid community workfare are funded by this approach. It has been criticised for being a 'numbers approach' driven by measures of throughput rather than successful transition. Five large employment brokers in British Columbia are contracted to place unemployed participants in Workplace Based Training (WBT) and receive a fee based on meeting targets. However this is not a straightforward throughput measure. As shown in Box 2.2, participants must be placed in *a job with a training guarantee lasting at least twelve months,* not just any job. One of the largest brokers in the Province has developed considerate expertise in canvassing employers and matching participants to their vacancies:

> Part of our job is to persuade employers they have a vacancy for the right person even before they have any plans to take on more employees.
> *(Executive Director, Community-Based Training Agency, British Columbia).*

Ontario's recent welfare reform programme is attempting to introduce a pay for performance model, where private and non-profit Employment Placement Agencies (EPAs) are paid a refundable advance and two subsequent payments if the client is still employed in an unsubsidised job three months and six months later. One problem with the Ontario Works model is that the distribution of risk bears little relation to the payment structure. While the EPAs bear practically all of the risk of moving people into jobs, two-thirds of any savings are shared by the Province and the Municipality (which will typically be charged with co-ordinating the mandatory job preparation phases) and only one-third will be paid to the agency. Yet the Province offers neither a wage subsidy nor a training credit. It is not self-evident why employers will choose to recruit from among the welfare caseload unless the screening and matching functions are particularly effective. The only other attraction for some employers will be the downward

Box 2: Employment Brokering in British Columbia: Work-Based Training

In British Columbia, unemployed claimants of Income Assistance (the main means-tested benefit) participate in three phases of activity according to how long they have been on benefit. The first seven months of Independent Job Search (IJS) is followed by two months of Assisted Job Search (AJS). If the claimant has not found a job by the ninth month, the third phase of active labour market programmes is opened.

Since 1996, claimants aged 19 to 24 have been required to participate in these options under the Youth Works initiative. Sole support parents on Income Assistance are also required to participate once their youngest child is aged seven. (In some provinces the requirement begins as early as six months following the birth of the youngest child. In British Columbia the previous requirement was when the youngest child was 19). Others aged over 25 are eligible to join the same programmes under the Welfare to Work initiative, as and when spaces become available.

Phase 3 offers participants six options according to how job-prepared they are considered to be. Around 60 per cent of participants join programmes focusing on the basic skills of literacy and numeracy in the first year. Other programmes include Bridging, providing victims of domestic violence with the counselling and support services needed to get back to work. For those considered ready for the labour market, Work Based Training provides a job with an employer training credit rather than a wage subsidy. Employers are eligible if they agree to pay 'a wage comparable to industry standards and commit to providing employment for a minimum of twelve months.' The Training Credit may be spent entirely on training the individual participant or divided between the participant and the existing workforce 'to encourage the development of a training culture and human resource development capacity within the employer community.'

The task of placing job ready participants in the workplace is done by five agencies covering the Province. These Employment Brokers are selected on the basis of competitive bidding and a track record in working with local employers. Contracts are issued for eighteen months in the first instance. The brokers are paid a fee on a placement basis, providing they reach agreed targets. There are also targets on the ratio of placements into work compared with registered participants.

impact on wages exerted by the entry of a large number of people paid at minimum wage. Unlike the BC model described in Box 2.2, this may succeed in moving people into low-paid jobs with very little effect on their chances of staying in work through skills enhancement. At best Ontario Works might be expected to succeed in reducing the caseload while increasing the rate of cycling back onto benefits after a relatively short period. Unless the costs, risks and incentives are shared more evenly between brokers, employers and government, any long-term gains from the contracting approach will be lost.

Australia's Coalition government pushed the employment services market further by expanding competition through a network of Employment Placement Enterprises (EPEs). Eligible participants (unemployed for more than twelve months) may choose which EPE to receive services from. The model is also one of payment by performance, the goal being 'sustainable, real jobs' (i.e. largely without wage subsidies). Payments for EPEs distinguish between primary outcomes (unsubsidised employment) and secondary outcomes (education and training), with final payments based on the client's position up to six months after the initial placement. Again, however, it is the intermediate brokers who carry much of the risk. There is no obvious incentive for private employers to recruit from such programmes in the numbers expected by politicians. In these circumstances there are probably only two ways to succeed: by building a reputation for first-rate screening, matching and job preparation services (where the agency is committed to raising human capital) or by cherry-picking the most employable clients who are likely to move into a job quickly and stay off benefit longer.

Incentives for cherry-picking

Whether private employment agencies do cherry-pick those who are job-prepared and in need of the least support before moving into work depends on the terms on which they are allowed to enter the employment services market. For-profit agencies like *America Works* have been presented to the UK policy audience as a model of competitive benchmarking for the Employment Service (Nye, 1996), although their critics have accused them of cherry-picking in order to maximise their fee income. In Australia, EPEs have been under intense pressure to prioritise unemployed claimants who are most likely to obtain jobs at least cost

(Finn, 1997). In Canada the architects of *Ontario Works* neither deny that cherry-picking takes place nor believe that it is a bad thing:

> What is the problem with cherry-picking? The whole point of the programme is to get the most employable of the caseload off quickly, to generate savings more quickly.
> *(Programme Director, OntarioWorks, Toronto)*

As with *America Works,* it is possible to design contracts where the agency has an incentive to place groups who have traditionally faced strong barriers to moving into work. Single parents with young children have faced particular barriers related to lack of affordable childcare and a disincentive to move into low-paid jobs which, unlike the benefits system, do not take into account family size. Because their benefits are higher than a single person, the savings from moving into a job paid at a decent wage will also be higher, providing higher fees for the agency as well. It is likely, however, that cherry-picking occurs *within* categories as well as between them, with the most employable lone parents preferred to those who need support with basic education and job preparation as well as help with childcare costs. If a pay by performance structure is established, it is difficult to see how cherry-picking will be avoided. Even where the public employment service used its power to regulate contracts tightly, private agencies would be tempted to focus their efforts on a faster throughput of the most employable.

Elsewhere in Canada the method of rationing employment services to those who have been unemployed for longest is thought to reduce the problem:

> If there are any 'cherries' left after nine months of unemployment and job search, our brokers are welcome to try and find them!
> *(Programme Manager, YouthWorks/Welfare to Work, British Columbia).*

In this case the provincial government uses both not-for-profit and private agencies to negotiate work and training placements with private employers. While pressure from employers to allow some recruitment after four months rather than nine months of job-seeking has paid off, and the risk of cherry-picking has therefore risen, the government's focus on creating more 'cherries' out of those who are left behind is critically important. Moreover the level of risk is not located entirely with the brokering agencies: participating employers are required to deliver in-work training for at least twelve months and in turn claim a Training Credit to cover their costs. There is also scope for any savings to be invested in training for existing employees. In other words there is some incentive for employers to recruit and retain some of the caseload, in turn generating income for the brokers. While private agencies could be allowed to deliver public service contracts in these circumstances, the case for private brokers to compete with the Employment Service in Britain has not been demonstrated.

As the New Deal unfolds, we expect more attention to focus on the delivery infrastructure. If the Employment Service is unable to deliver on target where the labour market is weakest, who should it form partnerships with? Can welfare-to-work be decentralised and delivered through community agencies which command more trust than the formal bureaucracy? Can public scrutiny and audit be maintained where the Employment Service is purchaser rather than provider of services? Our discussion here suggests that there is scope to develop service level agreements with community-based agencies on a not-for-profit basis. They should be given clear performance standards and subject to appropriate audit. During the early years of the New Deal the most effective way forward may be to use the infrastructure which is already in place in many of the most excluded communities, often funded through urban regeneration budgets.

Evaluation and Accountability

It is doubtful whether the recent wave of Labour Force Attachment models in the USA provide much of a guide to policy reform in the UK. However, the USA does have a tradition of evaluating welfare-to-work programmes in detail. While quality of evaluation varies, the work of the Manpower Development Research Corporation (MDRC) is extensively cited by US government and the policy community.

Britain should develop a commitment to long-term evaluation of the various strands of the New Deal. We should be cautious about snapshot measures taken a few months after the programmes have started. In particular it is important to have an ambitious set of outcome targets. As well as measuring Job Entry Rates (JERs), the rate of job retention should be measured at various intervals after a wage subsidy or training allowance has run out. Crossing the threshold and getting a job in the first place will not be too onerous a target where the labour market is relatively tight. Elsewhere it will be more difficult. Outcomes for the New Deal options should be measured and compared to the underlying rates of unemployment in different parts of the UK.

As well as collecting these key sources of data, government should co-ordinate an ongoing survey of a sample of participants. British Columbia's initiative in setting up a Longitudinal Panel Study of claimants might be instructive in this respect. Based on a sample of 2,000 Income Assistance claimants, and tracking them at six-monthly intervals, the Province is building up a comprehensive picture of the initial caseload as it moves through various welfare-to-work programmes. An accurate picture of the composition of claimants is emerging, suggesting a group of 'dippers' (who are on benefit for a short period, get a job and are unlikely to return within 6 to 12 months); 'cyclers' (a much larger group who get a job but lose it again within six months); and a group of 'long-termers' (who remain on benefit throughout the period, and make up a much smaller proportion than anticipated). A panel approach would provide greater insight into why people lost their jobs, found new ones or managed to keep them.

Projections for the cost effectiveness of existing welfare-to-work programmes in the UK suggest government could stand to save up to £7,000 or spend up to £8,000 in net terms, per additional person moved into work (Gardiner, 1997). That is a huge range. We will simply not know how much effect the New Deal has had unless we track participants' employment, earnings, taxes and benefits over a longer period than is typically chosen. Nor will we be able to assess the eventual impact of a programme unless we trace the various steps towards the labour market that will be necessary. Matched groups of non-participants should be included to provide a measurement of added value. While this will be straightforward for lone parents (since the programme will be voluntary), the under-25s programme will be mandatory. Following the approach used elsewhere, a second best option would be to draw the control sample for this group from projections based on previous years' data before the New Deal was introduced.

Beyond the New Deal

There are at least two pressing questions for government around eligibility for the New Deal. If a young person has not been registered unemployed and claiming the relevant benefit for six months, in most cases they will not be able to access the New Deal. Some face particular barriers related to homelessness, addiction and offending. Others have simply disappeared from the system. Only by adopting a flexible approach to Gateway entry will these groups be reached. And only by opening up welfare-to-work to 16 and 17 year olds when necessary will the flows into these categories be reduced.

At the other end of working age, unemployment among older workers is likely to worsen in relative terms. If under-25s have faced the highest rates of unemployment, the over-50s experience the longest durations. Where the labour market is weakest, many older claimants have been reclassified between unemployment and incapacity. These are also among the groups most at risk of dying early (Dorling, 1997). The best answer for many of them may be a programme of part-time job creation as proposed by Gerry Holtham, Peter Ingram and Ken Mayhew in the following chapter. If a dedicated New Deal for the Over-50s is out of the question, new types of activity test should be piloted where claimants who have been out of work the longest are encouraged to undertake some form of activity on at least a part-time basis. Marilyn Howard explores this idea in the context of disability policy in Chapter Four.

High quality welfare-to-work programmes must be crafted with care. Those which are heavily biased towards only labour force attachment, wage subsidies, social security reforms or employment service programmes will be less effective in helping people to get jobs and keep them. Those which fail to invest in effective job preparation, assessment and matching will not win the confidence of employers. Our conclusion is unsurprising: welfare-to-work programmes must include each of these different elements in appropriate measure in different localities. If the design is in the right direction, then the higher the investment the higher quality we should expect the outcomes to be.

References

Bernstein A and Trebilcock M J (1995) *Labour Market Training and Retraining*, Faculty of Law, University of Toronto.

Campbell M (1997) "Getting People into Jobs: Lessons from Local Employment Initiatives" LEPU Seminar, 21 May

Crighton M (1997) "Getting People into Jobs:Training that works,+ LEPU Seminar, 21 May

Department for Education and Employment (1997) *Design of the New Deal for 18-24 year olds,* DfEE, London

Dorling D (1997) *Death in Britain: How local mortality rates have changed: 1950s to 1990s* Joseph Rowntree Foundation York

Finn D (1997) *Working Nation, Welfare Reform and the Australian Job Compact for the long-term unemployed,* Unemployment Unit, London.

Gardiner K (1997) *Bridges from Benefit to Work: A Review,* Joseph Rowntree Foundation, York.

Gunderson M and Riddell W C (1995) *Training in Canada.* Labour Market Policy in Canada and Latin America Conference, University of Toronto, 7-8 December

Government of Ontario (1992) Briefings on *BC Benefits, YouthWorks and Welfare-to-Work* Programmes

Government of Ontario (1997) Guidance notes for *Ontario Works,* Toronto

McCormick J, Westall A, Gray T, Holtham G and Pearce N (1997) Designing the New Deal, IPPR Memorandum to the DfEE/Employment Service.

Moens L (1997) *Citizens' Service Pilots: An evaluation,* Joseph Rowntree Foundation / Price Waterhouse London

Nye R (1996) *Welfare to Work: The America Works Experience,* Social Market Foundation, London.

Peck J (1997) "Workfare in the sun: politics, representation and method in US welfare-to-work strategies", *Political Geography*

Robinson P (1996) *Labour Market Studies: United Kingdom,* Employment & Social Affairs Series No.1, European Commission.

Sheppard B (1997) "Getting People into jobs: What works?" LEPU Seminar, 21 May

Snower D (1994) "Converting unemployment benefits into employment subsidies", Discussion Paper No. 930, Centre for Economic Policy Research, London.

Walker R (1989) *Workfare: Evidence from the USA,* SPRU / Loughborough University

White M, Lissenburgh S and Bryson A (1997) *The Impact of Public Job Placing Programmes,* Policy Studies Institute, London.

3. THE LONG TERM UNEMPLOYED

What more can be done?

Gerald Holtham, Peter Ingram
and Ken Mayhew

Introduction

In early 1996 IPPR suggested a scheme for bringing the long term unemployed back into work and for a time the proposal was adopted as 'official' TUC policy (Holtham and Mayhew, 1996). Subsequently the new Labour Government has unveiled its New Deal programme. At the same time aggregate unemployment has continued to fall and is currently at its lowest level since 1980. Nonetheless, the problem of long-term unemployment remains acute, especially if viewed broadly to include discouraged workers who are not claimants. In this article we re-visit the original Holtham-Mayhew (H-M) proposal in the light of these labour market and policy developments.

The original proposal

The proposal related to the long-term unemployed defined as those who had been out of work for more than 12 months. They would be offered jobs in the local authority sector. These jobs would be part-time (no more than 25 hours per week) and would be paid at the going hourly rate. Local authorities would be asked to consider offering new services or improving the ones they already provide. For example they might decide to keep a swimming pool open longer or enhance their meals-on-wheels service or do more work on the upkeep of parks. In the case of extension of service the same organization already providing the core service would have to provide the extended one, whether the organization was a Direct Labour Organisation (DLO) or a private contractor from either the commercial or voluntary sector. The term 'service' is to be considered in the broadest sense to encompass all activities. The pay of the additional workers would be subsidised by central government as would the non-wage labour costs.

Participation in the scheme would be voluntary and would be for a maximum of 12 months for any individual. For the purposes of calculating costs, pay for 25 hours was assumed to be £95. However, such are the anomalies and inconsistencies in the social security system that some participants in the scheme would end up worse off or little better off than by remaining unemployed. Therefore we imposed a 'rule' that social security payments should be set such that every person on the scheme would be at least £20 per week better off.

The costs of the scheme would vary depending upon the

characteristics of the participants and upon the nature of the work they undertook. The public expenditure cost of the extra income for the average beneficiary we estimated to be £1,248 per annum. The administrative and direct costs were estimated at £2,000 per annum. Thus the total cost per place was put at £3,248 or £64 per week.

The scheme entailed a form of employment subsidy. In suggesting it, we were very conscious of the undistinguished history of such subsidies as a means of tackling unemployment. We considered the dangers inherent in this general policy approach and our design was intended to minimise them.

Classically, employment subsidies face the problems of deadweight, substitution and displacement. Deadweight describes the situation where the subsidy is used to hire people who would have been hired in any event. The H-M scheme involves little direct risk of this since local authorities in tendering to take part are required to specify the additional output that will result. The tender arrangements ensure that any local authority employment owing to the scheme would be truly additional. There would be a broader deadweight loss, in the sense that some of the participants in the scheme would have found work with other organizations. However this loss would be limited. Exit rates from unemployment fall with the length of time out of work and only a diminishing proportion of those who leave unemployment do so to take a job.

Substitution occurs when the subsidy displaces other workers in the employing organization. Displacement describes the possibility that the subsidy allows the recipient organization to undercut other providers thus causing an indirect loss of jobs. Again the tendering arrangements which are an integral part of the H-M scheme should allow monitoring to minimise the risk of substitution while displacement is limited by the fact that local authorities are almost the sole purchasers of many of the services they provide to citizens. The tendering arrangments would allow the authorities to check that the services being provided were genuinely additional.

If the argument against subsidies is not framed in terms of deadweight, displacement and substitution, then the accusation levelled against them is either that they do not create genuine jobs or that they do so only by engaging in unfair international competition. We deal with each of these accusations in turn.

On the issue of international competition, the argument goes as follows: by cheapening the cost of labour, far more is added to supply (in terms of additional output of goods and services) than is added to demand. Effectively the only way that the gap can be filled is by the firms using the subsidy to reduce the prices of internationally traded goods or services and under-cut foreign competition. The risk here is of retaliation or of accusations of unfair trading practices. It was precisely European Commission reaction of this sort which effectively destroyed the usefulness of the Temporary Employment Subsidy in the late 1970s. But without this foreign element, the critics argue, it is hard to see that many extra real jobs could be created - it is likely that the subsidy will simply redistribute unemployment amongst individuals. The H-M scheme avoids the international problem by concentrating mainly on the *non-traded sector*.

What about the issue of whether the new jobs are 'real' ones or not? In the short run the extra supply is clearly met by additional demand (we are told often by the local authorities themselves that there is significant unsatisfied demand for local services), and the price is covered in the costing above. But ultimately the critical test is whether or not the participants are able to stand on their own feet in the labour market once the subsidy is removed and whether they are able to do so without it being at someone else's expense. For this to be the case macro-economic policy has to ensure that there is sufficient demand for labour. If it can do so, then it is a matter of whether the people who have been on the H-M programme have something to offer to potential employers. With this in mind, we tried to differentiate the proposal from so many previous official programmes which effectively isolated the beneficiaries from the real labour market. This criticism, for example, could be levelled against the Community Programme which typically put the unemployed on isolated social projects run by voluntary groups, employing few or no regular workers. Under the H-M scheme the unemployed would find themselves working alongside the regular employees of companies (or local authority DLOs) who themselves are providing a commercial service. They would also be receiving the same terms and conditions of service. They would be part of the normal world of work and, we argue, would have a greater chance of obtaining jobs once their period of subsidised unemployment had expired. Of course none of this guarantees that they would find work and it would be foolish to ignore the inauspicious lessons to be learnt from employment subsidies across the OECD. But the public expenditure cost is relatively small even without accounting for the very real social gain from providing extra services for which there is clear unsatisfied demand.

Reactions to the H-M Proposal

Inevitably reaction to the proposal was varied, ranging from the supportive to the dismissive. The latter response was largely the product of the general suspicion of subsidies which we have already described. One particular comment from this camp, not least unofficially from civil servants, was the concern that the scheme was trying to do two things simultaneously – providing extra public services and bringing the long term unemployed back into work. If each of these was thought to be a desirable objective, then, it was argued, each should be tackled in separate initiatives. The implicit principle that it is impossible, or perhaps undesirable, to kill two birds with one policy stone we find wholly unconvincing.

Those who were more in sympathy voiced two worries in particular. The first was that many marginal groups who were anxious to work were not registered unemployed and therefore would not be eligible to participate in the scheme. Married women and single parents were especially mentioned in this context. The oddities of the social security system which are responsible for the dilemma of many such individuals are well known and need not be rehearsed here. Our response was not to deny the real problem but to argue that solutions should be found elsewhere than in this proposal. However, the fact that labour market conditions are now very different from two years ago encourages us to believe that the original proposal could be extended, for example to non-registered job-seekers from households where no-one has been employed for at least twelve months.

The second concern related to the scale of the proposal. The question is whether the local government sector is large enough to accommodate significant numbers of the long term unemployed. We considered this issue in the original proposal and concluded that, though in principle it could absorb significant numbers, it would be sensible to extend the scheme to other non-traded sectors such as hospitals and the prison service. We originally estimated that if we were to attract 500,000 participants this would add 25 per cent to the local authority workforce. We now believe that this was a significant under-estimate, caused by a failure to realise how many workers already employed on contract to local authorities are working limited hours. This strengthens our belief that the scheme could, usefully, be extended into other areas of employment.

In the last few months we have had informal discussions with officials of two local authorities about the viability of the H-M proposals. We were encouraged to do so by the Centre for Local Economic Strategies (CLES) whose extensive experience of local government economic strategies led them to think that there was merit in the proposals. We were left with four dominant impressions. The first was that indeed there was much work to be done in the areas we visited: environmental projets, the need to combat crime and vandalism and the need to improve the provision of parks and leisure facilities were frequently mentioned. So were school maintenance and extra provision of social services such as home helps. The second was that the local authorities were very receptive to special projects designed to fill these gaps. Work being done through Environmental Task Forces, Community Task Forces and pilots of Work Options were cited as examples. The third was that much effort was currently devoted to very small schemes - often involving no more than ten or twenty people - and this entailed the possibility that the return on the resources being deployed was lower than it need be. The fourth was that officials might at first find it difficult to countenance our more comprehensive scheme for one very specific reason. This is the worry that the extension of services we propose might become permanent commitments on an already strained budget. However, local delivery of the scheme together with careful design and delivery, ought to be capable of allaying these fears.

A further important issue was raised in our discussions. In our anxiety to ensure that participants were attached to the existing workforce by getting the rate for the job and working alongside regular workers on an equal footing, we may well have overlooked potential disincentive effects on permanent employees for three reasons. First, many local authority workers work fewer than 25 hours per week and would like to increase their hours. Second, it is possible that participants who require substantial training to get up to the starting line would be getting the same rate as experienced workers. Third, it is just possible that the £20 "top-up" that some of the participants receive would put them in an advantaged position compared with some existing workers. These are serious points which may indicate the need to fine tune our 'top–up' rule but seem to us not to threaten the basis of the proposal. They clearly underline the urgent need for significant reform of the present social security system to remove work disincentives, precisely the thorny issue explored in Chapter One.

Welfare to Work

Welfare to Work is a complex package, many elements of which are still unfolding. We consider only those elements which are relevant to discussion of the H-M proposal. As announced in the July 1997 Budget, the package had the following three elements. First a New Deal for the young and long term unemployed. Second, a New Deal for lone parents. Third, a New Deal for disabled people (explored in the following chapter by Marilyn Howard). It is largely the first of these which is relevant for our purposes. Taking first the young - 18-24 year olds on Jobseekers Allowance for 6 months or more. Four options are available:

1   A job with an employer attracting a wage subsidy of £60 per week for 6 months. The job is meant to be paid at the going rate and to carry normal terms and conditions. The employer is paid a lump sum of £750 to cover training expenses. The same amount for training is available under options 2 and 3.
2   A 6 month placement, with an Environment Task Force. Participants receive a 'trainee wage' which is £15 more than benefits.
3   A 6 month placement on a voluntary sector project, again at £15 more than benefits.
4   A place on a full time education or training course. Full benefits will continue to be paid. This place could last up to a year.

Initially local authorities were largely excluded. The major exception to this would have been their involvement with Environmental Task

Forces. It would also be possible for local authorities to act as trainers under option 4. However it seemed odd that subsidies could be paid to private employers and to charities but not to public sector employers. Subsequently it became clearer that they could be regarded as employers under the first option, though the Government gave the clear impression that it hoped the majority of places would be provided by private employers.

For those adults aged over 25 unemployed for more than two years, the New Deal offers employers a subsidy of £75 per week for six months as an incentive to recruit and train them. Consultations are still taking place about the details, but it is seem reasonable to assume that local authorities will be regarded much as they are under the New Deal for the under-25s. For this latter group the scheme was implemented in January 1998 in a small number of 'Pathfinder Pilot Areas' and goes national three months later. The over-25 dimension starts in June 1998.

Falling Unemployment

When we published the original proposal in February 1996, claimant unemployment was running at 2.3 million. Now, two years later it is 1.4 million. In early 1996 1.24 million had been unemployed more than six months and 0.82 million for more than a year, representing respectively 53.6 per cent and 35.3 per cent of the total unemployed. Today 0.67 million have been unemployed for more than 6 months and 0.44 million for more than a year, representing 54 per cent and 35.5 per cent of all the unemployed. Thus long term unemployment has fallen more or less in line with the aggregate. Some of this fall doubtless represents the impact of the new Jobseekers Allowance regime and some the impact of a general increase in the demand for labour. Nevertheless the existence of over 400,000 long-term unemployed after several years of continuous economic growth still represents a significant social and economic problem. This is particularly the case when the ratio of vacancies to those seeking work is so varied from area to area. The smaller absolute number of long term unemployed, together with their uneven geographical distribution, means that Government can both afford to be more selective and needs to be so in the policies it adopts to tackle the problem. It also gives the

Government more scope to consider the 'hidden' unemployed who for one reason or another do not appear in the claimant count.

New Deal Dilemmas

There are a number of problems.

1. Though the DfEE's Large Organizations Unit will conclude agreements at the national level, the Government has indicated that it expects much of Welfare to Work to be delivered locally by the Employment Service in partnership with a variety of local bodies, but predominantly the TECs (and LECs in Scotland). However, there are many other bodies who have made it clear that they want a say. These include the local authorities. There is a danger of turf wars, with obvious potential effects on the overall efficiency of the programme.

2. The New Deal also faces problems of deadweight, substitution and churning. Evidence from smaller initatives both in the UK and elsewhere suggests that deadweight effects could be as high as 50 per cent and substitution could be as much as 20 per cent. Indeed it is reasonable to suppose that at least some in Government circles do not much mind churning effects. Their reasoning is no doubt that churning reduces the average duration of unemployment for any given aggregate level, and thereby reduces the NAIRU,[1] on the assumption that the short term unemployed have more effect upon wage behaviour than do long term unemployed. There is some merit in this argument but it does ignore a potential political problem. This is to do with public acceptance of our proposals. There is some danger that publicity about substitution and churning will discredit the initiatives in the public mind.

3. There is some doubt about whether enough private sector employers will be willing to become involved, particularly in areas of the country where labour demand is weak. There is a particular concern about small employers amongst whom most job creation is taking place. If such doubts are realised, then the danger is that Welfare to Work will be seen as little different from the myriad schemes introduced by previous governments.

4. Yet there is a Catch 22 here. If private sector take-up is too high,

there could be a danger of the UK falling foul of its European partners and being accused of unfair competition. This could lead to pressures to significantly modify aspects of the programme, as happened with the Temporary Employment Subsidy in 1970s.

5. The Chancellor has stressed that individual youths will have a genuine choice between the four options, but that a further option of remaining on benefits will not be available. We believe it is important that the scheme should not appear coercive and that depends critically on the four options being genuinely available and upon the 'Gateway' programme of guidance and counselling being effective both in the eye of the client and the prospective employer. Depending upon the needs of the individual these programmes could last up to four months. The first Gateway interview will be conducted by the Employment Service. Subsequent interviews could be with other organisations and it is envisaged that the Careers Service will play a key role here. However, it is doubtful that all options will in fact be generally available in all areas of the country. Equally it is far from clear that the Job Centres are capable of providing adequate advice to participants in those areas where expectations are lowest.

6. It is uncertain whether sufficient funds have been set aside to cover a sustained training component. The balance between wage subsidies and in-work training credits may have to change over time if job retention is to be improved.

7. A question still not fully resolved is how Welfare to Work will fit in with other labour market measures. The Government is committed to replacing Youth Training with a new scheme, to be called Target 2000. Will Welfare to Work crowd it out?

8. Finally. there is the critical question as to whether six months is long enough to bring people back into contact with the labour market.

Perhaps the overarching problem is one of managing expectations. Active Labour Market Policy has a poor record of success. If Welfare to Work raises expectations which it is unable to fulfil, then it could quickly be seen by participants in a negative light - as a sort of crude workfare. This is a bigger danger than some advocates of the New Deal appear to realise. The government's emphasis on reciprocity and the citizen having matching rights and responsibilities is generally popular. It conforms to most peoples ideas of fairness. If in practice, though, the 'rights' were seen to be hollow because genuine opportunities were missing while the 'responsibilities' were being exacted nonetheless, participants would become disillusioned and public support would dwindle. There is abundant evidence from past and existing programmes to provide work for the long-term unemployed that willing participation is a sine qua non for success, as much from the employer's perspective as the claimant's.

The Holtham/Mayhew Proposal Revisited

Welfare to Work is an evolving programme. It is not cast in tablets of stone. It is being introduced at a time when long-term unemployment is quantitatively a smaller problem than for many years. Yet the problem is still considerable, especially when one remembers that the economy is at a cyclical high. Those elements which involve full-time work on the environment or for voluntary organizations may have a flavour of the failed schemes of the past. Subsidies for full-time employment are more promising. But here there are doubts about the availability of sufficient places and major churning effects. Deadweight could be a significant problem in a tight labour market.

The diverse labour market conditions in different parts of the country mean these dangers co-exist. According to official statistics [2] the ratio of notified vacancies to claimant unemployed ranges from a low of 13.2 per cent in Northern Ireland and 13.6 per cent in the North East of England to highs of 39.9 per cent and 37.7 per cent in the East Midlands and South East respectively. In other words there are two jobs for every five unemployed in some places but two jobs are contested by 13 unemployed elsewhere. Similarly, the ratio of those out of work for over a year to total unemployed ranges from a high of 38 per cent on Merseyside (where vacancies are also only 14 per cent of unemployment) to a low of 25 per cent in the rest of the North West and in the Eastern region. There is not much sign that these geographical differences are being ironed out. The most recent survey of employer expectations at the time of writing[3] showed the proportion expecting to increase employment exceeded those expecting to cut it by 19 points in the East Midlands and by 16 points in the Home Counties. In the North East the equivalent figure was minus one and in South Wales it was minus five points.

In this context the H-M proposal still has validity as a component of New Deal and as an alternative to private sector employment. Incorporation of the proposal into Welfare to Work could help avoid the negative image which it could attract in those areas where private sector vacancies are too few. One possibility would be to confine the full H-M scheme to pilot areas with unusually high unemployment. On a weekly basis it would be little more expensive than the subsidy to private employers which is set at £60 per week plus a grant of £750 to help cover expenses for training to NVQ level 2 or equivalent. In return we know that there would be a genuine addition to socially desirable output. Churning could well be avoided more easily than in private sector employment or the public sector, which under current arrangements would have an incentive to substitute subsidised workers for others in the performance of routine tasks. The H-M's emphaisis on additionality of output removes that adverse incentive. Moreover, the possible scale problems raised earlier are much less formidable than at the time we originally presented the proposal because of the fall in the number of long term unemployed.

In high-demand areas the H-M proposal has fewer advantages over existing New Deal measures. The government clearly believes that placing the unemployed with private sector employers is more likely to secure their real or perceived longer-term employability. Even in that context, the H-M scheme retains the advantage of being less likely to result in deadweight losses.

Certain features of H-M, if not the scheme in its entirety, could be considered for incorporation into New Deal measures. Under present rules the Employment Service could accept proposals from local authorities for six month programmes. In our view six months will often not be enough to bring many individuals back into real contact with the labour market. We would therefore continue to propose that participation be extended up to twelve months, subject to review at the end of the first six months.

As we understand it, the DfEE wishes to avoid a revolving door effect whereby private firms get rid of one group of participants after six months and bring in a second group. However, the discretion which Welfare to Work gives to local officers would allow them to continue particular local authority schemes, even if different participants were involved. This might well be desirable particularly if combined with the flexibility of allowing individuals to participate longer than the presently specified six months.

Conclusion

The fact that the number of long term unemployed has fallen, particularly in the government's first target group of young people, gives the opportunity to extend help within budget to other groups. There are several possibilities. It still seems desirable to us to define adult long term unemployment as one year rather than two. Then there are those who are seeking work but are not counted amongst the claimant unemployed. If this group were defined in a manner which was consistent with the H-M scheme, it would comprise those from households which had been without work for at least one year.

Welfare to Work is meant to be flexible, and we hope that this flexibility will be used to incorporate elements of our proposal that would reach further than the New deal is otherwise likely to.

Reference

Holtham G and Mayhew K (1996), *Tackling Long-Term Unemployment*, IPPR, London.

Endnotes

1. The so-called 'non-accelerating-inflation rate' of unemployment; when unemployment falls below this rate, inflation is thought to accelerate indefinitely.
2. *Employment Trends*, December 1997
3. Manpower: *Survey of Employment Prospects*, 1998:1

4. DISABILITY DILEMMAS

Welfare to work or early retirement

Marilyn Howard

Abbreviations used in this chapter

ATW   Access to Work
AWT   All work test
BA   Benefits Agency
CTB   Council Tax Benefit
DDA   Disability Discrimination Act
DLA   Disability Living Allowance
DWA   Disability Working Allowance
ES   Employment Service
EZ   Employment Zone
HB   Housing Benefit
IB   Incapacity Benefit
IMB   Income Maintenance Benefit
IS   Income Support
IVB   Invalidity Benefit
Isdp   Income Support disability premium
JIG   Job Interview Guarantee
JSA   Jobseeker's Allowance
NI   National Insurance
PACTs   Placing, Assessment and Counselling Teams
PHI   Permanent Health Insurance
SDA   Severe Disablement Allowance

Introduction

One in four of us will become disabled by the time we reach 65. The consequences of disability can be devastating: some people may never work again and may incur additional living costs because of their disability, like extra heating or payment for carers.Yet the risk of becoming disabled is little understood by the general public and provision of incomes in the event of ill health or disability is often left to chance.

The numbers of people excluded from the labour market and claiming benefit have grown. Successive governments have been concerned about the appropriateness of social security expenditure, leading for example to the reduction in benefit levels and a tighter test for Incapacity Benefit (IB). In effect, some people were re-classified from being incapable of work to being unemployed.

Stone (1984) has suggested that disability has been used by modern welfare states as a category of need giving eligibility for cash help, as well as exemption from some of the obligations of citizenship. However once so labelled, any pathways back into full citizenship have been relatively neglected: responsibility to fulfil them is located with neither society nor the individual. A simple de-labelling strategy which turns some disabled people back into "unemployed" is not enough. The challenge is to develop policies which aid a return to citzenship. The government's plans for welfare to work and the extension of rights under the Disability Discrimination Act (DDA) are both areas where this challenge arises. The principles of welfare reform applied to the field of disability will inevitably raise questions about the nature of obligation for individuals and society as a whole.

Benefit spending on long-term sick and disabled people now accounts for some £23billion–almost a quarter of benefit spending– and is expected to account for 25% of the increase over the next two years (Social Security Departmental report, 1997, Cm 3213). A serious look at the balance sheet is to be expected by any new government and a thorough review of current spending can be used to inform longer-term welfare reform. Rather than considering the social security budget in isolation, there is merit in examining the role of other departments and factors which may have a bearing on expenditure. Although disability can affect anyone at random, some of us are more vulnerable than others. People from manual occupations are more likely to become disabled than non-manual groups (DOH, 1997). Health risks *gradually* increase from professional to unskilled manual classes, suggesting that this is not merely an effect of extreme poverty, rather a form of relative deprivation in which childhood disadvantage and adult experiences interact (Power and Matthews, 1997). If the longer-term goal is to tackle social exclusion, identifying the points at which Government and other agencies can intervene to reduce these risks may well have an impact on public spending in the longer term, particularly social security. The establishment of the Social Exclusion Unit is a promising development which has the potential to act as a catalyst to bring together issues across departmental boundaries and consider how exclusion could be prevented.

Extending the New Deal to disabled people may help those who wish to move from benefits into work to do so. About a third of working age disabled people who are economically inactive have indicated that they would like to work; it is possible that under the right conditions, more may wish to do so (Sly, 1996). In the immediate future, though, the financial penalties within the current benefits system may well act as a disincentive to work. In the short-term the impact of the DDA is unlikely to increase the number of jobs available to disabled people, although the new government's announcements on extending the DDA and the setting up of a Ministerial Taskforce may result in more substantive changes in the longer-term.

Policy reforms would benefit greatly from a more consistent approach across public and private sectors in order to develop disability policies which both enable those who can work to do so, and offer an adequate income for those who cannot. This chapter develops some ideas for ways forward, including the appropriate balance between welfare to work and early retirement, with a particular focus on payments to replace lost income (rather than to meet the costs of disability). The three principles for welfare reform outlined by the Prime Minister are applied to disability policy.

Policy context
How many disabled people?

Disability can occur at any time: at birth, or from an injury, or associated with age, although most disabled people develop their disability during adulthood. Disability is not homogenous. It can be physical or sensory, involving a learning disability or mental health problem, or any combination of these. Major causes of disability are musculo-skeletal problems, accounting for 34% of disabilities, followed by deafness, representing a quarter of causes of disability (DOH, 1997). Around a quarter of disabilities are caused by accidents, but this is a more important factor in the younger age groups. Some occupations are risker than others with some 27% of those reporting deafness having been exposed to noise during work or military service (DOH, 1997). Conditions may also be progressive, particularly among older age groups, whether in employment or not. (These can include arthritis, respiratory conditions, musculo-skeletal problems and psychiatric conditions).

Part of the difficulty for policy-makers is that disability is not a neat category, although delivery of benefits and services is based on someone being categorised as 'disabled'. Disability is better understood as a continuum. Even estimates of the prevalence of disability depend on the precise definition used. The DDA now defines disability as:

> a physical or mental impairment which has a substantial
> and long-term adverse effect on (the) ability to carry out
> normal day-to-day activities.

Estimates suggest that that there are some 7.3 million disabled people over the age of 10, of whom 47 per cent are aged 65 or over (DOH, 1997). Whilst more than one in ten working age adults have a disability (3.9 million people overall), this rises to one in four between age 50 and state retirement age (Sly, 1996). Overall the number of households with at least one member who is long-term sick doubled between 1986 and 1996 (Bell et al, 1997).

Only a third of disabled people work. Unemployment is two and a half times higher and economic inactivity twice as high as for non-disabled people (Sly, 1996). Only 2% of people move from one of the incapacity benefits into work (Rowlingson and Berthoud, 1996). People with a mental health problem are much less likely to be economically active than people with physical or sensory impairments. Disabled people are slightly more likely to be self-employed or to work part–time, and are more concentrated in manual occupations (Sly, 1996). The levels of pay for disabled people tend to be low, and the expenses associated with disability (such as travel, heating, laundry and care costs) are often high (Berthoud et al, 1993).

Unemployment or early retirement: policy tensions

There have been some tensions between the policy goals of welfare to work on the one hand, and early retirement on the other. The association of Incapacity Benefit (IB) with areas of high unemployment has led some commentators to suggest that people who are early retired and sick can be counted as 'hidden unemployed' (Beatty et al, 1997). However, there is little evidence that it has been getting any easier to claim IB; rather, that people have been staying on it for longer (Berthoud, 1993).

The SERPS addition, on top of the basic rate of the former Invalidity Benefit (IVB) payable until 1995, equated the position of disabled people with that of pensioners 'early retired'. There was no expectation they would work again. Until 1995 IVB claimants could choose to continue to receive their (untaxed) IVB for five years after official retirement age in preference to claiming their retirement pension. This was estimated to account for a third of the increase in IVB claims in the 1980s (Berthoud, 1993). It was one of the elements abolished for new claimants with the introduction of IB, and the proportion of claimants over pension age has now almost halved. Between 1977 and 1988, the Job Release Scheme offered financial incentives to older and disabled workers to take early retirement in order to release a job with their employer for a younger unemployed person. However, the growing concern, reflected in other European countries, is that early retirement has contributed to the dramatic drop in labour market participation rates of older men and that the cost is likely to rise further as the post-war baby boomers near pension age. On the other hand, previous governments have stressed financial incentives to help people re-enter work, such as the introduction of Disability Working Allowance (DWA) in 1992 and benefit 'run-ons' for unemployed people introduced with Jobseeker's Allowance (JSA) in 1996.

The Government's Social Security Advisory Committee (SSAC) indicated that there is a case for re-examining the balance between levels of benefit between long term unemployment and long term sickness as current relative levels imply that IB is paid for a permanent situation equivalent to retirement (1997). From April 1998, the basic rate of JSA for people over 25 is £50.35, compared with IB rates of £48.80 for the first 28 weeks, £57.70 up to the first 52 weeks, and £64.70 thereafter. The extent to which people may be encouraged to claim incapacity benefits in preference to work or unemployment benefits is unclear. Older people may be more expensive to employ and may also have higher out of work incomes than younger people (especially through occupational pensions) but fewer will have dependant children.

Major disability benefits

There is a confusing array of benefits which a disabled person could be entitled to. For people over pension age, Attendance Allowance is intended to contribute towards the additional costs of disability, payable on the basis of care or supervision required. Except for certain premiums in means–tested benefits, there is no other help for people who become disabled after pension age, who are only eligible for the state Retirement Pension. People can also supplement their state pension with earnings without it being reduced, although both earnings and their pension are subject to taxation.

For people of working age, Disability Living Allowance (DLA) is intended to help with the additional costs of disability. The two components, one for care and the other for mobility, can be payable whether or not the claimant works, although only a small minority do. The main income-replacement benefits are payable on the basis of incapacity for work. This includes IB provided the person has paid sufficient National Insurance (NI) contributions; the non-contributory Severe Disablement Allowance (SDA) for people who are also assessed as 80 per cent disabled; and means-tested Income Support which is payable with an additional disability premium after a year (or six months with SDA). These incapacity benefits are only payable if people have passed or been considered exempt from the all work test (AWT): i.e. they are presumed incapable of any work. For people who do not fit any of these categories, JSA is payable provided the person can show they are available for work and actively seeking work.

Benefits are intended to compensate people for what they cannot do, placing a premium on 'inactivity'. People who are categorised as 'incapable' of work may be regularly reviewed by the Benefits Agency Medical Service, but are discouraged from keeping links with the labour market. People have to present themselves as incapable to the Benefits Agency (BA), but as capable enough to the Employment Service (ES) for work or training. Despite recent efforts at inter-departmental co-ordination, the DSS and the DfEE have tended to develop their policies in isolation from each other. Mainstream ES programmes can give priority to disabled people if they are considered suitable, but people on them could be placing their benefit at risk. A three-week Work Trial IB could lead the BA to review whether a participant really is incapable of all work; and a period on Training for Work can result in DLA being reviewed to see if the person's care needs had lessened. As one man told researchers,

> You are either really, really, deserving and half dead, and then you will be pitied and you will get [benefits], or you are treated as if there is nothing really wrong with you, and you could get off your backside and do things which, when you do that, you are really ill. (Rowlingson and Berthoud, 1996)

Disabled people may be able to undertake a limited amount of paid work whilst on one of the incapacity benefits, provided it is for fewer than 16 hours a week and below the earnings limit, but this is little used. For people who can work for 16 hours or more, there is a means-tested in-work benefit modelled on Family Credit. Disability Working Allowance (DWA), was intended to recognise that some disabled people could work but may have reduced capacity to do so for reasons such as pain or fatigue. However only one in five of the estimated 50,000 DWA caseload actually claims it (Rowlingson and Berthoud, 1996). This is largely because of the restrictive qualifying benefit rules, which mean that people on one of the incapacity benefits can only qualify if they have been in receipt of one of them within the previous eight weeks. The only other people who can claim DWA are those receiving DLA. Moving from a benefit payable for incapacity into a job supplemented by DWA may simply be too risky:

> The benefit system may therefore create or reinforce an identity based on total incapacity where some people might be partially capable of work. (Rowlingson and Berthoud, 1996)

Other payments for long term disability or early retirement

When out of work, people may be entitled to incomes from the state, their employer or insurance company. As with the state scheme, these have been based on the principle of compensating for incapacity for work.

Box 4.1 Income replacements for incapacity for work

Employers	Occupational Sick Pay, Occupational Pensions (ill health early retirement)
Insurers	Permanent Health Insurance
State	Incapacity Benefit, Severe Disablement Allowance, Income Support

Employers often provide some occupational sick pay, normally for up to six months (including Statutory Sick Pay, which is now a form of pay rather than a benefit). Some employers also have Permanent Health Insurance (PHI) schemes which can provide for longer-term absence from work. Individuals such as the self-employed can also take out PHI if they are not in an occupational scheme. Showing some similarity with state benefits, PH1 claims have risen and durations have been longer.

An occupational pension (OP) can be paid to someone below the usual retirement age if the scheme provides for permanent 'incapacity'. The maximum OP payable is commonly based on the employee's actual service and potential service up to normal retirement age. Employers therefore need a separate scheme (like PHI) if they are to provide for a prolonged absence rather than a permanent one. Applications to retire early with occupational pensions have been increasing over the past 15 years and about a third of people retiring early will do so for health reasons. Yet there can be considerable variations within and between organisations (Poole, 1997).

The Audit Commission has recently expressed concern about the standard of evidence and decision-making by local authorities around early retirement (Audit Commission, 1997). Local authority pensions are enhanced by not reducing the pension to take account of the longer period for which it will be paid; and by increasing the number of years on which the employee's pension is based ('compensatory added years'), which is mandatory in ill-health retirements. The cost of added years falls to the council's revenue account (potentially having a knock-on effect on the standard of service provision). In one local authority scheme, a 45-year old taking ill-health retirement after 14 years service could cost £313,750 *(Local Government Chronicle,* 5 July 1996). Whilst appearing to solve the short term needs of employers restructuring their workforce, early retirement raises costs to pension funds, results in the loss of company expertise, and costs the state through tax revenues foregone and increased benefit expenditure where people are also eligible for IB. (Around one in four IB claimants have a pension from their employment). The Labour Government's emphasis on work as the most appropriate form of welfare clearly signals a shift away from early retirement. What will it mean in practice?

Disability and Welfare to work

Whilst the focus on welfare to work represents a welcome shift of resources towards working age people who need help to get into work, the current structure of the various New Deal initiatives poses a challenge for disability policy. Both the mainstream New Deal options and initiatives for disabled people have been grafted onto the current web of benefits and employment services. The government itself has expressed concern that the benefit rules should not discourage participation in the welfare to work initiatives (HC Hansard, 17 December 1997, col. 242w). Further changes are required if the New Deal is to achieve its full potential.

Legislation only allows for piloting of benefit changes to IS and DWA. Early projects are likely to come on stream before significant changes can be made, so participants will encounter the present disincentives. In the short term, some benefit 'amnesty' may be required to encourage disabled people to join programmes which might otherwise put their incapacity status at risk and therefore lead to benefit withdrawal. Currently the ES has more powers than the BA to support people to move into work or stay in work; hence the importance of testing new ideas like the 'Jobmatch Plus' reform discussed in this chapter as soon as possible. This section considers the structure of the New Deal in relation to its possible impact on disabled people and barriers highlights some of the current benefit.

Disabled people have not been the specific target of the mainstream New Deal programmes, but anyone who is classed as disabled by the ES (using the DDA definition) will have early access to the Gateway period of job preparation without having to wait the required period of six months for young people on JSA.

The New Deal for 18-24s

Structure of the New Deal

The Gateway is likely to last up to four months, but disabled young people may need longer to improve their employability and it is unclear if the Gateway period can be extended without benefit penalties. Some disabled young people may need more flexible help than existing ES programmes allow, for example part-time or longer-lasting work trials. Options may also need to be supported by adapting current ES resources, such as making sure that disabled people on the Voluntary Sector Option or the Environment Task Force can be eligible for the current Access to Work (ATW) scheme, giving help with aids, equipment and support needs.

Benefit problems

During the Gateway, participants will have to satisfy JSA rules on availability and actively seeking work, although their Jobseekers Agreement may be amended to reflect participation in the New Deal (DfEE, 1997). Where people have placed restrictions on their availability for health reasons (such as reduced hours) these will apply to the New Deal options. An employer will receive the full subsidy even where the hours of work are reduced, provided the wages are at least equal to the subsidy. Young people who leave one of the options early, and who make a new JSA claim within three months, will be seen again by their ES personal adviser, and unless one of the 'good cause' provisions apply they will be sanctioned. (Disability can be considered a 'good cause').

Disabled young people who opt for the employer option after

receiving JSA for more than eight weeks are unlikely to be eligible for in-work help through DWA because JSA is not a qualifying benefit. This could particularly affect people who have failed the All Work Test by a small margin before claiming JSA. For the same reason, a four-month Gateway period would put someone outside the qualifying period for DWA. (This problem will also apply to the older unemployed).

Long term unemployed over-25s

Structure of the New Deal

People over 25 who have been unemployed for at least two years are the main target group for this stream of the New Deal. The options so far suggested for this older group are work with an employer (with a subsidy of £75 per week) or an employment-related course. Additional resources will be directed towards the older age groups, starting with a Gateway for the 25-35s, which may be gradually extended up the age range (DfEE press notice, 004/98, 5 January 1998).

This may present an opportunity to reconsider the definition of 'long-term' unemployment, perhaps eventually bringing it into line with the six-month period for the young unemployed. The risk of being long-term unemployed is greatest in the older age groups. Almost one in three men over 50 have been unemployed for two years or more, compared with only 7% of under-25s (JSA statistics, May 1997). Intervening at an earlier stage could be more cost-effective for the over-50s, and prevent them from sliding into long-term unemployment. Suggestions for testing alternatives are made below.

The New Deal and Employment Zone (EZ) programmes open opportunities to reconsider the distinctions between people who are long term unemployed and people who are disabled. Those who fail the AWT by a small margin and so have to sign on for JSA are nonetheless considerably more disadvantaged in getting work than most jobseekers, perhaps even more so than some people claiming IB. They tend to be older, to have been out of work for longer, have a disability likely to last at least 12 months, and are four times more likely than other jobseekers to have health problems which affect their ability to work (Davoud, 1996). An early ES tracking exercise showed that, when compared with other jobseekers, almost half of the over 50s who had left IB subsequently returned to reclaim benefit as 'sick', compared to 16% of other jobseekers (Knight and Fletcher, 1996). Merely shifting people from one benefit to another has not resolved the tension around the unemployment/disability boundary, nor offered sufficient assistance to make the difficult transition into work.

Benefit problems

Disabled people can sign on for JSA, but have to satisfy the labour market conditions of availability for work and actively seeking work. These conditions require a level of literacy and organisation which may be difficult for many claimants to attain. In one DSS study only around half of claimants kept written records (Bottomley et al, 1997). People with a long term sickness or disability signing on can restrict their availability for health reasons. In practice, however, there is evidence that some people who require treatment several times a week have been considered unavailable for work, and there are recent examples of disabled people with difficulty reading and writing failing the actively seeking work test (and so losing their JSA) (Allbeson, 1997).

A New Deal for disabled people

The ES has a history of offering specialist employment assistance to disabled people, currently organised through regional Placing, Assessment and Counselling Teams (PACTs), including specialist Disability Employment Advisers (DEAs). ES help includes occupational assessments, practical help through the Access to Work scheme, supported employment and the Job Introduction Scheme (Box 4.2). The ES also has a role in advising on the DDA and encouraging employers to become disability symbol-users (the "two ticks" symbol) which entails making five commitments linked to the recruitment and retention of disabled people.

Box 4.2 ES keep for disabled people

Access to Work provides help to employed, unemployed, and self-employed disabled people with the cost of special aids and equipment, adaptations to premises, communicator support for job interviews, support workers or personal readers for people with a visual impairment.

Supported employment is one option for disabled people whose productivity is reduced to between 30-80%. Clients are employed by sponsors (usually a charity or voluntary organisation) who place them in open employment with a host firm. The sponsor pays the client the rate for the job, and the host pays the sponsor for the value of the work performed. The ES pays the difference, plus a management fee.

The Job Introduction Scheme offers a wage subsidy in the open market to employers taking a disabled person for a trial period of at least six weeks.

Structure of the New Deal for Disabled People
The Chancellor announced in the 1997 Budget that £195 million would be made available during the lifetime of this Parliament for the New Deal for Disabled People to help people move from IB into work. Since then the DSS and the DfEE have developed a programme for bids from interested organisations with the intention of helping sick and disabled people move from benefits into work and enabling them to stay there. There are four main elements:

i.   Innovative schemes: to help people get jobs or to stay in work. Around 20 schemes are likely to be selected in two tranches, starting in spring and autumn 1998. The longer time scale for the second tranche is designed so as to allow organisations to form partnerships.

ii.   Personal advisers to co-ordinate a range of local services and provide a link to local employers, which will be the subject of a separate bidding process;

iii. An information campaign to improve knowledge of the help already available;

iv. Research and evaluation on the effectiveness of these measures.

The intention is for individuals on one of the key benefits to be taken onto a scheme on a voluntary basis (ie without compulsion). The key benefit groups are people on:

- IB (1.7 million claimants in total),
- SDA (0.4 million),
- Income Support with a disability premium (Isdp: 0.8 million),
- JSA but with health restrictions (360,000)
- Invalid Care Allowance, and
- People at risk of coming onto disability benefits (e.g. after eight weeks on Statutory Sick Pay).

The innovative schemes will be tested against whether they help people towards 'sustained employment', meaning a job or self-employment of more than 16 hours a week, for at least 26 weeks in a 52 week period.

Benefit problems

People on one of the incapacity benefits who attempt to work, study or train whilst on benefit currently risk a review of their incapacity status by the BA. People on IB or SDA are limited to working up to 16 hours a week, for no more than £48.00 per week (1998/9 figures); even earning 1p over this amount will mean that all of that week's benefit is lost. The work must be undertaken on the advice of a doctor and has to help improve, prevent or delay deterioration in the condition. (Supported employment is allowed.) People who are also receiving IS or Council Tax Benefit (CTB) Housing Benefit (HB) will see a pound for pound reduction in those benefits for any earnings over the disregard level (£5 per week, or £15 for those who qualify for the disability premium). Unsurprisingly, only an estimated 1 per cent of IB claimants undertake exempt work. For people on JSA (whether contributory or means-tested), any part–time earnings above £5 per week are deducted pound for pound from their benefit unless they are also in receipt of a disability premium.

For participants trying out 'sustained employment' of more than 16 hours a week, the current benefit rules allow a break of only eight weeks before having to requalify from the beginning. This means that people on IB or IS would have to wait a full year before requalifying for the maximum benefit. The exception to the eight-week linking rule is where people claim the in-work benefit, DWA and the linking rule is extended to two years. If they do not receive DWA, participants in 'sustained employment' will break the linking rule unless it can be extended to a year to cover the potential 'sustained' period. Evaluation of the New Deal could identify in more detail some of the precise effects of benefit disincentives and inform appropriate changes.

Testing alternatives

The challenge for the DSS and the DfEE is to develop cash benefits and services which are more flexible and responsive to the complex reality of disability. The New Deal provides a stimulus for new thinking on disability and benefits across departmental boundaries.

Encouraging part time work

The New Deal for over–25s and the £195 million initiatives for disabled people could develop several options for those who may need to work for less than a full working week because of age or disability. A strategy to encourage part time work might go some way towards helping some people who are presently in the 'grey' area between incapacity and employment, unable to sustain full time employment immediately and who may need assistance with that transition. Part-time earnings alone rarely provide a living wage before the additional costs of disability are considered. Even with a minimum wage set at £4 per hour, 16 hours of work would only attract gross wages of £64 per week, just on the lower earnings limit for NI but below the tax threshold. Part-time work could be encouraged by an extension of the existing ES Jobmatch scheme.

'Jobmatch Plus'

Jobmatch is a non-means-tested payment of £50 per week for six months payable to those who leave benefit and take up work of between 16 and

30 hours a week. Although currently only available to under-25s on a national basis, evaluation of the Jobmatch pilots for all age groups indicated that older and single men could be encouraged into part time work and increase their hours (Loyd and Hussey, 1996). Jobmatch participants also seemed to be more likely to stay in work and, interestingly, less likely to claim in-work benefits (Clemens, 1997). Participants also felt that Jobmatch had a positive effect on their motivation and confidence. When compared with other schemes Jobmatch appears to have most 'additionality' (that is helping people who would not have otherwise entered work) (Gardiner, 1997).

Given the obvious attraction of a simple, non-means-tested payment from the ES, extending the Jobmatch concept to older people, particularly those with an impairment, could be tested for effectiveness. It could be designed so as to help those, particularly men, over the age of 50, who are more likely to be on benefit for long periods whether currently on JSA or IB (or having moved between the two). What I have elsewhere called 'Jobmatch Plus' (Howard, 1997) could be payable for one year (rather than six months) to people over 50 who have been on JSA for six months, in particular those who have health restrictions on their work availability. The six-month period would be consistent with the definition of long-term unemployed for the under-25s New Deal and could prevent longer benefit durations. A period on Jobmatch Plus could be used as a qualifier for DWA for those who may subsequently increase their hours, but equally could be counted as 'linking' for the purposes of qualifying for IB, or for a more progressive alternative (as discussed below).

Jobmatch Plus could be piloted among the over-50s who:

- have received JSA for six months and may also have restricted work availability on health grounds;
- are on IB but have been assessed under one of the New Deal initiatives as wanting to undertake work on a part–time basis;
- are in work, but have been on sick leave for two months or more, or are at risk of dismissal/early retirement.

It is difficult to offer precise estimates on numbers or costs, but based on the previous Jobmatch pilots assuming a 10 per cent level of take up, this leaves some 14,000 people (11,000 men and 3,000 women) over-50s who have been on JSA for over six months who could be targeted for Jobmatch Plus.

Balancing work and welfare

In his speech on the 21st century welfare state in January 1997, the Prime Minister outlined three principles for welfare reform. He said, the new welfare state must:

- be active not passive;
- combine opportunity and responsibility as the foundation for community;
- be delivered through an enabling government in which private and public sectors work together.

In this section, the three principles are applied to some ideas for disability policy.

An active welfare state

Welfare to work raises the question of the appropriate policy balance between disability as unemployment or early retirement, and how to distinguish between the two. Some people with severe impairments are nonetheless capable of work, and others with less severe impairments may be capable of some types of work under certain conditions (Rowlingson and Berthoud, 1996). *There needs to be a clearer distinction between people for whom welfare to work strategies are appropriate and those for whom work is an unlikely prospect.* The AWT is a poor mechanism for making this distinction because it is intended to gatekeep IB, with a focus on functions rather than actual work capacity. Furthermore there is no link between the benefits system and help from the ES.

An interactionist approach

The polarisation between individual and structural issues in welfare has some parallels in models of disability. The individual or medical model of disability holds that disability is a result of impairment, and so is best resolved by clinical or other individual intervention. On the other hand, the social model views disability as society's failure to adjust to different impairments, locating the responsibility with society to adapt. The policy emphasis has tended to be on the individual model with the AWT firmly based in the medical tradition by reducing incapacity for work to a series of functional limitations. However, implicit in the DDA is the notion that impairments do not prevent work when adjustments can be made. Whilst the social model has gained greater acceptance in recent years, commentators have questioned the extent to which it can address the very real restrictions of some impairments (French, 1996) or equates disability with discrimination (Low, 1996). There may be a 'third way' to bridge the gap between the individual and social models. The *interactionist perspective,* developed earlier this century as a way of understanding how human identity is formed, can provide this bridge by allowing us to look at both the social barriers to employment, the impairment, and the relationship between them as a social process. The interactionist perspective, can explain how two individuals with the same impairment may experience the effects of that impairment in quite different ways.

Assessment, planning and identification
Earlier assessments

The lack of co-ordination between incomes and services provided by the ES, health and local authorities means that rehabilitation can be delayed, preventing or delaying a possible return to work. Fewer than one in 20 people with a personal injury claim following a work or road traffic accident were referred to Occupational Therapy or ES specialist services (Cornes, 1997). An assessment at two to three months instead of the AWT at six months could identify those with work potential early enough for an appropriate adjustment or retraining before delay makes rehabilitation more difficult.

Employability, not incapacity

A different approach could assess 'employability' rather than incapacity. This would include a focus on functions but, rather than scoring personal inabilities, would consider someone's abilities within a work context. This assessment would then form the basis for an individual plan to identify how the person's abilities could best be realised, entailing a far closer collaboration between the ES and BA than is currently the case. The individual plan would be managed by a key worker, perhaps an ES Disability Employment Adviser or another professional.

Identifying who really has work potential

There are probably three main groups of people who could be identified at this stage, although these are located along a continuum rather than rigid categories. The first group would be those who are *ready for work*, but need assistance from the ES to be matched to an appropriate employer, perhaps with workplace adjustments. (An assessment could help both employer and employee identify these). The second group would be those *not be expected to work immediately* but could enhance their prospects of work with employment rehabilitation or training. The third group would be those for whom there are no *real prospects of work* given the severity of their impairments or progressive nature of their condition based on a prospective assessment.

Evidence suggests that between a quarter and a third of disabled people would like to work if a suitable job was available (Sly, 1996; Rowlingson and Berthoud, 1996). Disabled people who have greatest attachment to the labour market tend to be younger, have fewer health problems, are less likely to have formally left their last job, have some formal qualifications and are slightly more likely to have a background in non-manual work (Erens and Ghate, 1993). So far, the 2 per cent of people on incapacity benefits who actually moved into work have tended to be younger, single men, and women with working partners, with less severe impairments or whose condition had improved (Rowlingson and Berthoud, 1996). Even for people with spinal injury resulting in severe physical and psychological impairments, where the chances of work are now limited, some people may nonetheless have the ability to undertake part-time or sheltered work – provided they receive early and co-ordinated intervention (Cornes, 1997).

Appropriate assistance

Individually-tailored help from BA and ES

For each of the groups outlined above, the benefits system would provide income replacement. In the short term, it would make sense to integrate IB and SDA, as they are both payable for the same contingency. They could form what I have elsewhere nominally called 'Income Maintenance Benefit' (IMB) to avoid the negative connotations associated with invalidity and incapacity (Howard, 1997). IMB could be payable during a period of training or rehabilitation, without having to satisfy other benefit conditions, and could also be paid on a long-term basis as this is the truly appropriate 'early retirement' group.

People who are ready for work
For people who are ready for work, benefit could be payable during the period of job search until matched with an employer, perhaps using supported placements for people with reduced productivity or using the ES to support work in the open market with workplace adjustments.

People who need a rehabilitation or training package
Where an assessment has indicated that some re-training or rehabilitation is required, customised training could be developed with rehabilitation providers. Currently benefit entitlement can be affected, depending on whether a scheme is technically Training for Work or supported by the European Social Fund. Instead, the proposed IMB could be payable without any added conditions for the duration of the course, and would then automatically link to DWA to help people make the transition to work.

People who have limited prospects of work
People who are assessed as having little prospect of employment should be treated as the 'early retired'. However once on IMB, contact with the labour market need not be discouraged. Some disabled people who are below retirement age may have little or no prospects of work because of the severity or nature of their impairments but could nonetheless make a contribution through voluntary or community work, or may be able to undertake small amounts of paid work on an irregular basis. This could be undertaken legitimately as part of the individual plan. Entitlement could be reviewed according to the likely

Box 4.3 BA and **ES** help combined for people ready for 'matching' with an employer

Access To Work: to include a payment to help employers with any additional training costs incurred when recruiting a disabled person

Work Trials, already found to be successful with some groups, could be developed by making the trial periods longer or perhaps part time, whilst benefit continues without the need to satisfy any additional conditions of entitlement or risking loss of benefit as a result of the trial. Some employers and disabled people may prefer this approach to a 'wage subsidy' like the Job Introduction Scheme.

The **Job Interview Guarantee,** which has also met with some success, could be adapted for disabled people.

The £200 **Jobfinder's Grant,** normally only available to long term unemployed people working more than 30 hours a week, could be extended to disabled people.
'Jobmatch Plus', the non-means-tested payment of £50 a week for a year, as above, could be used to encourage part time work.

Benefit **'run-ons'** could be extended. Where someone has been on JSA for 26 weeks and then finds work, they are eligible for HB or CTB for an extended period of four weeks to assist the transition into work. A similar rule could be extended to the mortgage interest element of IS, and to other benefits such as IB itself. For people moving from IB into work, the HB and DWA tapers could be reduced from 65% and 70% respectively to 50% for the first two years. Ireland's Back to Work Allowance, similar in concept to Jobmatch, allows a proportionate 'run-on' for three years after entering employment, a scheme which has 58 per cent additionality (Gardiner, 1997).

Disability Working Allowance could be made more effective through adding the disability test, now used at renewal stage, to the list of qualifying conditions for benefit.

The IB **linking rule** could be extended from eight weeks to at least a year, preferably two (for consistency with the DWA linking rules), in order to improve capacity to take and keep jobs.

prognosis of the condition, instead of either assuming a permanent condition or, conversely, sending people for regular AWT reviews for undertaking part time 'exempt' work. Currently exempt work can only be undertaken with prior GP recommendation and the hypothetical agreement of the DSS. Under a new system, combining part-time work with benefit would be integral to the individual plan. It would not require further verification or review. Any earnings could be assessed on a quarterly basis (ie a 'rolled-up' disregard), allowing for fluctuations in hours worked or wages, with earnings tapering off above the limit. (This could be done through the tax system rather than reducing the benefit. One suggestion is for a 50 per cent tax rate without any benefit taper where half of the 50 per cent share taken by the state is kept by the Inland Revenue, and half is reimbursed to benefit authorities (Bray, 1997).

Box 4.4 Summary of main 'employability' options

Assessment
|
Individual Plan

Ready for work	Rehabilitation/training	Limited prospects
IMB until matched	IMB for duration of	IMB (rolled up dis
ATW, Work Trials,	rehabilitation;	regard) plan allows
JIG	customised training/	prospective activity;
Full-time:	rehabilitation	voluntary contact
JIG, run-ons,		with ES; links to
DWA, tapers		DWA
Part-time:		
IMB, Jobmatch plus		

Active agencies

The present divisions between the BA and ES would become increasingly blurred under this new approach. Adopting an interactionist perspective means that external barriers like transport and employment opportunities are addressed. The ES is probably better placed to do this than the BA as it already has a specialist disability service as well as more localised offices than the BA. However it is likely that expertise would need to be recruited to the ES, or it would have to work in partnership with other organisations in order to fully develop this role. The time and resource implications for both agencies of adopting this approach should not be underestimated.

In practical terms it would involve greater liaison with employers, providing advice about DDA responsibilities and encouraging them to notify more vacancies through Job Centres or intermediaries with close links to disability groups. As employers indicate that they have few disabled applicants (Dench et al, 1996), personal contact with an ES 'employer liaison' worker could begin to change this situation, particularly if accompanied by information about the ES assistance available. Employers could be offered a cash payment for any extra training costs when recruiting a disabled person (Davoud, 1996). Small firms of fewer than 20 employees, currently not covered by the DDA, could be offered special help under ATW when recruiting a disabled person, say for a job coach to act as mentor. The use of the 'two-ticks' disability symbol by employers could also be monitored more extensively and recruitment of more employers as symbol-users increased. Each Job Centre could draw up plans to consult with symbol-users in that area with a view to offering the best deal for disabled people locally. The ES may need to recruit community workers to help with the outreach work to address local barriers with disabled people, such as transport and accessibility. Alternatively the ES may wish to purchase such a service from not-for-profit brokers.

Opportunities and responsibilities

The New Deal provides opportunities for people who have been excluded from the labour market to undertake socially useful work though the concept of Neighbourhood Match, to be tested in Employment Zones. The responsibilities of claimants to take up one of the New Deal options has been buttressed by sanctions for non-compliance. However this approach is unlikely to be effective or appropriate for many disabled people, and suggestions for how to develop a different style of responsibility are made below.

Opportunities
Locality

The natural concern about the New Deal is whether enough jobs exist for all target groups in the right places. The proportion of disabled people varies markedly by region, from 9 per cent in the South East to 15 per cent in the North and 17 per cent in Wales (Sly, 1996). The concentration of disabled people between 50 years old and pension age in the North of England (32%) and Wales (35%) is almost double that in the South East and South West (18%). In some areas down to the electoral ward level, pockets of inactivity exist particularly in South Wales. Taking one inactive person of working age, there is a 30% chance that a second person chosen at random from the same area will also be inactive:

> Such absolute isolation of those who are inactive/unemployed from the rest of the population is likely to reduce the chance (other things being equal) for inclusion of the non-employed in social networks including the employed (Green, 1994).

For disabled people in those areas, who may be unable to use public transport or travel more than a few miles, the employment prospects for even the keenest jobseeker are likely to be limited. Research on Invalidity Benefit also shows that work near to home is of particular importance to disabled people. In some cases this was more crucial than variable hours or rest breaks. Moving may not always be an option because of the difficulty in setting up care and support networks elsewhere. Neighbourhood match will therefore be of particular importance for disabled people.

Employment Zones
EZs have been set up in five areas of high unemployment to test new ways to raise employment levels and use money from benefits and training programmes within the limits of existing legislation. The target group are the over-25s unemployed for at least one year. Older and disabled people are categories for special attention. One of the EZs will look at the needs of disabled people, transport and childcare (DfEE

press release, 419/97, 10 December 1997). There may be scope to offer job opportunities to disabled people through extending the concept of supported employment, currently used mainly for people with learning disabilities. The merits of a more proactive role for the Employment Service could also be tested in EZs, (either directly or in partnership with others). In turn, this approach could inform how the Voluntary Sector Option and Environmental Task Force develop to include disabled people. Working with local authorities and the voluntary sector to look at how community care and community services could be developed is also worth exploring, expanding the pool of labour-intensive job opportunities and strengthening services available to disabled people.

Employers' role

Some of the savings attributable to the New Deal could be used to provide incentives for employers to locate or expand in these deprived areas rather than attaching to individuals in particular client groups (based on age for example). In the US a Wage Tax Credit scheme offers employers tax relief for recruiting local residents to work in areas where they live (Clark, 1996).

Many employers recognise that if they accommodate disabled employees, their services can be more accessible, in turn increasing their potential market. However, in the short term the DDA is unlikely to significantly increase the chances of disabled people getting work. The establishment of a government Taskforce to consider the establishment of a Disability Rights Commission, and to consult on the exclusion of firms with fewer than 20 employees, are encouraging developments but will take some time to make an impact. In the meantime, despite wishing to do the right thing, employers appear to be more aware of the DDA in relation to recruitment than retention (Infoseek, 1997). Many adjustments can be made at no or low cost, such as adjusting the height of a desk. An 'Employability' assessment as described above, could help identify what is required. Organisations including the ES could support employers in this way, and identify areas of service provision where better accessibility could expand the market to the benefit of employers as well as disabled people.

Responsibility

Consistent with the interactionist approach, the meaning of responsibility includes both society and the individual. Society's responsibility to assist the social inclusion of disabled people entails the development of community networks as well as assistance for employers to fulfil their DDA responsibilities to employ disabled people and accommodate disabled customers.

Disabled individuals, particularly those re-classified as unemployed rather than disabled, could be caught up in sanctions designed for unemployed people who fail in their responsibility to take up New Deal options. However, sanctions may neither be appropriate nor effective for disabled people, whether signing on or not. Motivation is a critical factor influencing the prospects of people who fail the AWT (Davoud, 1996) and the success of rehabilitation programmes (Lakey and Simpkins, 1994). The challenge is to enable people caught in the grey area between incapacity and unemployment, some of whom may have been on benefit for years, to develop enough confidence to consider a return to work.

An early employability assessment, with a personal adviser and individual plan, could change the culture for new claimants, but a more sensitive approach will be for existing claimants. Advisers will need to build motivation, backed up by the prospect of purposeful work and the security of having an income to fall back on if health fails. One approach, cognitive therapy, has been successful in promoting mental well-being and more effective jobsearch for the long-term unemployed and could be adapted (Proudfoot *et al*, 1997). For those whose prospects of work are limited, there would of course be no requirement for labour market attachment.

Enabling government: cross-sector links

The Government is rightly concerned to look across departmental divides, and initiatives like the Social Exclusion Unit could provide a catalyst for new thinking and practice. An enabling government will include private sector and public sector working together. Simply contracting out elements of public sector provision or administration may not be viable for disability insurance. Permanent Health Insurance (PHI) currently covers only 10 per cent of working adults who are relatively low-risk professional groups. The long-term target is only 35 per cent of the working population. When compared with state cover, commercial policies are expensive and the loading of high risk occupations increases the regressive effect for low income groups and those in poor health (Burchardt and Hills, 1997).

A co-ordinated approach to public, private and occupational provision of long-term disability incomes could include greater consistency of assessment and definition. The appropriate balance between sectors needs to be considered, especially in the light of developments for stakeholder and citizenship pensions and the distribution of risks discussed below. Some suggestions for a way forward are provided below.

Consistency of assessment

Lessons can be learned from the private sector and other countries where easy assessments and rehabilitation can prevent some claims becoming long–term. Insurers are increasingly using early intervention and rehabilitation *(Post Magazine,* 18 September 1997*)*. Some employers have adopted a similar approach; a return to work programme undertaken by Strathclyde Police involved occupational therapists undertaking assessments and therapy on injured police officers (Pratt et al, 1997). The numbers involved are small at this stage so it is hard to generalise from these findings, but the initial results are encouraging; nine out of 15 officers completing the programme returning to full operational duties, three to light duties and two were given medical retirement.

An assessment could help employers identify adjustments and determine a range of responses when an employee becomes disabled, as an estimated 3 in every 1000 do. These options include a period away from work to adjust to the disability (disability leave); minor adjustments to the workplace; full or partial retention in the same job; redeployment in a different job; or an expected absence from work which is prolonged or permanent.

One way forward could be to set up an independent agency to assess the impact of disability on employment, similar to the multi-disciplinary Employment Rehabilitation Centres (ERCs) previously run by the ES, but with a broader remit. It could be funded by all major stakeholders. Employers and insurers could have more confidence in a nationally recognised assessment procedure with universally agreed standards. Although there are a range of professionals with these skills such as occupational therapists, there have been no agreed standards for training or quality control. Unlike the USA which has hundreds of professional vocational rehabilitation courses and several professional bodies, these developments are in their infancy in the UK (Floyd, 1997). However, the National Vocational Rehabilitation Association (NVRA) has been established to develop accreditation and training. It could form the basis of a new profession which, in time, could be used by the state, employers, pension fund trustees and the private sector alike for employment assessments to indicate work and rehabilitation potential, and therefore the most appropriate income replacement benefit or pension.

Consistency of definitions

As described above, payments for 'incapacity' are now made by the state, employers and insurers. In the past PHI and pensions have tended to compensate for incapacity to undertake one's own occupation, although some companies in both sectors have offered reduced cover for a test of incapacity for any work (similar to the AWT). Whilst some companies may prefer to reserve the right to provide insurance or pensions under an own occupation definition, there may be scope for a common definition with a common set of criteria to be used across sectors.

The DDA as a baseline

The baseline for developing such a set of criteria could be the DDA as the overarching legislation in the area of disability. Although the BA and ES should be covered as employers and service providers, social security legislation has remained unaffected. The definition and purpose of financial support could complement DDA developments more closely than at present. The link between assessments to identify reasonable adjustments as part of an employer's DDA responsibilities and income replacement for retention or during prolonged absence from work, is an obvious complementarity.

Some disabled people with a pre-existing condition may be refused cover from a PHI or occupational pensions scheme. The DDA is unlikely to alter this position as it currently allows for less favourable treatment to be justified where there are actuarial reasons for doing so (such as a greater likelihood of retiring early due to Multiple Sclerosis for example). In such cases an employer or insurance company can lawfully provide a lower level of benefit or pension to a disabled person without having to make any reasonable adjustment, as is required with other employment provisions. This means that employers need not reduce the level of contributions an individual pays into a pension scheme in recognition of the greater likelihood of having to draw upon it. This provision may also have knock-on effects for the state scheme which may be required to pick up the tab for those people who are classed as more at risk. OPCS data show that some 57 per cent of men and 47 per cent of women with some disability had to retire early because of their own ill-health compared to 20 per cent and 18 per cent of those with no prior disability (Bone *et al*, 1992) indicating that substantial numbers could legitimately be treated less favourably.

The DDA is an important foundation for developing an enabling government across the sectors. This is an area which the Taskforce could consider in association with the finance industry and other experts.

The interface between sectors

Changes to state schemes like the abolition of the SERPS addition can have a knock-on effect on the occupational and private sectors, in definitions, coverage and the calculation of payments. Although the introduction of IB does not appear to have increased the sales of PHI significantly, some insurers have been prompted to introduce a more limited 'abilities test' to cover people unable to work in any occupation, similar to some aspects of the AWT.

Occupational sick pay and PHI normally take account of state benefits payable. If the rate of IB or the basis on which it is paid is changed, the employer or insurer is likely to have to alter its formula or payment. For instance, integrated PHI schemes have a target benefit (usually three-quarters or two thirds of salary), from which the actual IB received is deducted, with the insurer paying the difference. If the person does not qualify for IB, the insurer would pay the full target benefit. So, any moves to means-test or offset IB against other income could have knock-on effects on the private sector.

Across public, private and occupational sectors, greater flexibility of provision is needed to provide an adequate level of income for people who are likely to be on benefit long term or permanently, without excluding an eventual return to work. Pensions have tended to follow a fairly rigid format, with many schemes paying permanent incapacity at the maximum rate according to Inland Revenue rules. A minority of private sector companies offer a lower level of pension to accommodate less than total or permanent incapacity (IRS, 1995). Some PHI companies have a system of proportionate payments (to reflect partial loss of earnings) as a way to promote a return to work after recovery, but rarely as a measure to aid retention in work.

Similarly the problem of churning between low paid work and out of work benefits has already been identified in relation to the New Deal. This may be a particular problem for disabled people who may subsequently need to reclaim benefit after trying to work. Research shows that of those who do move from incapacity benefits into work by claiming DWA, two out of three subsequently leave because of ill health or disability (Arthur and Zarb, 1997). The same research also points to the importance of the two-year linking rule in encouraging people to apply for DWA in the first place. As PHI policies have 'linking' periods, the need for both flexibility and security of incomes across sectors should be considered.

People excluded from PHI, perhaps because of irregular work patterns, high-risk occupations or poor health, may have previously received the SERPS addition with IVB. With its abolition they are likely to be in the position of having no earnings-related cover. There may be some scope to fill this gap through the vehicle of stakeholder pensions so that people have some second-tier payments in the event of a prolonged or permanent absence from work due to disability or ill-health.

Towards social cohesion

The welfare-to-work programme has considerable potential to include disabled people in the labour market. But it is only one part of the policy response. Civil rights for disabled people need to be developed coherently alongside welfare reform, and a consideration of the distribution of risks between disabled and non-disabled can help us think of ways in which those risks can be better accommodated.

People in the lowest socio-economic groups tend to experience the greatest risks of illness which is broadly reflected in the distributing of insurance cover. Inequalities in health show a gradient rather than a sharp divide (Power and Matthews, 1997). The risk of ill health and early death is not only a matter for the poor in areas of high mortality such as described by Dorling (1997), but seems to be rooted in relative deprivation. Lack of control in the workplace linked to economic status can increase the risk of ill health as demonstrated in two studies of Whitehall civil servants, where death rates from heart disease were three times higher among junior than senior grades (Wilkinson, 1996). Policies to tackle this health gradient are needed in order to improve social cohesion, reduce risks and so save public spending on social security and treating preventable illness. Power and Matthews (1997) suggest areas where intervention could start to address early disadvantage and later adult experiences which compound poor health, education and employment practices respectively.

Factors outside the social security system can exert a strong influence over health, especially long-term unemployment. The growth of Invalidity Benefit is partly explained by employment practices and the decline of manual work. Research has shown that almost four in five claimants left their last job for reasons connected with their health, one third being asked to leave by their employer. Three-quarters of those working when their health problem began said their employer had provided no help for them to carry on working (Erens and Ghate, 1993). In contrast, early retirement is less likely where employers make workplace adjustments as in Germany for example (Thornton et al, 1997).

Accidents and work-related ill health alone have been estimated to cost the British economy between £6 and £12 million - equivalent to 2-3 per cent of GDP, or a typical year's economic growth (Davies and Teasdale, 1994). Some of the costs of poor health and safety are being borne by core health and education services. In NHS acute hospitals, the cost of accidents to both patients and staff has been estimated as of £150 million a year and could be well in excess of this figure (National Audit Office, 1996). Many of these incidents could have been prevented with better guidance and training on manual handling, dealing with clinical waste and violence against staff. Already one hospital trust has reduced sick leave by one fifth through better training to reduce the incidence of back injuries among staff.

Almost four out of ten teachers leaving the profession retire on the grounds of ill health, a figure which has grown by half during the period 1989 to 1996. This has occurred at a time when the education service is facing serious problems in recruiting sufficient numbers of good quality teachers. Given the stress involved at work which has contributed to the growth of early retirement, the potential impact of changing the distribution of work tasks and offering much wider opportunities for part-time work and job-sharing should be explored in more detail.

In the short-term, 'audit trails' could identify the knock-on effects of spending in other departments like Health and Education on the social security budget. Each government department could make 'disability impact statements' on the effect of its policies. These could be used to highlight positive developments in disability policy and to point up any potentially *disabling* effects in practice.

If preventive approaches can be developed, the imbalance of risks across current socio-economic groups may begin to diminish in absolute and relative terms.

With the an ageing population, it is unlikely that the proportion of disabled people will fall in the short term. The challenge for all income providers is then to consider the appropriate balance between the welfare to work and early retirement approaches. Key to this is early employment assessment, coupled with access to rehabilitation or training where appropriate, and a more flexible approach to income replacement across public and private sectors.

References

Allbeson J (1997) *Benefits and work: a CAB perspective on the welfare to work debate,* London, NACAB

Arthur S and Zarb G (1997) *Evaluation of the 1995 changes to disability working allowance,* in house report 25, London, DSS

Audit Commission (1997) *Retiring nature: early retirement in local government,* London

Beatty C, *et al* (1997) *The real level of unemployment,* Sheffield Hallam University, Centre for Regional Economic and Social Research

Bell I *et al* (1997) *Workless households, unemployment and economic activity,* Labour Market Trends, September 1997

Berthoud R (1993) *Invalidity benefit: where will the savings come from?* Research briefing, Policy Studies Institute

Berthoud R *et al* (1993) *The economic problems of disabled people,* London, Policy Studies Institute

Bone M, *et al* (1992) *Retirement and retirement plans: a survey carried out by the OPCS on behalf of the DSS,* London, OPCS

Bottomley D, *et al* (1997) *Unemployment and Jobseeking,* DSS research report no 62, London, TSO

Bray E (1997) *Arguments for a 50/50 disability earnings concession,* November 1997

Burchardt T and Hills J (1997) *Private welfare insurance and social security: pushing the boundaries,* York, Joseph Rowntree Foundation

Clark G (1996) *Budgeting for jobs: US tax-based incentives keep unemployment low,* Unemployment Unit Working Brief, Dec 1996/Jan 1997

Clemens S (1997) *The long term effects of Jobmatch: an evaluation of the Jobmatch pilots,* DfEE research report no 12, London, TSO

Cornes P (1997) "A follow-up study of accident victims" in Floyd, M, ed, *Vocational Rehabilitation and Europe,* Jessica Kingsley. London

Davies N and Teasdale, P (1994) *The costs to the British economy of work accidents and work-related ill health,* London, Health and Safety Executive

Davoud N, (1996) *Welfare to work: disability perspective: a report from the London North CEPD incapacity benefit working group,* London, London North CEPD

Dench S, *et al* (1996) *The recruitment and retention of people with disabilities,* report 301, Brighton, Institute for Employment Studies

DOH (1997) *On the state of the public health 1996: annual report of the Chief Medical Officer of the Department of Health for the year 1996,* London, TSO

Dorling D (1997) *Death in Britain: how local mortality rates have changed: 1950s-1990s,* York, Joseph Rowntree Foundation

DfEE (1997) *Design of the New Deal for 18-24 year olds,* October (1997) London, TSO

Erens B and Ghate D (1993) *Invalidity benefit: a longitudinal study of new recipients,* DSS research report no 20, London, TSO.

Floyd M (1997) *Vocational rehabilitation services in the United Kingdom,* in 'Vocational rehabilitation and Europe', London, Jessica Kingsley

French S (1996) *"Disability, impairment or something in between?"* in Swain *et al* eds, 'Disabling Barriers – Enabling Environments', London, OU/Sage

Gardiner K (1997) *Bridges from benefit to work: a review,* York, Joseph Rowntree Foundation

Green A (1994) *The geography of poverty and wealth,* University of Warwick, Institute for Employment Research

Howard M (1997) *Investing in disabled people: a strategy from welfare to work,* London, Disablement Income Group

Infoseek, (19970 *Employer attitudes towards the Disability Discrimination Act and employing disabled personnel,* Buckingham, Infoseek

IRS (1995) *Early retirement survey 1: ill-health retirement,* IRS employment trends 581

Knight M and Fletcher J (1996) *Tracking study of former incapacity benefit claimants,* Employment Service, RED 110

Lakey J and Simpkins R (1994) *Employment rehabilitation for disabled people,* London, Policy Studies Institute

Loyd R and Hussey D (1996) *Evaluation of Jobmatch,* DfEE research studies RS26, London TSO

Low C (1996) *Disability models... or muddles?,* Therapy Weekly, 1 February 1996

National Audit Office (1996) *"Health and safety in NHS acute hospitals",* HC 82, session 1996/7

Poole C (1997) *Retirement on grounds of ill health: cross sectional survey in six organisations in United Kingdom*, BMJ, vol. 314, 29 March 1997

Power C and Matthews S (1997) *Origins of health inequalities in a national population sample*, The Lancet, vol. 350, November 29 1997

Pratt J *et al* (1997) *A review of the initial outcomes of a return-to-work programme for police officers following injury or illness*, British Journal of Occupational Therapy, June 1997, 60 (6)

Proudfoot J *et al* (1997) *'Effect of cognitive-behavioural training on job-finding among long-term unemployed people'*, The Lancet, vol.350, July 12 1997.

Ritchie J and Snape D (1993) *Invalidity benefit: a preliminary qualitative study of the factors affecting its growth*, London, SCPR

Rowlingson K and Berthoud R (1996) *Disability, benefits and employment*, DSS research report no 54, London, TSO

Sly F (1996) *Disability and the labour market*, Labour Market Trends, September 1996

SSAC (1997) *Social security provision for disability: a case for change?*

Stone D (1984) *The Disabled State*, Macmillan

Thornton P *et al* (1997) *Helping disabled people to work: a cross-national study of social security and employment provisions*, SSAC research paper 8, London, TSO

Wilkinson R (1996) *Unhealthy societies: the affliction of inequality*, London, Routledge

5. PROSPECTS FOR PENSION REFORM

James McCormick

Introduction

When William Beveridge laid the foundations of a new pension system
fifty years ago, it was not unusual for men to live for only one or two
years beyond retirement. His system was constructed on the male
breadwinner model of full employment: husbands undertook the paid
work and wives did the unpaid work of caring (at least once the
children arrived). Contributions from earnings funded benefits to be
drawn upon when earnings were interrupted due to unemployment and
sickness, or ended with retirement.

Both contributions and benefits were flat-rate for two reasons. First,
low-paid workers could not have afforded the higher contributions
that would have earned more generous benefits; and second, to
encourage those on higher earnings to top-up the basic benefits
provided by the state from their own income. Although the new model
was conceived of as a social insurance system, a general subsidy from
the Treasury was written into the contract to ensure that benefits could
be paid early on. It was never an insurance system in the strict actuarial
sense. While the principles underlying the Beveridge system are
enduring - equity, affordability, comprehensive coverage - the
assumptions on which it was based have fundamentally changed.

Many of the changes are by now familiar to the British public policy
debate. The UK's population structure has aged but at a more gradual
pace and over a longer period than in most other OECD countries.
Although we can expect to live seven years longer than the generation
living and working in 1945, the increase has been highly uneven. The
average gap in life expectancy between the most affluent and poorest
neighbourhoods is eight years. There are new risks to be addressed if
expected levels of welfare are to be met, not least in the area of long-
term care. The composition of the labour market has altered
significantly, with women accounting for half the workforce in some
localities, working mothers becoming the norm (with the clear
exception of lone mothers) and 'atypical' working patterns becoming
typical in some sectors. At the same time, the duration of
unemployment has become a more relevant indicator of local labour
demand than the headline rate.

Each of these changes present hard choices for policy-makers.
Increased life expectancy is a success of the post-war years. It has at
least as much to do with high and sustained levels of employment for

most of the period as a secure benefits system or a comprehensive National Health Service. If some households and communities are persistently trapped outside opportunities to earn, we should expect standards of health to be affected. The cost of labour market failure as expressed in spending on means-tested benefits and tax revenues foregone has influenced a vigorous debate on 'welfare-to-work' strategies. Here we assess the impact of fifty years of change in welfare and work upon pensions. Considering the evidence based on a snapshot of today's population and projections for the future, we ask:

- How have retirement incomes changed and how are they expected to change?
- How does the welfare of pensioners compare with people of working age today?
- How can public policy best combine income transfers from the lifetime affluent to the lifetime poor (inter-personal redistribution) with income-smoothing between an individual's working age and retirement (life-cycle redistribution)?

Three Nations in Retirement

Beveridge assumed that being old meant being poor. Fifty years ago, it was a safe assumption. In 1998, it is an inadequate description of the retired population and a poor guide to policy reform. Concern about pensioner poverty was expressed in the idea of 'Two Nations in Retirement': one group of relatively well-off pensioners, likely to be married couples in their 60s drawing their supplementary income from occupational pensions; and another group of poor pensioners, likely to be single women in their 70s or 80s depending on the state almost entirely for their income.

Income inequality among pensioners narrowed between the mid-1960s and late 1970s as claims on state and occupational pensions expanded. By the mid-1970s, annual uprating of the Basic State Pension (BSP) moved from an ad hoc basis (Johnson et al, 1996) to track changes in either average earnings or prices (whichever was greater). Since 1980 however, the BSP has been linked to prices. Its relative decline in value has seen it overtaken by means-tested Income Support. Income from the state-run second pension SERPS has started to accrue to employees reaching the end of their working lives. However, changes in the calculation of entitlements - once in the 1986 Social Security Act and secondly in the 1995 Pensions Act - have reduced the return on SERPS contributions. Since 1988, government has permitted and indeed encouraged employees to opt-out of SERPS into personal pensions. This was significant not just in terms of opening up the possibility of funded pensions to employees who were unable to join a pension scheme at work, but in signalling the expansion of Money Purchase rather than traditional Final Salary Occupational Pensions.

How have these trends shaped the incomes of today's pensioners? The average retirement income is substantially higher than in previous generations, due largely to the accumulation of occupational pensions (and to a lesser extent the growth of savings and investment income, Downs, 1997). As more pensioners come to avoid poverty in retirement, they have become less represented among the ranks of the poor (replaced by lone parents, the long-term unemployed and their children). Maturing occupational pension schemes have brought a rising tide but they have failed to raise all boats.

The Commission on Social Justice (1994) suggested a threefold division to pension incomes - what we might now call the Three Nations in Retirement - with the incomes of the poorest third composed almost entirely of state transfers, a middle third just above the Income Support threshold but with very modest incomes from occupational schemes, and a higher income third paying tax on their pensions and investment income and able to draw on savings and other assets. The result has been growing inequality of income in retirement since the early 1980s, reversing the long-run trend of the previous two decades (Figure 5.1). Pensioners are no longer as likely to be poor. But those who remain poor are falling further behind the rest.

Fig 5.1 Retirement Income Inequality (Gini coefficients 1962 -1991)

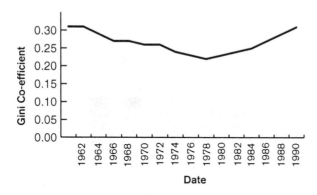

Source: Johnson et al (1996)

How will the pensioners of tomorrow compare with today's? The DSS has developed a model of pension incomes (PENSIM) with the Government Actuary Department and the LSE to compare the distribution and composition of pension incomes in 1994 with a projection thirty years ahead (Curry and Ball 1996, Figure 2).

Fig 5.2 Distribution of retirement income in 1994 and 2025, (adapted from Curry and Ball (1996)

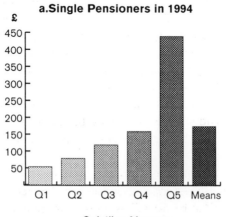

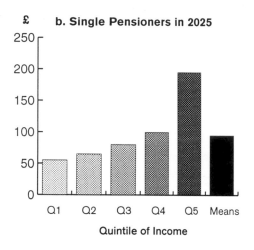

£   b. Single Pensioners in 2025

Quintile of Income

The average income is projected to rise by half over the next thirty years. Two points should be made here. First, the rise in income is smallest for today's poorest fifth of single pensioners (up by just 20%) and greatest for the highest income fifth (whose incomes are expected to more than double). Average incomes among the top fifth of single pensioners are currently around five times higher than at the bottom. On top of this, growth in income is expected to be six times faster at the top over the next thirty years. Where the BSP represents almost half of gross income today, this will fall to between one third and one quarter by 2025. The most significant relative growth is expected to be from personal pensions (which contribute a tiny proportion of the average income today), from SERPS (despite less generous accrual rates) and from investment income. The model forecasts no relative growth in income from occupational pensions or earnings. Second, the average income of all pensioners is forecast to grow by less than average earnings, except for the top fifth. In other words the Government Actuary expects a widening of inequality both between pensioners (intra-generational) and between pensioners and people of working age (inter-generational).

The DSS model cannot predict future working patterns, further changes in the state retirement age, or relevant changes in how state pensions are paid. What it does tell us is how current trends are likely to shape future retirement incomes assuming there are no major changes in the labour market or in welfare policy. The centre-left has to decide whether it is mainly concerned with a more secure and generous minimum for those facing the lowest incomes in retirement or whether the extent of relative inequalities above the minimum should be addressed. There is also a need to ask whether public policy actually contributes to widening inequality and if so how it can be reformed.

This Chapter considers how the first-tier flat-rate and second-tier earnings-related state pensions are currently unable to do an effective job of either relieving or preventing retirement poverty for those who rely on them most. It explores the case for switching from Pay-As-You-Go (PAYG) to funded state pensions. It then discusses how the twin goals of comprehensive coverage and adequacy above the basic first-tier can be achieved. Too often, analysis of pension policy has been rooted in a defence of the status quo: the basic state pension as we know it for fear of something worse being introduced; or the current structure of tax reliefs on private pensions for fear of savings being diverted into more tax-efficient products. It is our belief that neither a blind defence of what we have nor radical change for its own sake provide a useful starting point. It is also our belief that intelligent government intervention remains an essential element of effective pensions reform.

The First Tier Pension

How Basic a State Pension?

The Basic State Pension (BSP) is the foundation of retirement income provision. Paid at £62.45 to a single pensioner and £99.80 to couples, it is the single largest social security commitment by the state. In 1997-98 its cost is £33.6 billion. Disagreement over whether the BSP should simply be allowed to continue 'withering on the vine' (by maintaining the link with retail prices) or uprated in line with earnings has yet to be fully resolved. Until recently, however, the focus of policy debate was on how to reshape second-tier provision on top of it - whether SERPS should be wound up as part of a transition to universal funded second pensions for example. However it would be a mistake to assume that the fate of the BSP has been settled. The previous Conservative Government's proposal to wind up the BSP as well as SERPS, and introduce an integrated funded scheme called 'Basic Pension Plus', may never be put into practice but it does mark a departure in the debate. It signals that policy-thinkers must remake the case for a first-tier pension based on the Pay-As-You-Go principle.

Affordability

The starting point in the retirement income debate is usually affordability. An ageing society will make growing demands on the taxes of workers who, it is argued, are becoming less convinced of the case for paying contributions towards today's pensions in the hope that tomorrow's workers will do the same for them. Field (1996) is not alone in identifying "declining reserves of trust": towards governments which have hollowed out the BSP and SERPS; towards employers who are less likely to arrange occupational cover or contribute towards personal pensions; and towards each other. There is little doubt that pessimism is the order of the day when it comes to future expectations of the BSP (Box 5.1). Almost three-quarters of respondents believe that the state will be unable to provide a pension to all in the future. It is no surprise that references to 'the demographic timebomb' have fuelled this sense of fear, or that 80% of new employees opt out of SERPS in the search for a better return through a funded pension. In fact Britain is well able to provide a basic state pension to all, but we should distinguish this from the capacity or willingness to provide an *adequate* state pension.

There is no crisis of affordability for UK pensions. According to one influential study by an advocate of compulsory funded pensions, there is little doubt that a universal BSP paid at or above the level of Income Support can be sustained by current PAYG arrangements (Yarrow, 1997). If the BSP remains linked to prices, the combined National Insurance rate required to pay for it will fall over the next thirty years. Earnings growth will increase the tax base by enough to cover the costs, providing the rate of productivity per employee exceeds the modest target of 0.7% per year set by the OECD. Given the declining cost of state pensions relative to GDP, it is quite possible that the anticipated costs of health and long-term care for the elderly will be offset by growth (Davies, 1997). Unlike Germany, Italy and France, the UK is on course to meet all of its accrued pension commitments. Failure to do so would indeed damage remaining trust in state pensions, but that would be the result of political decisions rather than fiscal constraints.

Box 5.1 Public attitudes on pension policy (Birch 1997)

	Agree
The basic state pension should provide for basic need	95%
People should be encouraged to provide something towards their own retirement	75%
The government will not be able to provide a basic state pension to all	73%
The government should be mainly responsible for ensuring an adequate retirement income	51%
Workers should pay higher income taxes to pay for better state pensions for today's retired	28%

The real problem is one of adequacy. The Labour government has inherited a BSP worth around 15% of average male earnings, compared with over 20% when it left office almost twenty years ago. If its value continued to diminish at the current rate, it would be worth less than half that amount by 2030. To retain its real value at 15% of earnings, the combined National Insurance rate would need to increase by 7% to 25% over that period. Labour is no more likely to introduce a phased increase in NICs of this order than Conservative governments. Nor should it. There is more than one way to prevent the BSP trapping the poorest pensioners in a miserable retirement. We can be sure, however, that the BSP will be 'a benefit in search of a role' if pensions policy were to remain in its current form (Johnson, 1994).

Funding the BSP?

The fashionable answer to the problem of inadequacy is to shift from PAYG to funded pensions across-the-board, described by Butler (1997) as making "the great escape" from state-run pensions. There is a credible case for switching from PAYG by winding up SERPS and chanelling contributions into funded second pensions, which we consider below. But should we now go further and allow contracting out of the BSP as well?

The 'Basic Pension Plus' plan of the Conservatives has been developed further by the Adam Smith Institute (Butler et al, 1997). Their proposal of a Fortune Account would provide a voluntary lifetime savings and insurance account covering a range of risks. It might cover retirement income, long-term care, health insurance and unemployment insurance. It might come to replace the state-run social insurance system. Such proposals for an integrated package of insurance policies brings together very different risks which should remain firmly 'unbundled'. It is virtually impossible to envisage a privately-run unemployment insurance pool which is both affordable and comprehensive. The need for costly long-term care in old age is sufficiently uncertain to make social insurance a strong candidate for meeting the risk. It is a quite different proposition from building up adequate savings for retirement (a high-probability event compared with needing long-term care). There is no case for collapsing these different contingencies into one pot if affordability and equity remain important policy goals.

Our focus instead is on the specific case for funding the BSP. The ASI favours a target minimum in retirement set no lower than today's Income Support level but not so high as to impose an impossible burden on workers. They support the establishment of compulsory funded pension accounts for under-30s (rather than a phased introduction with new entrants to the labour market as proposed by former Social Security Minister Peter Lilley). Government would pay a flat-rate sum and a fixed proportion of earnings into each account, in place of the National Insurance rebate. A formula of £9 a week plus 5% of earnings was suggested. Funds would accumulate through the capital markets. In response to the criticism that this would concentrate all of the investment risk on the individual, the state would guarantee to pay the equivalent BSP if the eventual investment value fell below this level.

There are two problems with integrated funding. The most obvious problem is the cost of double payment. By definition, PAYG means that the contributions of today's earners are required to finance today's pensions. If employees took all of their contributions out of the state system, to be ring-fenced in their own retirement pots, who would pay today's pensions? Would today's workers end up as the transitional generation who had to pay twice over in order to safeguard the benefits promised to the already retired?

According to proponents of Basic Pension Plus, the problem of paying twice over is much less than assumed since the proposal relies on gradualism to spread the burden across more than one generation. Plugging the gap becomes manageable because it will take at least 50 years to complete the process. Accrued pension entitlements can be met through the 'savings' brought forward by reversing the tax treatment of pensions - that is, shifting tax relief to future pension benefits rather than current contributions. A more rapid transition to full funding could be made, according to the ASI, by issuing transition or recognition bonds to everyone who leaves the state system. It is important to note that their value would inevitably be rather less than the total paid in. Rather than getting involved in a complex and lengthy process of calculating who should get what, Butler et al (1997) favour a 'quick and easy formula' which need not pay out much because expectations of getting a decent return on past contributions are in any case so low:

> Even if this is only a rough settlement, even if it is payable only as an interest-bearing bond...and even if its value is far less than they are genuinely entitled to, many over-30s will choose to leave...because any future contributions will give them a very much better return than those same contributions put into the state scheme.

Expectations may indeed be low, but this cannot justify the state actively choosing to further diminish the value of past contributions. Another analysis suggests that the Government could issue gilts to cover part or all of the bill for rights accrued under PAYG, thus smoothing the transitional costs over a longer period of time. In practice this would mean the crystallisation of a massive amount of implicit government liabilities as conventional public debt - £30 billion a year initially if a complete gilt issuance went ahead (S. Davies 1997). In the unlikely event that cross-party support could be secured, this would be a considerable leap into the unknown without parallel in the OECD. The benefits of doing so are entirely unproven.

According to the ASI, the boost to economic growth provided by lifting the 'drag anchor' of the national insurance system should cover the entire costs of transition from PAYG within a single generation: 'We should expect a significant annual gain from transferring to a

funded system, perhaps as high as 3% of GNP per year in perpetuity'
(ASI, 1997). However, Davies notes that the economic benefits of a
switch to full funding would have to be much greater than those so far
modelled by US economists to justify such a move.

The case against full funding is made not simply on the grounds of
unproven economic benefit. Davies goes on to conclude that the best
way to avoid the problem of winners and losers may be to let the BSP
wither on the vine. This leads to our second objection: the basic
guarantee within Basic Pension Plus would offer a miserable retirement
income if it remained linked to prices. The additional benefit of a
modest SERPS supplement would not be part of the guarantee. Neither
full funding nor letting the BSP die a slow death is a serious option for
the UK.

Reforming the BSP

The BSP is the only element of pension provision capable of playing
a redistributive role, from higher income groups to those on lower
incomes and from men to women across the lifecycle. Whatever their
respective merits, neither SERPS nor funded second pensions are
designed to deal with inter-personal redistribution. If this remains a
serious goal, as we believe it is, earnings-related pensions cannot
achieve it for the lifetime poor and low-paid.

The BSP is worth more to those on lower incomes because they are
likely to have contributed less towards it across their lives and because
they do not pay tax on it. It is also cheap to administer. To repeat our
earlier point, the real drawback with the BSP is its growing irrelevance
to both the affluent and the poor. For those on high incomes, it offers
a diminishing return on fixed contributions. For those on low incomes,
its value has fallen behind income-related supplements (offering 20
per cent less than Income Support for the oldest single pensioners). In
the face of rising income inequality, the BSP is too low to tackle
poverty.

Closing the Gaps

The policies for improving pensions that we already know are
inadequate may well be different from those needed to reduce the risk

of retirement poverty in the future. It is often forgotten that the BSP is a contributory benefit rather than a universal entitlement according to age (like Child Benefit). Eligibility for the full pension depends on contributions for 44 years from men and 39 years from women. This points to the general proposition that having a full contributions record across working age is essential for achieving a reasonable pension from *any* scheme, whether funded or PAYG.

Few women and a declining number of men can meet that requirement due to care responsibilities and periods out of employment for other reasons. The provision of contribution credits towards the BSP for the registered unemployed, those claiming Incapacity Benefit and Invalid Care Allowance, and men aged over 60 was extended in 1978 by Home Responsibilities Protection (HRP), designed to compensate mothers claiming Child Benefit for under-16s.

The state therefore fills in some of the gaps in contribution records. However, there remains a group of workers who do not contribute anything towards their own BSP entitlements: approximately 3.1 million of them are paid less than the Lower Earnings Limit (LEL) at which National Insurance is liable (and do not satisfy any of the criteria for HRP) and 0.5 million are women paying a reduced National Insurance rate (the so-called 'married women's stamp'). Although no married woman entering employment after 1978 was able to pay reduced NICs, the number of workers failing to qualify for the BSP due to low pay has increased by 40% since 1978. This is despite the falling value of the LEL in relation to average earnings, and an expected reduction in the numbers earning below it. Low pay is therefore a persistent barrier against being able to contribute towards the BSP and it appears that the LEL imposes its own effects on the creation of better-paid jobs.

The introduction of a national minimum wage will help some of these missing millions to qualify for the BSP by bringing them within the contributions net. There will still be a core of workers who are unlikely to have the consistency of earnings needed to accrue an adequate pension. There are two distinct options to close the gap further.

The first of these is to abolish the contributory basis of the BSP and introduce a universal Citizens Pension, based simply on age and residence rules. This would have both immediate and ongoing effects.

In Australia and New Zealand the first tier pension is effectively a basic income for the retired, funded out of general taxation rather than employment contributions. Proponents of this option argue that the UK has already relaxed a number of rules to allow those without full contribution records to nevertheless qualify for the BSP. Virtually everyone who reaches retirement age in twenty years will be entitled to it - so why wait until then if a universal pension could be brought forward more quickly? Johnson *et al* (1996) ask whether, on the grounds of intergenerational equity, there is a case for improving the pensions of those who were unable to benefit from HRP for example, and who only qualify for the 'dependant's addition' to their partner's pension. They calculate that the net cost of widening the net by paying the single person's BSP to everyone of retirement age would be approximately £2 billion.

Universal benefits have practically every advantage over means-tested benefits. Universalism remains a valued goal of the left. But here is precisely the sort of tradeoff that will define a modern definition of universalism. The proportion of today's pensioners who would be better off with a Citizens Pension would *rise* with original income. The poorest would be little better off due to offsetting reductions in means-tested benefits. In addition, a non-contributory pension would weaken the solidarity principle of benefits being paid in return for contributions (B. Davies, 1993). If the language of priorities applies equally to pensions, a Citizens Pension cannot be a priority in the foreseeable future.

The second option is to extend the contributory principle rather than abolish it. This would affect people of working age rather than today's retired. Field (1996) sets out the clearest proposal for the near-universalisation of the BSP. His plan involves reducing the lower contributions limit to £10 a week, above which every worker would pay NICs. Those earning between £10 and £60 a week would pay 2% of their earnings towards the BSP, matched by their employer. Those earning between £60 and the Upper Earnings Limit (UEL) would pay 6% NICs (again matched by employers). Those earning above £100 a week would also be required to contribute a minimum share of earnings towards a funded second pension, as discussed later.

This would help to fund entitlement to the BSP for very low earners rather than raising much revenue for government. Removing the artificial block on earnings and working hours imposed by the current LEL should also have a beneficial impact on the pattern of job creation. It would result in a first-tier pension for almost everyone, at a relatively high replacement ratio for the lifetime low paid. For someone in a part-time or casual job earning at best £50 a week, a BSP of £61 would indeed represent a high replacement ratio. However it would still be an inadequate retirement income, in return for a tax increase on the very lowest paid. One of the few pension issues on which practically all commentators agree is the inadequacy of the BSP and Income Support supplements as the sole sources of income. Field's proposal to widen the net is helpful in its own right, but it does not address the question of what level the BSP should rise to or how it should be uprated. If the question of adequacy is to be addressed, especially for those who depend on the state for all of their retirement income, a level playing field is not enough. The state pension system must also be "tilted in favour of the low-paid" (B. Davies, 1993).

A More Effective BSP

The classic universalist strategy would be to increase the BSP across-the-board, in line with average earnings rather than prices. Although Labour was criticised for failing to reaffirm its commitment to earnings-linked growth in its 1997 Manifesto, there is a convincing case for finding other ways of improving the BSP. Earnings indexation based on 20% of average male earnings would result in a net cost of £4.1 billion, but cost is not the only reason for rethinking how to improve the first-tier. Indexing to 1.5% earnings growth per year would require a combined NIC rate of 25.3% in 2030 - a rise of seven points. Hills (1993) explains the modest cost (0.23% per annum) of slowly phasing in such an increase. There are other options. A balance could be achieved by uprating in line with an index based half on earnings and half on prices as in Finland for example (MacIntyre,1996). The earnings index could be based on net average earnings or median earnings (given that two-thirds of earners are below average income).

Although Minns (1997) believes there is strong public support for higher taxes to improve state pensions, we cannot assume that is the case if the figures in Box 5.1 are accurate. In any event, it would not achieve one of our key objectives: a reduction in income inequality through a BSP which more effectively tackled today's poverty and reduced the risk of it tomorrow. The reasons why an across-the-board increase may not be the first priority have been well rehearsed by the Commission on Social Justice (1994) among others. The most affluent pensioners would gain all of the increase minus the tax they pay on the BSP. The poorest pensioners would receive little of the increase as the higher BSP was offset by reduced Housing Benefit and Income Support payments. The richest 10% would gain twice as much as the poorest (making up around three-quarters of those who would see no gain at all).

The net result would be greater inequality. Townsend and Castle (1996) make the reasonable point that we could simply decide to disregard all of the increase for those already claiming means-tested benefits (the lowest income 'third nation in retirement'). Unlike people below retirement age, there are no work disincentives involved in doing so. It would ensure the poorest retired did not fall further behind, but it would not do much to reduce inequality.

Differential accrual rates

Payment of NICs is the main passport to the BSP. Because the lowest earners contribute much less across their working lives than the highest earners, and the BSP is flat-rate while contributions are earnings-related, an element of redistribution is implicit. All the evidence shows it is insufficient. One controversial option is therefore to rebalance the link between contributions and benefits, changing the period required to qualify for the standard rate of BSP. The result could be a banded pension where it is possible to earn a pension higher or lower than the standard. Unlike earnings-related second pensions, a rebalanced BSP would pay higher benefits to those making the lowest contributions.

The National Association of Pension Funds (NAPF) has proposed such a scheme. It suggested a lower threshold (perhaps set at the LEL) and a higher threshold (set at the UEL or the earnings point for the top rate tax band). Once the value of the BSP declines to 10% of average earnings, the earnings link would be restored and these thresholds introduced. For each year earnings are under the lower threshold, entitlement would be 2% higher than the standard rate. For each year earnings are above the higher threshold, entitlement would be 3% less than the standard rate. Someone on a very low income for twenty five years would accrue an enhanced BSP worth 50% more than the standard rate, and someone on a high income for twenty five years would qualify for a reduced BSP set 75% below the standard. Someone who was temporarily at either end of the income spectrum would earn a different level of pension only for the period they remained there. This would approximate the lifetime means-test outlined by Falkingham and Johnson (1993;1996) without requiring the 'big-bang' funded pension they propose. It would also be closer to *a test of capacity to save rather than willingness to save towards retirement,* tracked across working age. The eventual net cost is estimated by the NAPF to be £300 million more than retaining a flat-rate BSP linked to prices.

Any government introducing such a change would presumably wish to guarantee a minimum BSP below which no-one should fall, not even the highest lifetime earners. It would otherwise be politically impossible to justify some people having to pay NICs in return for next to nothing. It might be unwise to set the higher threshold at the UEL if it remained linked to prices. The UEL is currently worth 25% more than average earnings but it is forecast to fall to 40% below average earnings by 2030. This would result in a large number of workers who were by no means well-off accruing the reduced rate BSP. The UEL would either have to be linked to earnings or the higher threshold should be linked to the top rate tax band.

It is not necessary to agree with the precise model offered by the NAPF to explore the principle of ending a flat-rate BSP. The important insight is that offered by (Johnson *et al,* 1996). Over the next twenty to thirty years, the working poor would retire on substantially enhanced first-tier pensions and, if the thresholds and rates of accrual are set carefully, this might reduce the need to bring the lifetime low paid into funded second pension coverage. Moreover, any supplement to the standard BSP would be earned during working age rather than fixed according to the income one retires on (i.e. a 'snapshot' means-test).

A rebalanced pension could be introduced as well as or instead of Field's proposal for cutting the LEL to £10 a week. If the qualifying threshold was lowered in this way, those paying very low NICs could be entitled to the enhanced BSP. This option would still leave the majority of employees across their working lives earning the standard BSP uprated in line with earnings. The element of redistribution from highest to lowest income groups would increase, leaving most people unaffected.

There would certainly be in principle objections to a rebalanced BSP on the grounds that it weakens the contributory link and retreats from flat-rate universalism. The practical problem - that it will take the duration of working age from the point of establishment to fully work through - is a more compelling reason against choosing this as the only answer to retirement poverty. It does not resolve the question of what to do for those low income pensioners who cannot wait for solutions designed for today's workers to raise their standard of living.

Targeting based on income

This brings us back to a familiar dilemma for the centre-left. It remains true that universal, flat-rate benefits are the most efficient way of raising living standards for those on low incomes, without imposing stigma, costly administration or invidious distinctions between 'us' (the contributors) and 'them' (the beneficiaries). It is also true, however, that flat-rate benefits are spread too thinly to do a very effective job of helping the poorest. Means-testing of the BSP and Child Benefit is periodically offered as a badge of modernisation. Proponents ask how can we justify paying a miserable state pension or Income Support supplement when a substantial minority of the elderly no longer 'need' their state benefits? A number of countries including Canada have taken steps to tax back at least part of the first-tier pension from the high-income retired. It is a badge that neither the Commission on Social Justice (1994) nor Frank Field (1995, 1996) have wished to wear, reaffirming the numerous drawbacks of having to prove one's poverty in order to qualify for benefit.

More accurately, it is the *traditional British model of means-testing* that was rejected in favour of new ways of targeting the low-income without a selective test of poverty. As Falkingham and Johnson (1996) argue, "some form of targeting is an essential part of a socially-responsible welfare system." The problem with means-testing as we know it is its oppressive nature, resulting in some failing to claim what they are entitled to and others ensuring they fit the necessary categories one way or another. That means-testing imposes a penalty on honesty and savings is not in doubt (although the extent to which fraud has become a way of life is contested). How can the traditional model of targeting be reformed?

Various proposals have been made for a minimum pension guarantee to be paid automatically to those who retire on low incomes. The idea of a new guarantee was criticised by the previous government on the grounds that one already exists:

> Income Support provides a minimum pension guaranteed above the level of the basic pension. It means no pensioner couple need live on less than £100 a week plus their housing costs. (Lilley 1996).

There is a gap between theory and practice. Some pensioner couples and many single pensioners do indeed live below the Income Support 'guarantee', regardless of the availability of extra resources. The problem with a strategy based on widening the gap between the BSP and Income Support even further is that many fail or refuse to claim the supplement and remain in poverty. Those with modest savings find that they are no better off than those who were unable or unwilling to make the effort. While there is a strong case for targeting resources more closely on actual need, an extension of selective means-testing is an inefficient tool. The evidence of fifty years of income-related supplements to state pensions is a persistent shortfall in take-up, leading Birch (1997) to conclude that a dedicated take-up campaign would be thoroughly inadequate. There is no evidence that most who currently refuse to claim means-tested top-ups would start to do so.

All proposals for a more generous minimum pension recognise that it cannot be separated off from universal second pensions if new disincentives to save are to be avoided. With this crucial qualification in mind, would a guaranteed minimum pension relieve poverty and reduce inequality in a more cost-effective way than uprating across-the-board?

Let us assume a new Minimum Pension Guarantee (MPG) is to be set at 20% of average male earnings, implying an increase of around £20 a week on the BSP. We might wish to have increments at age 75 and 80. For administrative convenience we might also add a small earnings disregard. The question of investment income on savings is less clear. It accounts for a modest proportion of retirement incomes at the moment but is forecast to grow most for those who will have higher incomes. To have a generous disregard would be unfair (Falkingham and Johnson, 1996), and would provide an incentive to 'hide' savings in Building Society and Bank accounts or PEPs in order to qualify for the MPG. The incentive would be particularly strong the nearer one is to retirement (Johnson, 1994). A modest exemption may again be appropriate. The MPG would presumably become the new point at which eligibility for full Housing Benefit starts to fall (replacing the current Income Support line). There is then a decision to be made on the effect of income from second pensions. We could choose to set a 50% taper, meaning £1 paid from an occupational pension would reduce MPG by 50p until no top-up was paid. Alternatively we could impose a 100% taper, effectively taxing all MGP income back pound for pound. That would mean a net MPG of zero as soon as the second pension element equalled the state top-up.

The more gentle the taper, the more expensive the MPG. Johnson et al (1996) calculate that a 50% taper applied to the MPG described above would have a net cost of £4.4 billion compared to just under £3 billion with a 100% taper. The decision here should be political rather than technical. Although a 100% taper would target the gains more closely on the poorest pensioners who have few additional sources of income, it would also impose a steep loss of supplementary income on pensioners with very modest second pensions. The threshold between gaining at least something and losing should be pushed upwards as resources allow.

S. Davies (1996) raises three objections to a guaranteed supplement. First, it would provide an incentive to save through other vehicles in order to claim the state top-up. If there was not a clear disregard, the MPG would simply extend the traditional means-test even further, imposing disincentives to save at all. Second, it would be an expensive way of adding to pension incomes and imposing a substantial retrospective tax on those who had saved enough towards their own retirement. Third, and more significant, Davies simply doubts the need for a state supplement. While lower-income pensioners have not shared in the general rise in living standards, he argues that they have benefited from low inflation and from indexing to the RPI which overstates the real level of inflation. In other words, the BSP is rather more generous than assumed. Davies' view is shared by few who would agree with his other objections.

A different approach to a guaranteed minimum is offered by Field and Owen (1993). If universal funded second tier pensions were well established, perhaps twenty years from now, a new minimum (their Guaranteed Minimum Pension, GMP) should replace the BSP as the first-tier building block. They would set it around 20% above the current BSP, providing a total minimum of around £3500 for single pensioners in today's prices. In addition, the first £5500 income from second pensions would be disregarded, setting a total threshold of around £170 a week before any clawback of GMP occurred. This would raise the means-test starting point to virtually double the current level. They proposed taxing GMP income back at the rate of £10 for every £1000 of additional income, to a limit of 60%. Thus someone with a second pension income of £6500 would qualify for a 90% GMP top-up, while anyone with a second pension income above £11,500 would qualify for the lowest entitlement of 40%. This would represent half the amount currently paid through the BSP.

Since they proposed that all would retire with some second pension income (including state contributions for periods of non-employment), no-one would retire solely on GMP. As a result its cost would be frontloaded and decline over time. Field and Owen expected this would be a less expensive way of delivering a secure state pension than retaining the current BSP. In order to pay for the GMP and contribution credits for at least some of the non-employed, they favoured scrapping all tax relief on pension contributions (a suggestion discussed below).

One further variant on an automatic higher entitlement was proposed by Dilnot and Johnson (1993). By integrating the BSP with Income Support, a higher combined pension could be set and financed by a clawback on the IS element. This would leave low-income pensioners with higher basic pensions. There may be in principle objections to targeting lower income pensioners, although this form of targeting could be based on an affluence test rather than a selective poverty test. More significant is the practical difficulty of using the income tax system to clawback part of the pension, as is done in Canada and Denmark (Johnson *et al* 1996). Taxes are based on the individual whereas the intention here would presumably be to pay a couples' allowance based on joint assessment of income. The majority of pensioners in the UK are not taxed at all, and many who do pay are taxed at source on their savings.

These approaches seek to target limited extra resources on lower-income pensioners in different ways. However, each starts from the assumption that an across-the-board increase in the BSP cannot be the best response to wide and growing inequality in retirement. Each retains the concept of targeting and seeks new ways of applying the means-test. A Minimum Guarantee could be introduced quickly and reduce future pensioner poverty, providing it is allied with wider take-up of adequate funded pensions. Whether this approach is more effective and politically feasible than an ongoing adjustment to accrual rates should be fully debated.

Targeting based on age

An alternative form of targeting is based not on assessed income but on age. One's age cannot be hidden in the way that income can. Basing entitlement on age bands within retirement does not carry any moral hazard or particular disincentive to save. It is certainly true that being old no longer necessarily means being poor. Yet being very old still carries the risk of being poor. Figures for 1992 show the majority of those aged over 75 with an income of less than £5000 a year.

Pensioners aged over 75 had no chance to benefit from SERPS or HRP. They are likely to depend wholly on the state for their income. Field and Owen (1993) are right to say they should be among the highest priorities in short-term pension reform. Their proposal was to pay them a higher pension in the form of a 'late endowment', restricted to those already in this age group. The costs would peak upfront since enhanced entitlements would die with them. Such an endowment could be delivered through the machinery of SERPS, perhaps set equal to the difference between their current income and the average SERPS benefit in payment. It is one of the few policy proposals that involves new net expenditure in the short-term.

Targeting on the basis of old age can be justified on the grounds of equity between generations of pensioners, but criticised because it delivers extra money to some non-poor individuals. Whether a late endowment should be once-and-for-all, or remain an option of last resort for those who will soon reach age 75 is an open question. We do not know for certain whether today's generation of oldest pensioners are poorer than the younger cohorts who will replace them in years to come will be, or whether the relative link between old age and poverty is likely to endure. Waiting for the oldest and poorest to die may reduce the level of inequality in a crude sense if poverty is better explained by cohort-specific effects, and if rising incomes in retirement succeed in 'lifting more boats.' Yet this is no feasible response. By definition the oldest poor need additional support quickly.

We should state a general principle to guide pensions reform. Given the savings already made to state pensions since 1980, and Britain's ability to meet its pension commitments, the country can well afford to improve both the coverage and adequacy of basic retirement income for those who currently have least and those whose earning patterns suggest they will end up with least. Whereas the former Social Security Minister argued that "Britain should not put its position at risk by undermining our funding system or underwriting additional unfunded liabilities", the type of focused improvements discussed so far would neither pose a threat to competitiveness nor to future generations. There can be no absolute ban on new methods of spending public resources through changes in the tax and benefit systems (Taverne, 1997).

There has been no shortage of weighty policy reports on pensions, but they have tended to gloss over what to do with the first-tier pension. There is general agreement that it should remain as the PAYG foundation on which second-tier pensions should be based, with most of the focus then on how to extend funding and how to raise the contributions rate. Although firm conclusions cannot be drawn in isolation from second-tier pensions, neither allowing the BSP to wither on the prices vine nor increasing it faster than prices when resources allow, nor even improving Income Support levels, will secure adequate provision for those who depend on the state pension most. Making progress towards an improved basic pension for the lifetime poor depends crucially on how we reform second pensions. Only if working people are convinced that the second-tier contributions they make towards their own retirement are secure, are protected from raids by government, and that others are making an effort related to their ability to pay, is there a chance of gaining support for a more generous insurance element to compensate for periods when contributions genuinely could not be made. This may mean removing choice over *whether* to have a funded second pension but wider choice over what type of scheme to join.

More and better second pensions

The first tier of pension provision was never viewed as anything more than the foundation on which other sources of income would be built. A common part of the male breadwinner model of full employment was the occupational pension, offering a more generous return to loyal employees who served their firm the longest. The spread of occupational coverage is the single most important reason for the link between poverty and retirement being substantially weakened. Over 60% of the retired and two-thirds of the recently retired have some income from an occupational pension compared with 40% in 1979. Nevertheless, the most significant problem remains one of uneven access. Fewer than half of today's employees are covered by an occupational scheme. Personal pensions, recognised by government since 1988 as approved vehicles for second-tier coverage, are able to accommodate some of the employees who cannot join a work-based pension scheme but there are clear limits to how far they can reach.

In theory, everyone in employment should be contributing towards a second pension. Proposals to introduce a compulsory second pension, as well as minimum pension guarantees, have been criticised by Conservative politicians:

> We already have a compulsory second pension. We require all employees to save nearly 5% of their income to supplement their basic pension. They can save within SERPS, or opt-out and put the money into an occupational or personal scheme. But that element of everyone's earnings must be saved to provide a second-tier pension. The proponents of (compulsion) are already well aware of this (Lilley 1996).

Whatever the merits of compulsory second pensions, this position misses the point that the UK certainly does not have universal second pensions in practice (Box 5.2). At least three million workers, let alone the non-employed, are without any type of second-tier cover because they earn too little to contribute. Once those claiming Job Seekers Allowance move onto Income Support, there are no credits towards SERPS. The two key tests for policy proposals are:

- whether they manage to extend the benefits of second tier coverage more widely;
- and whether those who are contributing are saving enough to secure an adequate second pension.

Before considering the potential for new forms of occupational pension and reforms to personal pensions, how can the state assist with these two goals?

Box 5.2 Second pension coverage for employees 1991

EMPLOYEES (EST. 23 MILLION)	100%
SECOND TIER PENSION	85%
NO SECOND TIER PENSION	15%
FUNDED SECOND PENSION	
49% Occupational Pension	
24% Personal Pension*	68%
UNFUNDED (SERPS) ONLY	17%

* There is some overlap between OP and PP coverage.
(Source: Johnson et al, 1996)

By definition second-tier pensions aim to redistribute an individual's savings across his or her lifetime, deferring pay in order to generate a higher pension. Higher contributions earn higher benefits, unlike the BSP. In the case of SERPS the link is at least as proportional as in the average Occupational or Personal Pension scheme (although it is not transparent). Understanding this principle was vital if average and higher earners were to be attracted to SERPS and to remain in it. The obvious corollary of any earnings-related system is that the low-paid receive low pensions.

Changes to SERPS

The purpose of SERPS was clear enough when it was established twenty years ago. Those employees with low and irregular earnings, unable to maintain contributions to an occupational scheme but expecting to retire on more than the BSP, would be covered automatically by the state scheme. In addition those employees who were too old to make a personal pension worthwhile would be able to gain a secure return on their contributions. SERPS has a number of advantages:

- It established the principle of a compulsory second tier pension for those above the lower earnings threshold (LEL).
- Most benefits will go to the low-paid who have no access to occupational pension schemes.
- It set a minimum standard to be matched by the private sector: contributions to occupational and personal pensions must at least match the proportion of earnings going into SERPS.
- It represents a lower-risk than personal pensions for the low-paid and its administrative costs take up a low proportion of contributions compared with other second-tier pensions.
- It is fully portable, carries no penalty on changing jobs and allows members to stop and start contributions in line with earnings. In this respect it is well suited to an increasingly flexible labour market.

Yet the story of SERPS has been a disappointment compared with the reforming ambition of its architects:

- It does not reach the lowest-paid workers nor the self-employed. Unlike the BSP, there are as yet no contribution credits through HRP.
- For most contributors the returns are relatively low compared with occupational and personal pensions - low-risk also means low return.
- Its affordability is secured by its inadequacy.
- The low-paid are only the beneficiaries because others have opted out – further reducing its long-term sustainability.
- The benchmark (a total contribution of 4.8% of relevant earnings) is too low.

● Although SERPS is portable, its benefit structure is far from transparent. Few members know how much they can expect to receive from SERPS.

Johnson *et al* (1996) describe SERPS as extraordinarily complex. This is partly because actual entitlement depends largely on when contributions were made and when the first benefits were paid. The accrual rate is 1/80th of eligible earnings. In other words, someone retiring in 1998 after 20 full years of paying into SERPS would qualify for a pension worth one quarter of average earnings. This reflects changes announced in 1986, cutting the more generous accrual rate established in 1978. Changes in the 1995 Pensions Act will eventually reduce entitlements further: the rate will fall again from 1999, reaching only 1/244th within 30 years. Someone retiring then after a full working career of fifty years would qualify for only 20% of average revalued earnings. The average replacement ratio from state pensions (BSP plus SERPS) by 2030 is expected to halve to only 18%.

Fewer than 20% of employees remain contracted in to SERPS, the bulk of whom are women in low-paid work. The majority of people with incomes below £10,000 in 1991 had no private provision at all and are much more likely to be contracted-in, while three-quarters of those with incomes above £15,000 did have an occupational or personal pension. Most of the future benefits will therefore flow to the lifetime low-paid, although this does not mean SERPS is redistributive. The average benefit will be low, less than 10% of average earnings for the worker who has experienced a few periods of unemployment. Most beneficiaries will not receive enough to float them above the Income Support line.

More seriously, as Taverne (1997) notes, the contributions of those who consistently earn just above the LEL are likely to be wasted because other means-tested benefits will be reduced in line with eventual SERPS payments. For those facing means-testing in retirement, SERPS has the hallmark of a regressive tax. In the meantime, the great majority of employees have contracted-out to funded second pensions, either through the workplace or a personal pension. In return the state undertakes to pay the equivalent SERPS NI contribution as a rebate to their second pension (providing a base contribution of 4.8% of earnings).

Whatever the arguments against PAYG pensions, the 'hollowing out' of SERPS is not an inevitable design feature in the system. It was the result of political decisions, aimed at reducing the public expenditure costs and pushing employees into funded second pensions (particularly personal pensions, Crawford, 1997). The result of earlier raids on the system is that the status quo cannot be a serious option. *Either SERPS has to be improved for those who remain within it or a better second pension system must be devised.*

Revival or closure?

Few believe that the clock should be turned back prior to the reforms of 1986. Yet the case for closing SERPS to new entrants is not without critics. A number of commentators argue that the anti-SERPS rhetoric which is now commonplace reflects the political risk of governments choosing to renege on past commitments rather than the economic risks associated with PAYG pensions and future generations being unwilling to pay for accrued entitlements. Minns (1997) for example points to the irony that compulsory funded pensions would require an expansion of state tax reliefs - which he describes as one of the most substantial PAYG schemes underwritten by government in order to subsidise private welfare.

Most supporters of SERPS do tend to agree on one point however: that it must be made more transparent. Proposals include showing the contracted-in element as the second pensions premium which is bought by National Insurance Contributions (Crawford 1997), issuing an automatic yearly statement of accrued rights (B. Davies 1993), and uprating the UEL by earnings rather than prices. The range over which earnings were counted for SERPS could then rise, providing a carrot for some higher earners to stay in it and be encouraged to make higher voluntary contributions in return for higher benefits.

Given that there is no scope for inter-personal redistribution within SERPS, the legitimacy of the system depends on being able to 'gear-up' the return on relatively low contributions by those on low incomes. It is possible that government could support a new second pension to replace SERPS, funded rather than PAYG but offering a secure and low-risk return to those otherwise likely to retire on a low income. The prospects of such a scheme being available are discussed below. At this stage however it should by now be clear that the *lifetime poor and low-paid cannot secure an adequate second pension without some ongoing element of government support.*

If there are clear limits to the reach of funded second pensions, there is no case for closing SERPS unless an enhanced BSP could be designed for those with persistently low incomes. For example, Field's (1996) proposal to close SERPS and require funded second pensions for all with earnings above £5,000 might only be considered equitable if the BSP was reformed along the lines proposed in the first section. If the decision were made to restrict membership of SERPS to those with incomes below a new threshold, such as £10,000 a year, it could be better targeted. The relevant earnings band could be narrowed to that between the LEL and £10,000. Above this, NI contributions would be paid at a new flat-rate, while benefits accrued only to those on low incomes. This would make SERPS more progressive for low earners. The alternative could be to allow all to remain contracted in if they wished, but only allow SERPS benefits to be accrued on earnings up to £10,000. This would avoid having to move in and out of SERPS as incomes fluctuated around this level (Johnson *et al*, 1996).

Even if the disadvantages of SERPS outweigh its benefits, the case for its closure cannot be made simply on the grounds of cost. If it was to be abolished tomorrow, existing commitments would still have to be paid out more than forty years from now. Those employees approaching the end of their working lives would simply not be in a position to accumulate an adequate personal pension, resulting in pressure for state compensation for lost SERPS benefits.

There are two approaches to closing SERPS. One is to allow all existing employees to continue contributing if they choose to, but with more generous rebates to attract workers to opt out at an earlier age and to remain contracted out. The next generation of workers would have to join a funded pension scheme. This proposal for a cohort-specific closure of SERPS was part of the Basic Pension Plus supported by the previous government. This would not result in significant savings for at least forty years. The other approach is to close SERPS for those below a certain age and/or above a certain level of income, directing equivalent contributions into recognised, funded second pensions.

The NAPF (1997) among others has proposed closing SERPS to under-50s. This would bring forward the date when SERPS matures by twenty years to 2010, providing net savings of around £2.3 billion by 2030. In order to reach that point, however, there is the double payment problem to be addressed. Accrued benefits will not vanish if SERPS is closed and members take their NICs with them to pay into their new funded accounts. Who will pay for those already claiming SERPS benefits and those expecting to when they retire?

The likeliest result would be a marginally higher flat-rate of employee National Insurance Contributions. All would have to pay the same extra proportion of their earnings: SERPS members would pay 10.24% instead of 10%, with 1.8% being ear-marked for the funded pension (the equivalent of SERPS contributions), and 8.44% being paid as the 'core' NI rate including accrued SERPS rights. Those who have already left SERPS would pay 8.44% NI instead of the rebated level of 8.2% (Taverne, 1997). The effect on the income distribution of requiring all workers above the LEL to save at least the standard 1.8% employee rebate (plus the standard 3% employer rebate) in a funded account would be small because the rebate is so low - set at a rate to provide "woefully inadequate pensions for the low paid" (Johnson *et al* 1996). This would widen the coverage of *funded* pensions but not of second pensions overall (since those paid below the LEL would still be without a second pension).

Compulsion – or the New Universalism?

The centre-left tends to be suspicious of calls for compulsion. Proposals for compulsory contributions to second pensions are commonly presented as part of a new radical turn in public policy. In fact the UK already requires a minimum level of contributions to a second-tier pension for all earning above the LEL. What is an extension of compulsion for the political right could be claimed as part of the new universalism by the left.

Extending the net

On the question of second pensions coverage, around one in seven employees are not contributing towards any type of second-tier pension, largely explained by the number of workers paid below the LEL. Of the majority covered by the second tier, three-quarters are members of a funded pension (Box 5.2). Occupational pensions are twice as common as personal pensions: almost half of all employees are members of an occupational scheme compared with around a quarter who contribute towards a personal pension. However occupational coverage for men is around 20% higher (at 57%) than among women (at 37%). The number of employees covered by an occupational scheme has been stable for two decades despite an expanding workforce, and there is little evidence of further expansion through newer and smaller employers establishing their own schemes.

To give some impression of the position of younger employees, only one-third of women employees aged under 25 have access to any kind of occupational pension and only half of all employees aged under 35 are covered by a funded second tier pension. The life insurance industry believes it is essential to address 'the low priority given by today's adults - tomorrow's pensioners - to the necessity of realistic pension planning.' Too many workers leave it so late to start saving that the contribution levels necessary to reach the target retirement income they will expect are unaffordable. One recent survey among full-time workers and the self-employed pointed to a 'retirement misery gap' between expectations and the likely reality of retirement incomes based on current saving patterns (Barclays, 1996). Yet there is no evidence that exhortations by government or pension providers to save more will close the gap and raise the level of savings. Arguments about compulsory second pensions tend to obscure the fact that, above an earnings threshold, we already have them. But it is a thin requirement.

On this second question of adequacy, it is usually assumed that members of an occupational scheme will receive a decent pension. The growth of occupational pension incomes has successfully weakened the relationship between old age and poverty, but a majority of contributors to personal pensions do not make any additional payments on top of the minimum rebate of just under 3.4% of earnings. According to one recent survey, more than 40% of pension scheme members make monthly contributions of £50 or less (Barclays, 1996).

We also know that those contracted in to SERPS are unlikely to earn a second pension worth more than 20% of average earnings. *Thus, up to four in ten employees (approximately 10 million in total) are currently in line to qualify for an inadequate second pension, if they qualify for one at all.* Significantly this includes a minority of those who are covered by a funded pension, as well as all who are not. In other words the twin tasks of extending coverage and tackling inadequate contribution levels affect more than the minority for whom the labour market has failed to cater.

Our key questions in the remainder of this section include:

- Should the switch be made to funded second pensions without the option of a PAYG supplement?
- If funding is preferred, is the private sector always better at doing the job of funding?
- Should we require contributions up to a defined proportion of earnings (maximum compulsion) or only up to a fixed absolute amount (adequate compulsion?)
- How can we extend the benefits of second pensions to some of those with incomes below the LEL?
- Should government encourage group rather than individual pension schemes or remain neutral, and should the tax treatment of second pensions be changed?

Is Funding the Magic Bullet?

The UK's switch away from PAYG to funded pensions has resulted in a larger funded portfolio than in the rest of the EU member states put together. The UK is expected to have negligible pension-related public debt in the coming decades. It is little surprise that funding is seen as the answer and that pressure to close SERPS has become so strong. By paying individual contributions into funded accounts rather than paying taxes and contributions into the general public pot, the risk of governments reneging on past commitments may be avoided and the pool of savings available for productive investment can provide an ongoing boost to the economy. Funded second pensions appear to offer a rare double dividend.

The case for full funding of first and second tiers has been discussed earlier. Restricting funding to second pensions and retaining PAYG for the first-tier is often considered a reasonable way of spreading both market risks and political risks. The assumption that funding provides us with a 'magic bullet' to escape the constraints of PAYG has been challenged by those who support funded second pensions as well as those who are opposed.

The first principle to bear in mind is that the cost of supporting the retired is met by the output of people in productive work whenever pension commitments are met. Contributions towards a funded pension for thirty years will accumulate and be converted into a pension through the purchase of an annuity on retirement. The value of that fund will depend on the real productivity of working people age thirty years from now, even if the claim will not be upon the direct taxes they pay. *Funding does not enable contributors to 'get away from it all' and eliminate the dependence of tomorrow's pensioners on tomorrow's workers.* If it is to raise the rate of return on contributions, high growth rates and low levels of unemployment remain the key policy goals (Yarrow 1997).

Whether funding makes a real difference turns on whether it generates a net increase in GNP between the time contributions are paid and benefits are received (Crawford 1997). The evidence here is more mixed than usually assumed. Despite the UK's huge privately funded pensions sector the level of national savings does not necessarily bear much relation to the pattern of economic growth in recent decades. It has not resulted in any step change in economic performance. Despite having large PAYG commitments, France, Germany and Italy do not have lower rates of saving than the UK. Downs and Stevens-Ströhman (1995) estimate that up to half the contributions made to compulsory funded pensions are offset by reduced savings in other forms, and Davies (1993) cites favourable studies suggesting that the net increase in capital formation is a smaller proportion of contributions (around 20% in the USA according to the OECD). Once the cost of various tax reliefs and administration are accounted for, the net advantages over unfunded state schemes may be much less significant (Crawford 1997). It is not self-evident that compulsory funding can be justified on the grounds of economic growth alone.

The case for funding has also been made on the grounds of greater security of contributions. According to this view, governments will always be tempted to renege on previous commitments. Across Europe and not just in the UK, governments have been raising the state retirement age, requiring longer contribution periods for the same benefits, freezing the rate of benefit and restricting eligibility. In the UK, linking the BSP to prices rather than average earnings has been criticised on the grounds of ripping up the contract laid down by Beveridge. In fact there has never been a clear commitment on how the BSP should be raised. In the early 1970s it was raised in line with either prices or earnings depending on which rose faster. Between 1974 and 1980 uprating was linked to earnings. When the Conservatives switched to price indexation they were reversing the practice of recent years and certainly offering pensioners a less generous return, but not tearing up a contract signed by generations of workers.

However, the decision to reduce SERPS entitlements on two occasions can be said to undo the deal struck between the state and the contributor as recently as 1978. In any event, it is the belief that government is willing to provide less generous pensions than expected that really matters. No British government is going to make a deliberate raid on more transparent funded pensions. Funding therefore reduces some of the political risk. Yet it remains the case that any government will wish to retain the option of changing the rules on the tax treatment of pensions for example. Few of us can afford to save enough towards an adequate pension without the support of an employer or government (through the NI rebate and tax relief on contributions). *As long as that is true, there can be no absolute guarantee that the expectations we start with will be met when we retire.*

A third argument that may tip the balance in favour of funding is that it opens up the possibility of a greater stake in pension savings. If we are to maintain collective support for a redistributive BSP, Field (1996) is correct to argue that we must also increase the sense of individual ownership over pension schemes. The link between contributions and benefits must be made more explicit. It would be possible to improve the transparency of SERPS, but it would still be the victim of perceived political risk. People are also more likely to regard funded second pensions as an extension of savings towards their own retirement rather than taxation (the benefits of which may or may not flow back to the contributor at some future date).

The centre-left should therefore support stakeholder arguments for wider access to capital ownership through funded second pensions, as long as it does not expect a switch to funding to provide an easy answer to the difficult questions about adequate pensions for the lifetime low-paid. We support the principle of closing SERPS for those aged under 50. Whether there should also be an income threshold, below which SERPS membership can be retained, depends on our ability to deliver value-for-money funded second pensions even for those with low and intermittent earnings. Decent occupational pensions and appropriate personal pensions will not be available to all those who remain in SERPS today. Closure cannot be an option if part-time, low-paid women workers were to end up worse off either by having no top-up to their BSP or having to take out a poor value personal pension which cost more and performed no better than SERPS. Without an adequate replacement it would be disastrous. The success of government and industry in developing a new range of stakeholder pensions, pooling the costs and risks across a large number of contributors, is therefore critically important.

A National Savings Pension: A New Bond with Government

One reason why the Conservative Government decided against closing SERPS in the 1980s was the category of people with low and volatile earnings and disrupted employment patterns who are costly for pension providers to service. It is not clear that many more of the new and small employers without any pension provision are prepared to offer a work-based personal pension, nor that growth in this area would close enough of the gaps in cover.

Instead SERPS could be relaunched as a vehicle through which contributions are invested in a new class of government bonds held in individual accounts (B. Davies, 1993). These would earn a lower return than through stocks, but pension savings would be at lower risk. The (post office counters) Commission on Social Justice (1994) favoured greater competition to force high-charging/low return personal pension schemes to improve their performance. One of the options it proposed was such a low-cost funded scheme to take the place of SERPS - possibly in the form of a National Savings Pension Plan (NSPP). It would take a low proportion of contributions in charges and administration and offer a secure return on contributions. It would meet the tests of simplicity, flexibility, value for money and portability, encouraging higher voluntary contributions. Although the marketing and selling of NSPPs could be combined with existing National Savings products, the CSJ argued that investment management would be done at arms-length from government. Contributions would be invested in index-linked funds, which could include government bonds as well as a fund tracking the FTSE 100. This mixed portfolio would mean the NSPP would not be based on government funding and would fall outside the usual scope of National Savings products.

A National Savings Pension Bill was brought before Parliament in May 1996, with support from members of the Social Security Select Committee. It proposed two types of plan. In Scheme A, the accrual rate would be set at no less than the rise in prices over the previous year, and should be higher when the expected rate of return on government stock is taken into account. In Scheme B, interest on a pension plan deposit would be set in line with changes in the value of dividends paid on listed market securities. Thus, a very low-risk/low return product would be offered alongside one likely to generate a higher return but with less security. The choice of pension might be influenced as much by age as income. Young workers might be advised to contribute to Scheme B and switch to Scheme A nearer to retirement, offering a 'smoothed' profile aimed at minimising risk and maximising return.

Arguments against
The Conservative Government opposed the Bill to establish an NSPP for three reasons. First, it would open the door to a very large increase in the volume of unfunded public liabilities: although annuities might technically be funded by an issue of gilts, it was argued there would be no real wealth backing them. Second, the legislative framework underpinning pension provision in the UK (based on the EU's First Council Directive on Life Assurance) makes it difficult for governments to engage in any business involving the issue of annuities. Under the Insurance Companies Act, annuities must form the main business of the company offering them. This condition would not currently be met by National Savings. Third, there are technical and financial constraints implicit in a pension scheme likely to attract small contributions from the relatively low-paid on a regular basis. Transaction charges on contributions paid over the counter would raise administrative costs.

Each of these criticisms has been challenged (B. Davies 1997 for example). The chosen definition of 'real wealth' for example seems spurious. Although NSPP contributions may not be invested in company securities, they would support investment which would appear on the public balance sheet and would therefore be funded. The same principle is accepted for public sector occupational pension funds. Second, it is by no means impossible for government to issue annuities. If it proves politically unfeasible, the task of investment could be shared or transferred to the private sector, with a separate 'National Savings Life' company being established to oversee the move. Third, employees could have their contributions paid directly by their employers, or the Contributions Agency could bank the appropriate contributions and transfer them to NSPP accounts twice a year in order to reduce transaction charges. The facility for one-off top-ups should be available.

Arguments for

One clear advantage of an NSPP is that it could be introduced quickly by packaging together existing National Savings policies designed to meet the requirements of saving for retirement. These already bring saving within the reach of many low-income households. By extending the range of products to include a pension, a low-cost incentive for the insecurely employed could be offered. The principle underlying National Savings products – index-linked returns to provide protection against inflation – would apply.

The NSPP could be marketed and sold through the Post Office, offering wide access which does not depend on much employer commitment of time or administrative effort. Passport style savings books could be devised to enable every contributor to know how much they can expect in return, providing incentives to contribute more than the minimum as incomes rise which SERPS could probably never offer. Moreover top-up relief on contributions could be provided enabling contributions to go further than they do under SERPS. There is a question mark over how best to target relief to those who pay little or no income tax. We discuss the relative merits of tax relief over state credits into NSPP and other schemes below. At this stage however, *the principle of bringing the low-paid within the net of government relief, by extending or targeting the support taken for granted by higher earners, should commend itself.*

It is likely that greater competition for low-income contributors would attract many of those still contracted-in to leave SERPS. Bryn Davies (1997) assumes that 10% of the 10 million or so facing an inadequate second pension could switch to NSPP in the early years. Assuming an average wage of £12,000 and an additional contribution rate of 2%, up to £250 million would be paid in. (We address the question of whether such a low contribution rate would produce an adequate return below.) If joining a funded second pension is made a requirement - at least for those currently earning above the LEL - perhaps three times as many employees would opt for the NSPP as for any other particular scheme. It would provide wider choice based on a well-established and trusted brand.

If the barriers facing an NSPP can be tackled, it might serve as the obvious successor to SERPS. It could provide greater competition in a part of the market where it is weak or based on inappropriate choice - not least for lower-paid women workers. It would also represent a major step forward in terms of simplifying a sales process which is complex and expensive. The product must be kept simple and sold on a high volume basis. Although it would not provide a suitable pension for higher earners, it would be designed to 'gear-up' the contributions of low earners more effectively than other pension products currently do. It is ironic that some advocates of universal funding who stress the importance of choice and competition, rule out any involvement of government when it might secure those objectives more effectively. The NSPP would sit comfortably with the development of other stakeholder pensions.

Other Second Pensions

Government and employers have a central role to play in partnership with individuals if more and better second pensions are to restore confidence. In this section we consider the main types of funded pension – the traditional Final Salary schemes and the emerging Money Purchase schemes – and ask whether policy-makers should take a view on which is more appropriate. In a later section we also explore how government seeks to influence savings decisions through tax incentives and how a more discerning use of tax reliefs could result in a more efficient pattern of saving.

Not surprisingly, the National Association of Pension Funds

believes that Occupational Pensions (OPs) are the most cost-effective means of providing for retirement: "Wherever possible, second-tier pensions should be provided by employer-sponsored schemes" (NAPF 1997). A notable tradition of the British system for decades has been the strong voluntary partnership between employers and their employees in favour of OPs. There are signs that the willingness to continue this partnership is faltering (or rather not being renewed) in Box 5.3.

Box 5.3 Employees in Occupational Pension Schemes, UK

Year	Occupational pension Scheme Members (m)	Total employees (m)	Proportion
1953	6.2	21.9	28.3%
1956	8.0	22.7	35.2%
1963	11.1	22.9	48.5%
1967	12.2	23.2	52.6%
1971	11.1	22.5	49.3%
1975	11.4	23.1	49.3%
1979	11.6	23.4	49.6%
1983	11.1	21.1	52.6%
1987	10.6	21.6	49.1%
1991	10.7	22.5	47.5%

(Source: NAPF, 1997)

Until 1988, employers had the right to make membership of their pension scheme a condition of service. Where there is no employer-organised pension, alternative personal pensions attract few employer contributions. Neither these nor SERPS have filled the gap. Requiring membership of particular schemes is not the way forward. We do not wish to force everyone into occupational schemes which may in any case turn out to be inappropriate. Instead our focus should be on developing pension schemes which go beyond the 'one size fits all' approach and reflect the reality of periods of employment and unpaid work across the life cycle.

Most members are in OP schemes of the Defined Benefit variety, where up to two-thirds of pre-retirement earnings are paid out (the so-called Final Salary schemes). Trade unions tend to prefer Final Salary schemes because pension entitlements are defined and ultimate responsibility for meeting the cost of the promise rests with the employer. The employer takes on most of the costs and risks of running the scheme, with a premium placed on length of service. Additional benefits are often built in, such as eligibility for early retirement on the grounds of ill health, spouses' benefits and life assurance. The costs may be substantial, requiring combined contributions of 20%-25% of earnings. The problem in today's labour market is that a declining proportion of workers remain in full-time jobs with a small number of employers across their working life. The enduring criticism of occupational schemes has been the penalty they impose on 'early leavers' – the majority of employees who switch jobs and associated pension schemes. Enhanced final salary payments may have rewarded employee loyalty but at the expense of colleagues who left before retirement and failed to benefit from the uprating of their earlier contributions in line with average earnings. Indeed it is the saving gained by not offering the full return to early leavers that funds the 'bonus' to the employees who remain.

The assumption is that OPs backload benefits towards final salary in order to encourage workers to stay with the same employer, and to allow the employer to capture the benefits of training paid for by the company. However, as Johnson *et al* (1996) note, there is no clear evidence that Defined Benefit schemes have such productivity-enhancing effects. It is more likely that they continue to be structured in this way because they always have been. A growing number of employers are now interested in alternative plans for their employees which reduce the management costs and levels of risk borne in-house.

Where traditional schemes tend to be linked to an era of full employment and employer-supplemented welfare, Money Purchase schemes based on set contributions are considered to go with the grain of labour market change (with all the uncertainty that implies). Some argue that the premium placed on employee loyalty and employer paternalism in Final Salary schemes is anachronistic in a labour market with rapid turnover and the expectation of numerous job changes in the future, certainly for younger employees (Field and Owen 1993).

Defined Contribution pensions (usually known as Money Purchase

Schemes – or COMPS when Contracted Out) require a defined level of contributions with no explicit commitment to the level of pension to be received. One key advantage of Money Purchase schemes is their portability. They do not penalise employees who change jobs frequently in the way that most DB schemes do. However they are often viewed with scepticism because, in practice, employers share little of the investment risks and charges borne by the individual. In one analysis of small employers, four out of five who ran a scheme offered a Money Purchase/Defined Contribution scheme rather than the traditional Final Salary type. Employers are likely to make a lower contribution to occupational Money Purchase schemes (and are less likely to provide additional benefits such as life cover). These receive an average of around 8% of earnings compared with 15% (Birch 1997). In the case of Personal Pensions and some Group Personal Pensions (which are also Money Purchase) the employer may well make no contribution at all.

If there is no support from the employer or the government, there is no subsidy to be reneged upon later. Ironically, some employees may therefore be attracted by the chance to 'pay their own way'. Yet, *it is essential that individuals are not left to bear the full administrative costs in addition to the capital market risks inherent in personal pensions.* While Money Purchase pensions cannot insulate the individual from investment risk, the costs of administration and of contributing should be shared more widely.

There has been a significant shift towards Money Purchase pensions in the USA. Although the shift has been slower in the UK and relatively few employers have actually switched an existing Final Salary scheme to Money Purchase, one analysis for the CBI shows that a substantial number of employers would have chosen the second option if they were able to start again. A further survey of large employers looked at the reasons why they might consider moving from Final Salary to a Money Purchase scheme employers (Investment Week, 1997). The most common responses referred to expense (seeing DC schemes as potentially less costly in terms of company time and finance) rather than the nature of the product or the workforce (Box 5.4).

Box 5.4 Reasons for considering a switch from Final Salary to Money Purchase (ranked)

1. Uncertainty of cost of DB schemes.
2. Increasing cost of DB schemes.
3. Opportunity to reduce company contributions.
4. Increasing costs of regulation in DB schemes.
5. Lower running costs of DC schemes.
6. Changing workforce.
7. Requirements of 1995 Pensions Act.
8. Complexity of FS schemes.
9. Members better understand MP/DC schemes.

(Source: Alexander Clay/Investment Week (1997)

Contributions to Money Purchase schemes by large employers were generally higher than from small employers. The majority of schemes had a combined contribution rate of between 10% and 12% of earnings. More surprisingly two-thirds of respondent firms supported compulsory contributions to funded second pensions by employers as well as employees, even though this could result in higher non-wage labour costs.

The debate around employer participation in second pensions need not conclude with a return to the position before 1988 when employers could make membership of their own occupational scheme mandatory. *All employers could however come to be required to contribute a higher minimum amount to their employees' pension fund whether they are company schemes or not.*

Should the state have a preference for a particular type of funded pension? There is no convincing reason why a DB pension should be superior to a DC plan or vice versa, and no reason why the state should favour one over the other. The appropriate type of pension depends not only on the different labour market risks faced by individuals but on their stage in the earnings cycle. Someone with an individual personal pension while employed on a short-term contract might be well advised to join the occupational scheme offered by a new employer for example. Johnson *et al's* (1996) cautious conclusion offers a sound guide for policy-makers: "We should be sceptical about claims that one type of plan generates a better return than another for all (or even most) individuals". The centre-left should reclaim the idea of appropriate choice as it embarks on pension reform. The right to choose from a number of pension schemes should be matched by access to appropriate advice. A reputable pension provider would not advise those on low and unpredictable incomes to take out a high risk/high return pension.

It may not be the type of pension scheme that matters so much as the degree to which its management costs, funding and level of risk are shared or passed onto the individual. If employers do not contribute towards Money Purchase schemes and there are few discretionary benefits built in, that is not necessarily a criticism of the pension instrument itself - any more than the reduction in SERPS benefits in recent years is inherent in the design features of SERPS. It is the behaviour of employers, the state and individuals that has to be considered more closely. Retaining and improving the BSP while expanding access to funded pensions is often presented as a way of pooling the political risks and the capital market risks. There is a need to share costs and risks within the second tier as well.

Even if the scale of labour market change tends to be exaggerated by advocates of Money Purchase pensions and the continuing significance of coverage by 'traditional' occupational pensions is underplayed, there is an important point here. We should have neither an a *priori* preference for Final Salary schemes nor an implicit distrust of Money Purchase pensions. Trying to shore up a pensions model designed for a very different labour market will not result in its return. Nor will it improve the pension prospects of those low-paid employees who were never able to access secure occupational schemes in the first place.

Stakeholder Industry Pensions: Safety in Numbers

The evidence we have discussed so far points to a sizeable group of employees who do not have access to an occupational scheme and would be ill-advised to take out a personal pension. They will be hardest hit by the declining value of the BSP and SERPS. Typically this group is earning no more than £12,000 a year. How can the benefits of funded pensions be extended to them if their employers are unlikely to establish company schemes?

There is considerable interest in group-based pension schemes where administrative costs must be much lower than the 20% typically taken up by personal pensions (and aim to be no higher than the 10% cost of most occupational schemes); pension rights must be portable and protected for the majority of employees who will be early leavers; transfer within limits should be free of penalties; value for money for the lower paid must be improved; and employee representatives must have a central role in stewardship of the pensions funds. Industry Pensions may be the best way to achieve these goals, by pooling the costs and risks of running a scheme across an affinity group based on employment sectors (B. Davies, 1993). They would be based on 'safety in numbers' rather than shifting all of the administrative charges onto the individual. While Industry Pensions are not new nor a British invention, they may offer an appropriate alternative for employers between the traditional in-house scheme and doing nothing. They also form the core of Labour's strategy for extending occupational coverage in the shape of stakeholder pensions.

B. Davies (1993) sets out the key characteristics of Industry Pensions (IPs) and how they might be widely established. Unlike most occupational schemes, IPs would be run on a Money Purchase basis. This should not prevent final pensions being based on some defined final earnings target. Such a hybrid approach is compared with a with-profits endowment policy where the sum assured is secure but bonuses can be expected on top. To make IPs attractive to employees and employers, Davies states that secure benefits must be combined with the cost constraints that increasingly attract employers to other Money Purchase arrangements.

Encouragement for employers to offer their workforce access to new pension schemes (not necessarily run in-house) is uncontroversial. Employers remain the obvious vehicle to include many of the excluded. In the USA, a system of pension schemes known as 401(k) Retirement Plans is supported by employers. They establish the scheme and make contributions for their workers (who usually contribute in addition). If and when they change jobs, they are free to transfer to the scheme of their next employer or to an Individual Retirement Account (the equivalent of a personal pension).

Cost is the dominant reason why employers are not sufficiently interested in providing pensions for their workforce, particularly among small and newly-established companies. It is not self-evident that they can be persuaded to offer membership of an Industry Pension to their employees. While many agree that new group schemes could represent a significant step forward and a gradual build-up of schemes with a proven track-record is one feasible option, they are ultimately only likely to flourish against the background of a requirement on more employers and employees to contribute to a funded pension scheme (Colonial/Unity Trust Bank, 1997). Providing the condition is observed that Industry Pensions should not be offered to employees if an existing scheme provides better benefits (Davies, 1993), the requirement to contribute would provide a significant stimulus. Any requirement on employers and employees should be to contribute towards some funded second pension, including a National Savings Pension Scheme, rather than one specific alternative to a traditional occupational pension. Industry Pensions as part of a range of more appropriate funded pensions could widen choice and avoid the problem of being left with only a much-reduced SERPS entitlement.

Personal Pensions

Personal Pensions were recognised as approved vehicles for pension savings to offer a better deal for those without access to any type of occupational pension or who were likely to change jobs on frequent occasions. Here we consider the scope for personal pensions to increase take-up of second pensions rather than as third-tier savings vehicles for those on high salaries (who may pay 'Free Standing Additional Voluntary Contributions'–FSAVCs–into personal plans as well as receiving the benefit of a secure occupational pension).

Unlike most occupational schemes, personal pensions in the UK are of the defined contribution variety. The final benefit depends on how much has been paid in, the performance of the fund over time and the rate at which the fund is converted into an annuity on retirement. The individual bears the investment risk of the capital markets rather than the political risk of governments reneging on accrued entitlements.

Despite being appropriate for some, personal pensions have come in for heavy criticism. Since they are not designed to redistribute from higher to lower earners, it is particularly important that low and irregular contributions achieve a decent return. However, personal pensions are mostly sold as individual contracts. Charges and management costs are passed on to the individual rather than shared. As the Commission on Social Justice (1994) noted, "Every reputable life company will confirm that personal pensions are wholly unsuitable for the two million men and six million women earning less than £10,000 a year." Unfortunately it has taken years of hard experience for this view to become accepted. Early attempts in the 1980s to encourage opting out of SERPS and occupational pensions were wholly inappropriate for many of the low-paid and insecurely employed. The 600,000 cases referred to the Personal Investment Authority (PIA) on the grounds of mis-selling have been processed slowly. By the summer of 1997, three per cent of those who had outstanding claims had died without compensation. It is no surprise that the government has set tougher guidelines for the backlog of compensation claims to be dealt with. If these are consistently breached, the risk of companies losing their approval to provide pensions should be clearly understood.

The fallout from mis-selling has been a halving in the number of personal pensions taken out each year. Although there are now stronger disincentives to engage in mis-selling, there is evidence of another stain on the track-record of personal pensions. We discuss the extent to which the state ends up subsidising high-cost providers in the following section.

We have considered the current failure of the pension system to accommodate low income contributors and those who lapse or transfer at an early stage. While noting these criticisms, some are nevertheless optimistic about the willingness of the pensions industry to provide low-cost products such as tracker funds - relatively 'safe haven' products offering lower returns but lower risks than other Money Purchase schemes. S. Davies (1997) believes that costs can be reduced through compulsion, since people would then be looking for the right pension provider rather than the other way round (which ought to cut some of the marketing budget which contributors end up subsidising). *It may be a triumph of hope over sober expectation to believe that individual personal pensions can be adapted to accommodate most of those who are currently outside the net of adequate second pensions.* For the life-time lower paid, less costly and risky schemes are essential. These should include the National Savings and Industry Pension options discussed above.

Group Personal Pensions (GPPs) offer another alternative - clusters of Money Purchase pensions set up for a workforce. These provide employers with a means of extending pension cover without incurring the management time and costs associated with occupational pensions. They offer employees who do not have access to an appropriate occupational scheme a group-based pension which should provide better value for money than an individually-based personal pension.

There has been a surge in the popularity of GPPs in recent years, particularly in parts of the retail sector where a majority of employees are in part-time jobs. Regulatory tightening in the 1995 Pensions Act may be responsible for much of the growth. Since GPPs are not officially classed as occupational pensions, they fall outside the scope of the legislation. Many employers looking for a low-cost alternative will therefore see GPPs as a way of avoiding Pension Act costs and legal liabilities. This has led the Occupational Pensions Advisory Service (OPAS) to warn that GPPs existing in a regulatory black hole are "the next pensions disaster waiting to happen." There is already evidence from the new regulator for occupational pensions (OPRA) of small company pensions schemes operated by businesses that have gone bust. Thousands of members are unable to access the money they expected or transfer their savings to another fund. In these cases, life companies are unable to pay out to a recognised trustee because the former employer was the sole guardian of the fund. If an employer was to renege on its obligations under a GPP arrangement, by failing to pay contributions deducted from employee salaries to the provider for example, the employee's only comeback under current rules would be to take civil action for breach of contract through the courts. The possibility of employer risk must therefore be added to our discussion of pension risks.

Industry Pensions and similar Affinity Group schemes should be able to pool the costs and the risks on a wider basis than many GPPs. However, their growth probably depends on a greater commitment from employers than required by a typical GPP. A problem with GPPs arises if employers see them as a way of reducing their own responsibilities. Some may blame 'over-regulation' in the Pensions Act for providing incentives to move out of occupational schemes. The first step towards simplifying the regulatory structure is to apply the same principles across the board. Members of GPPs should therefore enjoy the same protection as those in long-standing Final Salary Schemes. They are more appropriately treated as occupational than personal pensions.

Considerable progress can be made towards the design of more and better pension products for those who are currently without a good value second pension. It is not the task of government to design the new products but it does have a responsibility to draw the boundaries for reform, on the point at which charges and the cost of registration and maintenance are considered unacceptable for example. The principle of pooling costs, risks and benefits on a group basis is an old one but an enduring one. Assuming the supply-side can be reshaped, how do we make progress on the second of our key objectives – adequacy of saving for retirement?

How Adequate is 'adequate'?

A stakeholder pension system can bring many more people into lower-cost, more secure second pensions. Yet it will do little to cut the risk of poverty if only minimum contributions equivalent to today's contracted-out rebate are made. The new settlement would suffer precisely the same problem as the traditional model: the required amount would be spread too thinly to make a difference at the bottom. There is a clear gap between the current pattern of saving for retirement and public expectations of future living standards. Among full-time workers and the self-employed who have not made any pension provision, almost one in three expect to retire before the age of 60 (compared to 40% overall, Barclays 1996). Three-quarters expect to retire on an income which will be at least as high as their maximum earnings. Moreover, the proportion is *higher* among those without any pension scheme, those contributing least to their pension, among younger people and among lower income workers. While one in three of the retired say they now find life difficult financially, just 6% of workers anticipate financial problems in retirement – compelling evidence for compulsory savings at an earlier age and at an adequate level. What contributions should be required of employees, their employers and the state?

Most proposals for universal funded pensions define the proportion of total earnings that should be saved in order to earn an adequate second-tier pension. In addition to the new rate of NI that would result from closing SERPS, Taverne (1997) argues that a minimum contribution of 10% of earnings should be required of everyone above the current LEL shared between employers and employees. This would not affect those who already contribute to an adequate occupational pension or those who make sufficient additional contributions to a personal pension. However, it would affect the large proportion of employees and their employers who are currently paying no more than the SERPS equivalent of under 5%. The increase could be phased in, reaching 10% within three years. Other recent reports (for example Colonial/Unity Trust Bank, 1997) agree that the level of contributions should rise from 5% to a total of 10%, although they suggest a phased increase over ten years. Davies (1993) proposed that the eventual contribution rate should be 12% of each member's relevant earnings, split 8% from employers and 4% from employees, phased in over ten years. By comparison the introduction of compulsory occupational pensions in Australia will eventually require a combined rate of 12%, split 9% from the employer and 3% from the employee.

Should such changes be universal? One way to extend funded pensions is to close SERPS and bring all employees within the net irrespective of pay levels (Field and Owen 1993). They would be required to pay 4% of earnings and their employers 6% towards a funded pension account as soon as they started earning. The minimum total contribution would thus be 10% as proposed by Taverne (1997), but with a much lower entry level. Contribution credits for the non-employed would be paid by the state. Perhaps because of the burden of having to pay even 4% on very low earnings, Field's proposal by 1996 was for a near-universal second pension. Both the qualifying threshold and the minimum contribution were increased, such that everyone earning above £100 a week would contribute to a funded pension. This would be the new Lower Contributions Threshold, LCT. The eventual target rate above this threshold would be 16% of total earnings rather than 10%. The contracted-out rebate would be paid into each pension fund.

A similar proposal by the NAPF (1995) is for a Private National Pension Scheme (PNPS), with contributions set initially close to the contracted-out rebate and rising to between 10% and 20% of earnings. This is expected to achieve a pension worth 50% of average career earnings. More recently, the introduction of mandatory contributions at twice the LEL (earnings of £124 a week in 1997) was proposed, on the grounds that it may not be in the interests of the lower paid to be included in second-tier pensions (Colonial/Unity Trust Bank, 1997). The main problem with these proposals would be to exclude workers who currently earn between £61 and any higher entry level to the second-tier. This group currently contributes to SERPS if nothing else. The effect of closing SERPS and failing to provide an appropriate alternative would be to leave them without any second-tier cover, on the promise of an enhanced state pension. Access to a funded second pension should begin no lower than the current LEL, with the possibility of employer and government-funded top ups for the working poor to secure an adequate fund in retirement.

There is no dispute about the problem of under-saving, but a misleading impression about its extent can be projected by the pensions industry. One report, designed to dramatise the extent of under-provision, implied that a fixed contribution rate was required according to age rather than earnings. It suggested that under-25s should be saving £250 a month, rising to £500 for those aged 45-54. Actual average contributions are closer to £80 to £110 a month. In fact these recommended amounts would be more appropriate for people earning from £30,000 up to £60,000 a year. Such a contribution rate would not only be impossible for the young employee earning £15,000 – given the maximum allowable contribution of 17.5% of earnings for under-35s - it implies a wholly unrealistic replacement ratio. Nor is it clear if such calculations take account of expected income from state pensions, which funded pensions are designed to build on rather than replace. While a new partnership between government, employers and the industry is a high priority, misleading recommendations are unlikely to do anything to restore confidence or gradually increase the amount that is saved.

Other supporters of compulsory funded pensions argue that there is no case for the state to require earnings-related contributions. Lower-paid contributors need to save a higher proportion of their earnings to achieve an adequate pension than the higher-paid. In this case 'adequacy' is not defined in relation to income before retirement (where one might argue all should be aiming for a pension no lower than 50% of earnings), but the absolute amount of money required for an adequate retirement. By definition this would represent a much lower replacement ratio for the higher paid. Someone earning on average £10,000 across their working life might well be advised to save between 10% and 16% to earn a decent pension. But does this justify the state also requiring someone earning an average of £30,000 to also save up to 16% (S Davies, 1997)? In other words, is it the state's responsibility to require minimum/adequate funding or maximum/proportional funding?

If the case for compulsion is made largely on the grounds of reducing disincentives to save, this justifies people having to save enough to ensure that they retire with an income above the poverty line (Income Support) but no more than that. If the higher-paid are required to carry on contributing the same proportion well above this point of adequacy, other routes to saving for retirement (by starting a business, accumulating property and saving through PEPs for example) will be closed off, diverting too high a share of productive assets into pension funds.

A more salient point is that a fixed minimum proportion of earnings during working age is increasingly out of step with the capacity to save at different stages of the life-cycle. There may be times when only a low level of contributions can be afforded, and other times when a higher level is feasible. A young couple in their late 20s - repaying student loans and tuition fees, taking on a mortgage and starting a family - will rarely be in a position to save 16% of their earnings towards pensions. The likely result would be a higher rate of borrowing in order to compensate for reduced disposable income. It should be possible to devise pension schemes that set a target contribution rate as an average of lifetime earnings, with 'milestones' after every five years. This would imply that the minimum contribution could be accumulated over time, composed of lower than average rates at one stage of the life-cycle and higher than average rates at other times.

It is difficult to take issue with Davies' (1997) conclusion that "there is no obvious reason why high earners should have to contribute the same proportion of their earnings as the lower paid," providing some minimum is set and adhered to across-the-board. We might therefore think in terms of an absolute target contribution in the form of a lump sum rather than a proportional contribution. This does not necessarily mean that Davies is correct to call for the lowest minimum possible to ensure a retirement income just above Income Support levels. Yarrow (1997) believes there is an incentives-based case for requiring contributions rather higher than the bare minimum to enable people to avoid the net of means-testing (including Housing Benefit and Council Tax Benefit where possible) rather than just Income Support. The decision here is a political one not a technical one.

The real policy dilemma is not whether we are asking the affluent to save too much of their earnings in pension funds, but how we ensure that the lowest income groups are included and retire with adequate incomes. According to an NAPF analysis, a lump sum contribution of £550 a year would earn a second pension worth 30% more than the Income Support level. Someone earning around £11,500 would expect to earn a second pension of this order by contributing the minimum rebate of 4.8% into a well-run funded pension. Workers earning rather more would need to contribute relatively less to secure this level of pension, although it would be in everyone's interest to clearly stress that minimum contributions earn minimum benefits. However, at the second pension qualifying salary of £5,000 suggested by Field (1996), this would require a contribution rate of around 11% of earnings. A minimum 5% rate would leave the lowest paid with wholly inadequate pensions. We consider how low contributions can be 'geared up' in our following discussion of tax relief and pension credits.

This brings us back to a simple first principle of pensions policy: the lowest-paid employees (in addition to the non-employed) cannot earn an adequate income through the market without some level of state support. Not only does adequacy exact an unreasonably high savings rate, charges on low contributions and high administrative costs with personal pensions mean accumulation takes longer and the return is lower. The general principle of widening the benefits of funded second pensions as far as possible is one we support, but we should be under no illusions about the how far this can be achieved without cost to the Exchequer.

If we wish to have something closer to a genuinely universal system, as opposed to the near-universal system normally proposed, the case for contribution credits must be considered for the second-tier. If we conclude that for a group of persistently low-paid and insecurely employed workers funded second pensions are probably inappropriate, we must then ensure that access to an enhanced BSP is secured. For those who are temporarily low paid or non-employed, there must be appropriate routes back into contributing.

Contribution Credits

Although Home Responsibilities Protection and credits for the unemployed provide entitlement to first-tier pension provision, the principle of credits for the non-employed has not yet been applied to SERPS. Labour has announced the possibility of a Citizenship Pension based on the machinery of SERPS to improve the pension rights of those, mainly women, who undertake caring tasks outside the labour market: "Without further action, they may face a retirement on means-tested benefits which are costly to operate, reduce the incentive to save and represent a demeaning reward for many years of hard work" (Labour Party, 1996). Whether or not SERPS survives for the minority who remain members, the case for contribution credits is likely to be explored.

There are a number of barriers to the extension of second-tier credits for the non-employed. Probably the most important is the question of cost. Yarrow (1997) argues that there is no case to credit the non-employed through second pensions: the goal of redistribution should be achieved through some form of basic income, paid at a higher rate to disabled people unable to work and those with caring responsibilities for example. Most other commentators agree that some form of crediting is needed if second pension coverage is genuinely to be widened. There are two key questions: to whom should credits be extended; and at what rate should they be paid?

Who would qualify?

Few have argued in favour of universal crediting for all groups of non-employed. The NAPF (1997) and Field & Owen (1993) are among those who have, the latter seeking to extend credits for all non-employed by scrapping tax relief on new pension contributions. There is certainly scope for some reallocation of tax reliefs but no case for outright abolition. More recently Field (1996) has argued for starting to credit in *target groups* of the non-employed. Contributions would be paid for full-time carers and the non-working disabled, using existing benefits (Invalid Care Allowance, Incapacity Benefit and relevant disability benefits) as a passport to credits.

There is some debate as to how far this would create incentives to adjust to the new contribution categories. There is little evidence that existing credits to the Basic State Pension provide any incentives to deliberately remain unemployed, because there is a very low level of awareness about benefits that may accrue years in advance. One might argue in any case that second-tier credits ought to provide a positive incentive for more people to undertake the unpaid work of caring (although clearly not to register as disabled when in reality the claimant is long-term unemployed and unable to find a job).

This leaves us with the question of how to treat people who are registered as unemployed. Some favour time-limited credits for the unemployed, running out after two years (Taverne, 1997). Others would exclude them from credits on the grounds that it is a higher priority to provide assistance with finding the next job through a more active Employment Service/Benefits Agency infrastructure (Field, 1996). A better approach may be to pay credits to target groups of the unemployed, such as those who have been out of work for more than two years and are aged over 55. As discussed towards the conclusion of this paper, there is evidence of very low labour market activity among lower-skilled people in areas with restricted job opportunities. Without targeted support for this age group (as proposed for the under-25s for example), they are unlikely to get jobs. There may be a strong case for allowing second-tier credits to be paid to those who are engaged on at least a part-time basis in other forms of activity. This would require a new approach to the definition of 'legitimate' work.

How much would be credited?

The NAPF proposed that a low level of contribution, around £300 a year, should be paid on behalf of the non-employed and increased in line with earnings. The cost has been estimated at £2 billion a year. Although that amount of money could be found from savings on tax relief, the real problem is that this rate of contribution would not earn a pension high enough to escape means-testing in retirement. A contribution rate closer to £600 a year is needed to raise retirement income clear of the Income Support threshold. This second pension entitlement would reduce eligibility to top-up benefits unless there was a large enough disregard.

A more expensive but effective option would be to pay credits at the rates of perhaps 6% and 3% of average earnings according to the time commitment taken up by care responsibilities. Field and Owen (1993) suggest a higher rate for non-working parents whose children are below school age for example. At today's earnings this would result in a maximum credit of around £1030, significantly less than the maximum amount of tax relief available on contributions paid by higher earners. The cost of only crediting in full-time claimants of ICA would be under £500 million. There is a convincing case for paying credits for non-employment, but the rate at which they are paid can only be decided after consultation. Rather than making the decision simply according to what resources might allow, it would be better to consider how much tax relief should be available on contributions from earnings and for government to then decide what value it wishes to place on unpaid work in comparison. We discuss priorities for tax relief and how to support the low-paid who may not be in a position to benefit in the next section.

Tax Relief In Sharper Focus

The need for a genuine sharing of risks and costs between the individual, the state and the employer must be grasped. Pension-planning requires a uniquely long-term commitment to attain the full effects of fund accrual. In Britain, both contributions to funded pensions and the interest earned as funds grow have attracted tax relief. There is common agreement that the tax system should compensate for deferred earnings in this way. Income has not been taxed until benefits are drawn on retirement. Even then, a lump sum worth up to 25% of the value of the fund can be drawn free of tax. This is the Exempt-Exempt-Tax (EET) model. The previous government's proposed Basic Pension Plus would have reversed this order, with pension contributions being taxed, interest accrual remaining untaxed and benefits being drawn free of tax (a T-E-E model). This would have brought forward a huge amount of money, helping to pay the costs of transition to full funding. The present government's changes to Advance Corporation Tax (ACT) mean fund accrual will not be fully exempt. It will be an E-P-T model where P stands for only Partially Exempt.

Perhaps more important than the redistributive effects between income groups is the individual life-cycle effect. The problems of requiring younger people to contribute a higher fixed proportion of earnings to their pension were discussed above. The pattern of savings, borrowing and expenditure for the average thirty-year-old is different from the average fifty-year-old. If the retirement savings rate is to be raised, incentives are required during working age. If tax relief were to be switched to retirement, there is virtually no prospect of persuading younger age groups to save more and save earlier. *Tax relief should remain for contributions rather than benefits as recognised by the current government.*

This does not imply that the current approach to tax relief is efficient. The tax-free lump sum may be drawn and put into savings. It would therefore be hidden from any calculation of entitlement for a Minimum Pension Guarantee (unless all savings were assessed). One option would be to remove tax relief while retaining the option of a 25% upfront share of the fund. This would eventually raise around £1 billion (Johnson 1994). Tax relief on part of the pension benefit seems anomalous, given that the contributions and interest on that element were untaxed. Yet abolition of tax relief on the lump sum has few supporters. The more common view appears to be that tax relief provides some compensation for the illiquidity of pensions compared with PEPs which can be drawn on without age restrictions. An appropriate reform might be lift the limit on how much can be saved in the form of pensions and reduce the amount of the lump sum that is untaxed to 15% for example (Colonial/Unity Trust Bank, 1997). The 'rational' response of abolishing the tax-free lump sum looks less feasible following the tax changes announced in the 1997 Budget.

Proposals to change the tax treatment of pension contributions have been more common. Someone who contributes £100 a month from net income while paying income tax at the basic rate ends up with a contribution worth £130. That rises to £167 for someone earning at the top rate. The higher the contribution, the greater the value of the state's support, up to earnings of £82,200. Yet tax relief is worth nothing to lower-paid employees who earn too little to pay income tax, but might benefit from an appropriate second pension scheme. SERPS contributions are deducted at source. There is no scope for paying additional contributions which might attract tax relief. Minns (1997) describes tax relief on private pensions, at a cost of more than £8 billion a year, as one of the most substantial PAYG schemes yet devised. He notes the irony that advocates of compulsory private pensions assume that the state will under-write part of the cost through generous tax relief and calls for tax relief to be switched to SERPS contributions instead. In a similar vein, Crawford (1997) argues that "the recipients of tax relief are not on the whole people who need state subsidies."

If the state's responsibilities are to widen access to funded second pensions and to raise the adequacy of savings, *the question of tax relief cannot be ignored.* Assuming there is a political commitment to cast the funded second-tier as widely as possible, and develop a better targeted first-tier pension, is tax relief still necessary? In other words, once the question of *whether* to save towards a funded pension is no longer a consideration, what is the case for tax-based incentives?

Field and Owen (1993) take issue with those who believe that "the irresponsible public will squander its resources and be left high and dry come retirement" if tax relief on contributions and the lump sum were to be removed. They proposed scrapping all relief as well as the limits on how much can be saved in pension funds (abolishing the 'earnings-only' rule). The savings would not be used to revive SERPS however. Instead they would be used to pay for the proposed guaranteed minimum pension and contribution credits for second pensions. This would relieve the cost of general tax welfare towards occupational and personal pensions, and refocus state support towards life-time low earners.

Although the position adopted by Field and Owen is logically sound, there is a strong case for retaining tax relief on contributions in order to encourage a higher level of savings where it is currently low (and not just ensuring that all are covered up to a minimum). The responsibility of an active welfare state will be to encourage a level of saving that produces an adequate second pension (free from the means-test trap where possible). If contributors are required to save towards a target amount rather than a fixed proportion of earnings, the distribution of tax relief should observe the same principle. Churchill and Hindle (1997) argue that any reduction in tax incentives will result in the increased use of short-term savings vehicles such as PEPs instead of pension funds, and for that reason should be avoided. However, if a restriction of tax relief for higher earners results in savings being channelled towards other vehicles, it is not self-evident why this should be a concern for policy-makers. It may encourage the perception that additional voluntary contributions are relatively less attractive than PEPs, but as long as an adequate level of pension savings has been achieved (with the help of tax relief), government should be neutral on how genuinely additional savings are made.

Government should therefore retain tax relief on contributions but sharpen its focus. A useful starting point might be to reduce the ceiling on contributions which qualify for tax relief to £6,000 a year and restrict the rate at which relief is paid to the basic rate (as proposed by Colonial/Unity Trust Bank and Field for example). Many who receive 40% tax relief in working age will pay tax on their pension at the basic rate. *Tax reliefs for high earners are unduly generous set against the minimal support available to the low-paid. They should be changed.* Field's new limits would mean a maximum value of tax relief of just under £1,400 a year. Someone earning four times the average salary and paying 10% of their earnings into a personal pension (rather less than the maximum allowed) would currently receive twice this sum. This would save a considerable amount that could be used to improve the pensions of lower earners. The new limit would still be relatively generous. For most people, contributions will be limited by ability to pay rather than this maximum amount.

Tax relief is currently worth nothing to the very low-paid because they do not pay income tax or because they are members of SERPS. While the large majority of earners will continue to benefit from tax relief, and some of the non-employed will qualify for contribution credits, low-income earners would be the 'excluded middle'. Some will be temporarily in low-paid jobs before moving up the earnings ladder, but others will remain low-paid in the long-term. *If pension reform is to be sustainable, support for the working poor must be improved.* A national minimum wage, combined with in-work benefits, should improve their current incomes. The same principle needs to be applied to their future retirement incomes.

The priority here is probably that group paid between £61 a week (the LEL) and twice that amount. They are currently covered by SERPS if nothing else but are probably not earning enough to switch to a personal pension. Field (1996) proposed that they should pay lower NICs towards the full basic state pension rather than a poor value second-tier pension. While there is no case for requiring those below the LEL to contribute towards a second pension, those earning a modest income above it should have access.

Drawing on the debate in North America, the position of the working poor has improved because they receive a wage supplement in the form of an Earned Income Tax Credit (EITC). The EITC is presented as a tax cut to low earners who pay income tax, and as an in-work benefit to those who do not. A parallel Earned Income Pension Credit (EIPC) could be designed to assist Britain's low earners. Instead of giving tax relief to the low-paid, pension credits could be banked in the second-tier scheme of their choice (Birch, 1997). Pension Credits might be paid on wages between the LEL and twice that amount (between £62 and £124 in 1997) for example.

Such a reform would have to be designed carefully after consultation, but the hurdles are more likely to be technical and cost-related rather than in principle objections. Even the Adam Smith Institute (1997) accepts that state-financed supplements might be required for the persistently low-paid. The real argument turns on whether government should assist this group once they reach retirement or on a regular basis during working age. Pension credits should probably be paid on an annual basis, in the form of an income-tracking mechanism. Individuals will therefore receive credits only while they are on low earnings. In this way, credits would be funded and accumulate over time. The goal would be to yield a return which means most of the beneficiaries are free of means-testing when they reach retirement, and that the cost of any Minimum Pension Guarantee would then be reduced.

There are of course new risks associated with any new government initiative. The level of pension credit could be reduced, eligibility tightened, or even abolished by a future government. The return on credits might be lower than expected. However, political risk can be used as an argument against government doing anything. One way to reduce the risk of a future government eroding the new system is to introduce transparent and popular reforms, with clear ownership rights and expectations of future returns. Having none of these, SERPS became a soft target despite early political consensus.

Box 5.5 Earned Income Pension Credits

Alison is 35, divorced and has two children at school. She earns £85 a week as a part-time sales assistant in a small shop. Her employer does not offer an occupational scheme. She does not feel there is a personal pension for people like her but is concerned that her SERPS contributions will not add up to much when she retires. She decides to take out a new National Savings Pension through the Post Office. The contracted-out rebate is paid in but on its own this will earn a low pension. She does not earn enough to pay additional contributions at the moment, so gets no tax relief from the government, but she does qualify for the new Pension Credit. New rules mean she is able to pay in occasional top-ups over the counter. She receives a statement twice a year showing how much has been paid in, giving encouragement to save a bit more when she can.

John is 20, has been unemployed for a year and, despite having completed an IT training course and had some temporary work, has not found the kind of job he would like. He qualifies for a new work and training placement with a local software company as part of the New Deal for under-25s. He has never thought about savings or pensions before. When his parents arranged a visit from a life insurance rep, he told them he would think about a pension when he was older. His new employer does not run its own pension scheme, but does contribute to a Industry Pension. John chooses to join it. On top of the contracted-out rebate, the government pays a starter credit for under-25s.

Conditions on where tax relief goes

In addition to asking who should get how much in the way of tax relief, there is also the question of which pension funds should benefit. Given the substantial amount of public money used to subsidise personal pension contributions, it is surprising that a proper audit of how it is invested has not been a higher concern for government before now. Indeed a large number of personal pensions - estimated to be 3 million of 5.1 million in 1992 – do not receive any additional payments beyond the minimum rebate.

We do not have much information about the return they can expect. An analysis of personal pensions by The Independent and World in Action (1997) calculated the return on premium payments of £100 a month (equivalent to a 10% contribution rate on annual earnings of £12,000). It found a substantial variation in the impact of upfront charges, lapse rates, transfer values and the implicit subsidy by government with some well-known life companies front-loading their charges in the early years to the extent that very little of the contributions paid in that time is saved towards a retirement fund.

The worst companies did not achieve the break-even point where money paid in begins to earn a pension for seven or eight years. Those who remain with the same company until retirement may earn a reasonable pension, but only because other contributors have lapsed - precisely the problem in occupational schemes that personal pensions were supposed to tackle. Indeed some companies may end up making the bulk of their profit on personal pensions from those who lapse providing a perverse incentive - even if it is not consciously factored into the company's decision-making - to sell unsuitable policies to people who are unlikely to maintain them until retirement. More detailed analysis by Chapman (1997) reveals a much higher lapse rate than anticipated: 25% lapsing within two years was not unusual, due to unemployment or switching to an occupational scheme for example.

Of the new policies taken out in 1996, Chapman estimates that one-third are likely to lose money for these reasons. The concern is not necessarily that high-charging pension providers exist. In a well-developed market place, where we all have accurate information about how much companies charge, such companies should be subject to competitive pressures: reduce charges or go out of business. Yet disclosure of such information is still in its early phase. There is every reason to assume that pension policies will remain shrouded in confusion for many. Although we may be encouraged to shop around and the process of selling, advising and paying is likely to become easier, the stakes are high. The consequences of choosing the wrong personal pension are profound. How should policy-makers respond?

Perhaps the most significant finding from Chapman's work is the extent *to which the state underwrites poor value private welfare.* All approved personal pension schemes attract tax relief on contributions, regardless of their performance. Government in effect subsidises the highest-charging companies. Of new policies in 1996, £157 million of tax relief will have been paid directly to companies which fail to deliver a positive fund value at the point of transfer or lapse.

None of this means that we should give up on personal pensions. Too much has already been invested and too many gaps exist in the rest of the pensions market to simply withdraw support. Instead, the Government should instruct the regulator to publish an annual league-table of a range of indicators, showing administrative costs and charges for every £100 invested in a personal pension for example. This would be an advance on the league tables currently produced by individual companies, which consistently select different measures of performance in order to show themselves in the most favourable light. These could further undermine consumer confidence. It would however take some time before the market adjusted and the high charge/low return personal pension was squeezed out or forced to adapt. More immediately, the Government should review how it chooses 'approved' PP schemes in order to allocate tax relief (which accounts for almost one-third of the money invested in personal pensions, Table 5). *All schemes should consider tax relief status as a benefit to be earned not taken for granted.* Perhaps the most compelling incentive would be provided by a new range of targets on lower and better smoothed charges, higher transfer values and the disclosure of 'paid-up values' to allow those transferring to assess the costs and benefits of doing so. A market-based approach would see persistently bad performers face relegation from the approved league table and the loss of all tax relief, provided that pension holders were then able to transfer to a more secure scheme without penalty. This would still leave unacceptable risks in the system. A better approach would be to use regulation instead of relegation. Targets on product performance would be clearly-defined in order to eliminate the risk of confusion among providers. Where standards were breached, those products would simply lose their approved status.

Box 5.6 Personal Pensions Income 1995/96

National Insurance Rebates	£2.43 billion	(35%)
Personal Contributions	£2.35 billion	(34%)
Tax relief on contributions above minimum rebate	£2.10 billion	(31%)

Source: Inland Revenue Statistics 1995/96; Chapman 1997.

Second-tier pensions should not attempt to redistribute income between members of society. However, it is the responsibility of an active welfare state to ensure that the resources it does commit tackle market failures where appropriate and extend value for money to those least likely to benefit. Tax relief clearly can be an instrument of redistribution. It currently provides much more to the better-off. A system which spends a substantial amount of public money to subsidise savings which would largely have been made anyway, and which encouraged people to move their savings in ways that were against their own interests, is clearly ripe for reform. We argue for a refocused system of tax reliefs rather than scrapping relief on personal pension contributions. The tax system could be a useful instrument for government to encourage people to invest in companies with low charges and high transfer values (to protect those who have to interrupt their contributions). A new system of pension credits, paid for by restricting tax reliefs to the better-off, may enable the low paid to save more towards retirement.

Second Pensions Plus

The 'basic' guarantee in the Basic Pension Plus proposed by the former government would indeed have been paid at a fairly miserable level while the 'plus' element was supposed to have delivered most of the pension income to most of the population. The idea of additional benefits through pension savings is already familiar through the discretionary benefits funded in part by employers through traditional occupational schemes. As these come to cover a declining share of the workforce however, benefits like life insurance are much less likely to be provided.

There is a general problem of the number of low-income households without any form of life cover falling sharply in recent years. They are least likely to have adequate pension funds to draw upon in the event of a partner dying unexpectedly. There is also the particular problem of young families who are least likely to have cash to spare for additional insurance products. Even having sorted out their pensions, there will be little in their funds to pass on to their families if one partner dies prematurely (Field and Owen 1993). The benefits system is poorly geared towards such low probability risks which carry a high cost.

Saving for retirement may be best done through a pension, and insuring against premature death through a life policy. Many in the industry may be reluctant to consider 'bundling' options which allow both risks to be covered in one product. However we already know that young people put off starting to save enough towards a pension. The establishment of Individual Savings Accounts (ISAs) from 1999 could enable those saving for retirement to contribute towards other financial services including life insurance at the same time.

The Government should therefore consider the Australian experience, where around 10% of the employee's pension contribution is ear-marked for life cover which will pay twice the average industry earnings in the event of a claim. In Britain a small proportion of the contribution to a stakeholder pension could automatically pay towards a basic life policy. That amount could be front-loaded to peak in the early years and decline as the value of the pension fund accrues. There would be every encouragement for individuals to top up this level of cover with a separate policy, and there would be the choice of opting-out. Government should consult widely with the industry on the best way to close the gap in life coverage and on whether this is the best way to do it. The key principle of retaining some of the added benefits of having a pension - making sense of 'Second Pensions Plus' - should commend itself however.

Future Trends

We conclude this chapter with a discussion of some of the trends in work and retirement that are likely to have an important bearing on pensions policy. Just over two-thirds of the UK's population is of working age (defined as between 18 and 65). The remainder is now divided fairly evenly between children and pensioners. Economic and demographic forecasts usually refer to the Dependency or Support Ratio, measured as the balance between people of working age and the retired. As the numbers of elderly increase the ratio deteriorates. The scale of the so-called demographic crisis turns on how far the balance shifts away from working age. The UK began the ageing process earlier and at a slower pace than Japan, Germany or Italy for example. A more telling measurement is the Contributory Support Ratio (Downs and Stevens-Ströhman, 1995). This reflects the actual rather than notional levels of economic activity across age groups including people of working age who are not in employment (because they are studying, caring, seeking work or have retired early) and people of retirement age who carry on working. Although the ability to alter long-term demographic change is largely beyond governments, policy choices on employment, the structure of pension funds and official retirement age may clearly affect the Contributory Support Ratio.

Employment Patterns

The level of labour market activity among British men has been falling for more than two decades, explained more by a drop in the participation rate than the number of hours worked. The drop is particularly marked among those aged 50-65 where inactivity reflects early retirement. Some of it is involuntary retirement disguising the true problem of long-term unemployment. Each new cohort of women tends to work longer hours in later middle age than previous generations did. At the aggregate level, these higher participation rates for women have compensated for falling male participation rates. The trend towards early retirement appears to have slowed in recent years. This may provide a hint of things to come, as the prospects for well-pensioned early retirement diminish (Churchill and Hindle 1997).

Men spend much more of their working age in employment than women. According to a study of economic activity across working age by Johnson *et al* (1996), men who have retired on higher incomes spent less time in absolute terms in the labour market than men with low incomes. This reflects later entry to the first job (due to spending longer in education) and the likelihood of earlier exit, due to greater opportunities to retire with a decent occupational pension. However, the same men spent a higher proportion of their effective working life in employment. Only 1% of time was spent out of work compared with 6% for the lower income retired men. Despite a later start and an earlier finish, higher income men will have faced fewer interruptions to their earnings. Women spent significantly less time in the labour market. Higher income women spent 34% of working age outside employment compared with 52% for lower income women.

Considering the reasons for non-employment, it emerges that men are divided according to income much more than women. For lower income men, more than 70% of time spent out of work was the result of registered unemployment compared with only 45% for those with higher incomes. For women however, up to 80% of time spent out of work was due to 'not seeking work' – largely explained by caring responsibilities – irrespective of the income they retired with. The amount of time spent outside employment has in the past been a key determinant of retirement income for men rather than for women. However this may not provide us with a reliable guide to the future.

Families no longer provides the secure means of life-time redistribution assumed by Beveridge. Legislation to require the splitting of pension entitlements on divorce was a long overdue recognition of this fact. Nevertheless women cannot rely on a decent retirement income based on a partner's earnings. Long-term reliance on means-tested benefits is likely to lead lone mothers towards retirement poverty and women living in households with no earner will be little better off unless at least one of the adults gains employment. Time spent out of employment is as likely to become a determinant of retirement income for women as it has been for men in the past. Contribution credits to second pensions for some periods of non-employment will assist but higher levels of employment for those who face the strongest barriers to work must also be a priority.

Age-related credits: The Over-55s

The over-55s are much less likely to be in work than they were twenty years ago. Some have the benefit of a decent occupational pension. Having chosen early retirement, they are likely to find themselves in the first of our three nations in retirement. Others have retired early on the grounds of ill-health and might combine a second pension income with Incapacity Benefit. The focus for public policy should be that group of the semi-skilled unemployed who are able to work but live in areas with poor job prospects. Box 5.7 outlines the significant regional differences in employment rates. Long-term unemployment among this group differs from the under-25s. First, a higher priority is likely to be attached to moving the young into jobs. Even with a package of wage subsidies to encourage employers to take on older workers, there is a common perception that losing your job when aged 55 cannot compare with never having had one by age 25. Second, unemployment may eventually show up as incapacity.

Box 5.7 The Regional 'Twilight Zones' for the older unemployed

Area	% of men aged 55-64 not working	% of women aged 50-59 not working
Britain	43	39
South Yorkshire	59	44
Wales	57	46
Strathclyde	55	53
Greater Manchester	55	42
West Yorkshire	40	41
London & S. East	39	37
South West	34	35
East Anglia	34	36
Range	25	18

(Source: Rogers, 1995)

A serious debate on the work prospects of this group is overdue. There is a clear age effect but there is also a gender effect. In those areas with the highest non-employment rates, many new jobs are likely to be viewed by men and by employers as 'women's work' because they are part-time and low-paid (Commission on Social Justice, 1994). Uneven competition for the new jobs between the sexes explains much of the changing labour market in these localities. A real shift in perceptions may take a generation. In the meantime, policy-makers should accept that this group of older men faces particularly strong barriers to getting a job. Some form of 'benefits amnesty' might be piloted where barriers to paid work are formidable. The aim would be to encourage more of the cash-in-hand activity that goes on in the shadow economy for relatively small amounts of money to be recognised and taxed (Holtham, 1997).

There is also the question of pension provision for those who will retire in the next ten years. While second pension contributions should probably not be credited by the state for unemployment, the over-50s may be a special case. The Government should recognise the extent of labour market failure for many in this age group and consider how a system of enhanced pension credits could be paid for those who undertake activities of benefit to their communities. There is no shortage of help required in schools, hospitals, community and voluntary groups, which many of the older unemployed could provide if the welfare state actually encouraged them.

The Under-25s

A universal pension savings net beginning at an early age should allow today's young workers to achieve higher pensions in the future. As part of the Government's New Deal for the under-25s, starter credits to funded pensions could be paid either during the period of their work or learning opportunity or on moving to the first job thereafter. Many in the pensions industry supported the last government's proposals to bring financial advice into schools. Whatever the merits of such an approach, it is highly unlikely to affect attitudes or behaviour. Most young people want to earn money and then spend it. If they do have savings, a pension is low on the list. The first job offers a rare opportunity to make a start on lifetime savings. Paying starter credits would also provide some compensation for an age group who are expected to pay income tax and national insurance at the same rate as everyone else, but receive benefits at a lower rate because of their age. Faced with limited resources, government would be better advised to signal a long-term commitment to better pensions in this way than to restore the level of means-tested benefits (which young people should in any case be given every support to avoid).

Pension Fund Structure

Periods spent in and out of employment and indeed the effective length of working age are not driven simply by changes in the pattern of demand for labour. The existence and type of pension coverage is critical. As a general rule, we are a country of workers who want to retire at the earliest date possible. Those who continue working the longest have generally been those who need to for financial reasons. While early retirement remains the aspiration, many are likely to be disappointed as opportunities for well-pensioned early retirement diminish. As the pensions paid out for twenty five or thirty years' contributions become spread more thinly across longer periods of retirement, and enhanced final salary schemes become less common, a harder actuarial reality will hit home. As Money Purchase schemes grow in importance, the link between contributions and benefits will become clearer. Benefits will come to more closely reflect how much has been paid in.

Flexibility in Retirement Age

Higher pension commitments as a result of living longer in retirement, coupled with new uncertainties in the labour market, have persuaded many countries to tighten pension provision. Governments in Europe and North America have reduced the rate at which state pensions are accrued, increased the required contribution period for the same level of benefit, and increased the official retirement age. It is the last of these that has been significant in the UK. Different retirement ages for women and men were always difficult to justify. When the state pension system was introduced, men typically lived five years less than women. Despite a significant increase in life expectancy, the gap has not closed. A pensions system expected to pay out for only one year to men and eleven to women now covers an average of eight years and eighteen years respectively (Box 5.8). The decision to equalise at age 65 is therefore wholly justified from the Government Actuary's point of view.

Box 5.8 Living longer across the sexes

	Averages for Men		Averages for Women	
Year	Life expectancy	Years in retirement	Life expectancy	Years in retirement
1945	66 years	1	71 years	11
1993	73 years	8	78 years	18

(Source: Field and Owen 1993)

The debate about state retirement age only provides a partial glimpse of actual retirement behaviour. In the ten years before the Basic State Pension can be claimed, non-employment is often as common as having a job. There is a long-standing argument for recognising the reality of labour market experience for this age group by reducing state retirement age to 60. That argument has been lost. A more promising set of proposals has emerged around the idea of retirement as a phased process rather than an event. A flexible decade of retirement would not allow the full state pension to be drawn early, but it would allow a reduced payment to be made according to how early it was claimed. This could enable more workers to combine part-time retirement with part-time employment, and eventually reduce the significance attached to the official retirement age (Colonial/Unity Trust Bank, 1997).

It is the age at which flexibility should be offered that is in dispute rather than the principle of flexible retirement. The last government opened the door to flexibility in retirement . A bonus of 7.5% is added to the basic State Pension for every year an initial claim is deferred *beyond* retirement age. A woman wishing to work until age 65 or a man until 70 would therefore receive a basic pension worth 37.5% more than normal. From 2010 the deferral rate was planned to rise to 10% per year. The calculation is of course that the later one claims the less will be paid out. In practice only 2% of employees reaching retirement have taken up the offer. The option is not widely known about. Those who can afford to retire early on the strength of a decent second pension income will continue to do so. Those who cannot afford to retire early probably have least opportunity to work beyond retirement age. There is simply no culture of working longer than is absolutely necessary in the UK (unlike Japan for example).

The Conservative government criticised proposals for flexibility from age 60 because it would mean most people wishing to take their state pensions at that age (Lilley 1996). Assuming the BSP was reduced by 7.5% for each year it was claimed before age 65, this could result in many of the early retired having to claim means-tested benefits on top if they were unable to combine pension income with part-time earnings for example. It is more likely that flexibility in retirement age will be encouraged through the second tier than the BSP. It is here that moves towards part-time retirement combined with part-time work should be considered learning the lessons from other countries which have moved in that direction (MacIntyre 1996).

Working Later not Longer
The official retirement age set by the state has a declining influence on when people actually leave the labour market particularly in Britain.

Raising the retirement age to 67 as in the USA and some of the Scandinavian countries cannot be dismissed as simply a way for the state to reduce its spending commitments. If people are living longer, lengthening the years of employment may make some sense. Judged against the policy goal of equity however it may be regressive in its impact. Although people are living longer on average, in many communities life expectancy has barely improved for two decades. Unless prospects for employment or alternative forms of activity are suitably accredited, raising the retirement age will simply lengthen the 'twilight zone' before the BSP is claimed. *Further changes in the state retirement age beyond 65 are an unnecessary distraction from the task of raising employment in work-poor communities.*

There remains a paradox however. If we can expect to live longer and healthier lives, why do we want to retire earlier and earlier? One answer is to be found in the changing nature of work. The high and rising expectations we have as consumers and employers must be met through our work as employees. The need to achieve more with the same resources is resulting in longer working hours and more stress-related illness. Although the extent of insecurity in working age is contested, the reality of 'burnout' associated with long working hours is not. In at least some sectors retiring early may reflect the push factors (related to our capacity to adjust to stress) more than the pull factor of a well-pensioned retirement. Esping-Andersen (1995) explores how working age could become less hectic if individuals had the choice of more time out of the labour market in return for retiring later - the amount of paid work undertaken may be the same but its phasing could change. If an extra two years could be 'borrowed', state pensions could then be drawn at age 67 for example.

Governments will be reluctant to run the actuarial risks involved in such a proposal. However, a practical example of what we might term better time-smoothing in working age is already underway in Canada. British Columbia's Deferred Salary Leave Programme (DSLP) allows government employees to save part of their salary in order to buy themselves out of their job for a year on full pay (Province of British Columbia, 1993). Money is invested in government bonds and with fund accrual the full deferred salary can be drawn on within five to seven years. The contract requires that the employee returns to work for at least one year so that it cannot be used as an early retirement mechanism. The benefits are clear: employees are able to draw down a block of paid leave freeing up work for others to do. It therefore has the potential to improve upon existing job-sharing methods. It has been hugely popular in practice.

There are clear limits to how far this approach can reach. Those who have taken advantage tend to be more securely-employed public service workers. Lower-paid employees would be unable to accrue an adequate fund from low contributions. The true innovation would be to develop groups of private employers prepared to offer a similar scheme to their workforce. However, government as a major employer can send a signal to the private sector just as it could in reforming working hours. Programmes like DSLP are likely to be of more value to older employees in a position to save more of their salary once earlier financial commitments have been met. To that extent they could offer a degree of flexibility to those in the 45-55 age group that might begin to ease the pressure for outright early retirement at no net cost to the employer. Some employees might be better able to work later and closer to the official retirement age rather than being pressured to work longer hours and end up retiring early on the grounds of illness.

Conclusion

No one is happy with the pensions system as we know it. Pensioners who rely on the state for all their income have fallen behind their own expectations as well as the progress shared by people in work. Younger workers expect to retire on decent pensions but they start saving late and typically do not save enough. The life industry has been bruised by its own mistakes over personal pensions. And a new government is eager to draw a line under the failures of its predecessor and find new ways of putting the enduring principles of equity, transparency and above all security into action. There is a strong mood for change.

This chapter has not attempted an exhaustive review of all the reasons why the current system is failing too many, or explored all the strategies for improvement. It has instead focused on the need to deliver better support to the retired poor, and upon the twin tasks for people of working age: to widen access to good value second pensions and to raise the level of saving for retirement. We have to recognise that the trends driving both a lower level of retirement poverty overall and a sharply rising degree of inequality cannot be tackled by doing more of the same. The traditional policy instruments will have their place in the new settlement, but they must be used in new ways:

- The Basic State Pension should be retained on a pay-as-you-go basis, but automatic top-ups should be made more generous and targeted towards the retired poor. Over time the rate at which the first-tier pension is earned could be adjusted in favour of the lifetime low-paid. Better targeting can be achieved without an extension of selective means-tests of the poor. They don't work. Nor must the better-off be excluded from state provision.
- SERPS fulfils a role which no private pension does. But it has not been allowed to perform that role well enough to lift all its contributors free of poverty. The development of low-cost and fully portable funded pensions, sold to affinity groups on a high-volume basis, could attract many of those who currently have no choice but to stay in SERPS. A National Savings Pension scheme could stimulate competition to serve the low-paid as part of a broader stakeholder pension reform.
- We would expect good occupational and personal pensions to continue to serve their appropriate parts of the labour force. Where they are not performing this role well, a new tier of products will be in place to compete with them.

Assuming the supply side of the pensions infrastructure can be improved, and the weight of competition used to serve lower-income groups, the question of adequacy remains. We have not prescribed how far the savings rate should be raised in order to secure decent second pensions for their members. But we do make the following points:

- Schemes should set periodic milestones for contributions rather than carving in stone how much should be paid on a regular basis to allow contributions to vary with the individual's place in the life-cycle.
- The requirement should be to save up to an amount rather than a set proportion of earnings which is expected to float contributors free of means-testing in retirement.
- And most importantly, the resources paid through tax relief on

pensions contributions should be reallocated. Contribution credits for some forms of unpaid work should be improved. Earned income pension credits should be targeted to the working poor to ensure their modest contributions are adequately topped-up by the state. They are a higher priority for subsidies than those who earn enough to pay income tax at the top rate.

Throughout our analysis, we have been guided by two simple propositions: that creating the conditions for appropriate pension provision cannot be achieved without the active involvement of government through a judicious combination of regulation and fiscal incentives; and that responsibility for facing the risks and costs must be shared rather than shifted between individuals, employers and government. The government's task now is to set out in detail its own understanding of an enduring pensions settlement, covering the challenges of today as well as tomorrow.

References

Barclays Life Assurance (1996) *Closing the Misery Gap,* Barclays Life, London

Birch R(1997) 'Educating the Consumer', *A Changing Nation: Retirement Provision for the 21st Century,* NatWest, 28-49.

Butler E(1997) *The Great Escape: Financing the Transition to Funded Pensions,* Adam Smith Institute, London

Butler, E Pirie M and Young M (1997) Beyond Pensions Plus Adam Smith Institute, London

Chapman J (1997) 'Pensions: The Facts', *The Independent,* 5 April, 23-26

Churchill L and Hindle J (1997) 'Manifesto for Change', *A Changing Nation: Retirement Provision for the 21st Century,* NatWest, 8-25

Colonial/Unity Trust Bank (1997) *Pensions: Time to Act,* Colonial/Unity Trust Bank

Commission on Social Justice (1994) *Social Justice: Strategies for National Renewal* IPPR/Vintage, London

Crawford M (1997) 'The Big Pensions Lie', *New Economy,* Spring IPPR, London 38-44.

Curry C and Ball J (1996) 'Pensioners' Incomes in the Next Century', *Insurance Trends* 11 ABI, London, 6-13.

Davies B (1993) *Better Pensions for All,* IPPR, London

Davies B (1997) *The National Savings Pension Plan - A Proposal* CPSA, London

Davies S (1997) *Future Provision for Retirement: Options for Reform* IoD Economic Research Paper, London

Denham J (1996) 'Security in Retirement - The Stakeholder Pension in Practice' (Speech)

Downs C J (1997) 'Pensions for an Older Population', *Benefits* January, 9-12.

Downs C J and Stevens-Ströhman R(1995) 'Providing Fair Pensions Efficiently', *Risk, Insurance and Welfare: The changing balance between public and private protection,* ABI, London, 53-68.

Esping-Andersen G (1995) 'Equality and Work in the Post-industrial Life-cycle' in D Miliband (ed) *Reinventing the Left,* IPPR, London, 167-185.

Falkingham J and Jonson P (1993) *A Unified Funded Pe.* *(UFPS) for Britain*, STICERD Welfare State Programme Paper WSP/90 LSE, London

Falkingham J and Jonson P (1997) 'Public Pensions and the Private Secto. A new way forward', *Soundings*, 159-167.

Field F (1995) *Making Welfare Work: Reconstructing Welfare for the Millennium*, ICS, London

Field F (1996) *How to Pay for the Future: Building a Stakeholders' Welfare*, ICS, London

Field F and Owen M (1993) *Private Pensions for All: Squaring the Circle*, Fabian Society, London

Holtham G (1997) 'Amnesty for self-starters', *Financial Times*, 15 June.

The Independent/World in Action (1997) TV documentary, April.

Investment Week, (1997) 'Funding the Future', 21 April, 59.

Johnson P (1994) *The Pensions Dilemma*, (Commission on Social Justice/IPPR, London)

Johnson P, Disney R and Stears G (1996) *Pensions: 2000 and Beyond*, Volume 2 IFS/Retirement Income Inquiry, London

Labour Party (1996) *Security in Retirement Labour Party*, London

Lilley P(1996) *Providing for Pensions*, Politeia, London

MacIntyre K (1996) 'The Finnished Article? Pensions in Finland' *PMI News*, 2-3.

Minns R (1997) *Pulp Fiction: Pensioning Off the State*, PERC, Sheffield

NAPF (1997) *Agenda for Pensions* NAPF, London

Province of British Columbia (1993) *Deferred Salary Leave Programme* PBC, Victoria Canada

Retirement Income Inquiry (1996) *Pensions: 2000 and Beyond, Volume 1*, Retirement Income Inquiry, London.

Rogers R (1995) 'The age of discontent for millions' *The Herald*, 12 April.

Taverne D (1997) 'The Next Steps to Better Pensions', *A Changing Nation: Retirement Provision for the 21st Century*, NatWest 82-105.

Yarrow G (1997) 'Towards an Inclusive Society', *A Changing Nation: Retirement Provision for the 21st Century*, NatWest, 51-79.